Pick A Pocket Or Two

Pick A Pocket Or Two

A History Of British Musical Theatre

ETHAN MORDDEN

OXFORD

UNIVERSITY PRESS

OXFORD
UNIVERSITY PRESS

Oxford University Press is a department of the University of Oxford. It furthers
the University's objective of excellence in research, scholarship, and education
by publishing worldwide. Oxford is a registered trade mark of Oxford University
Press in the UK and certain other countries.

Published in the United States of America by Oxford University Press
198 Madison Avenue, New York, NY 10016, United States of America.

Library of Congress Cataloging-in-Publication Data
Names: Mordden, Ethan, author.
Title: Pick a pocket or two : a history of British musical theatre / Ethan Mordden.
Description: New York : Oxford University Press, 2021. |
Includes bibliographical references and index.
Identifiers: LCCN 2021027770 (print) | LCCN 2021027771 (ebook) |
ISBN 9780190877958 (cloth) | ISBN 9780190877965 (updf) |
ISBN 9780190877972 (epub) | ISBN 9780190877989
Subjects: LCSH: Musicals—Great Britain—History and criticism. |
Musical theater—Great Britain—History and criticism.
Classification: LCC ML1731 .M67 2021 (print) | LCC ML1731 (ebook) |
DDC 782.1/40941—dc23
LC record available at https://lccn.loc.gov/2021027770
LC ebook record available at https://lccn.loc.gov/2021027771

DOI: 10.1093/oso/9780190877958.001.0001

1 3 5 7 9 8 6 4 2

Printed by Sheridan Books, Inc., United States of America

Illustrations courtesy of The Billy Rose Theatre Collection, New York Library For the Performing Arts,
Astor, Lenox, and Tilden Foundations; and private collections.

Contents

Acknowledgments

To those who enriched the manuscript with pertinent information: Jason Carr, Jon Cronwell, David Firman, Ian Marshall Fisher, Ken Mandelbaum.

1

Beginnings

In the Days Of My Youth

It's one of the most quoted remarks in British theatre history: dramatist John Gay is talking to Jonathan Swift about the lurid reports of highwaymen operating on Hounslow Heath along the Great West Road (today part of the A4). And Swift says, "What an odd pretty sort of thing a Newgate pastoral would be."

Now, Newgate was London's most notorious prison and the pastoral originated as music theatre about shepherds and their coterie, so a "Newgate pastoral" would seem to be the most discordant of oxymorons. However, "pastoral," through common usage, denoted also any more or less light-hearted musical drama, whatever its setting. The ninth edition of *The Oxford Companion To Music* defines the pastoral as "a type of stage work embodying music, ballet, &tc.," even as "a forerunner of opera."

So Swift was being facetious, as if someone from our own time suggested doing *The Boy Friend* with serial killers or *Jesus Christ Superstar* with atheists. Nevertheless, Gay saw the possibilities: in a comedy of Restoration wit about the criminal class, spiced with familiar tunes given new lyrics fitted to the story. And when Gay showed the finished work to William Congreve—the cleverest of all the Restoration playwrights, sharp as a diamond—he predicted that Gay's show was so innovative, so beyond what the public knew and liked, that it would "either take greatly, or be damned confoundedly."

The Beggar's Opera (1728) took greatly. It is not only the first musical (as we know the term today) but one still stage-ready as written, a wicked, hilarious, and melodious piece. It centers on an anti-hero, Macheath, surrounded by enemies and allies grouped in twos—the fence and thief-taker[1] Peachum and the Newgate jailer Lockit; Macheath's sweethearts Polly Peachum and Lucy

---

[1] A thief-taker could earn £40—a tremendous sum at the time—for "impeaching" a criminal (i.e., turning him in to the authorities for the reward). Peachum rules an outlaw gang with the threat of informing on them, which meant execution or transportation to Australia. He is amorality perfected, sociopathic to a fault.

Lockit; the Beggar "author" of the show itself and A Player, who together establish Gay's concept of a big thing (opera) for little people (beggars) in an
Introduction; and Macheath's gang and a suite of bordello ladies.

Peachum was modeled on a real-life fence and thief-taker, one Jonathan
Wild, who similarly ran a gang by intimidation, sent many a henchman to
the gallows, and was ultimately hanged himself after his Pecksniffian front
collapsed and his true nature became a national scandal.

But author Gay was really using Peachum as an attack on Robert Walpole,
at the time the most powerful politician in England as Prime Minister. An
able statesman who nevertheless ran the government on a buy-and-sell basis
from almost his first days in power, Walpole tells us that the famous line that
"power corrupts" is inaccurate. Rather, power attracts the already corrupt.

Ironically, Walpole did not take bribes: he offered them. Still, he ran the
state as a disorderly house, and this is how Peachum runs his crime family:

PEACHUM: Why, Polly, the Captain [Macheath] knows, that as 'tis his
Employment to rob, so 'tis ours to take [i.e., denounce for the reward]
Robbers; every Man in his Business.

Thus, even though his daughter has married Macheath, Peachum turns him
in, because all the world is lawless scum. At the end, Macheath is facing the
hangman, but the Beggar is talked out of so dire a conclusion, as operas—
meaning those aristocratic Italian things that Handel was putting on, to the
delight of the rank and fashion of London—always ended happily. "In this
kind of Drama," the Beggar now agrees, "'tis no matter how absurdly things
are brought about," and the Player explains that they must "comply with the
Taste of the Town."

But who is the work's protagonist, the character whose ego needs drive the
action? It is not Macheath, though he is the designated alpha male, charisma
bait for idols from Laurence Olivier to Roger Daltrey. Macheath is love and
laughter: the merry ease of his first solo, "My Heart Was So Free [it roamed
like the bee]," and his almost immediately ensuing duet with Polly, "Were
I Laid On Greenland's Coast," are irresistibly seductive. In three words: it's his
story. Yet he never quite accomplishes anything.

His two lady loves, Polly and Lucy, are more industrious, quarreling over
him like kids sharing a cookie. Still, it is Peachum who runs the story, incidentally seasoning the continuity with observations about politics, gender,
human nature:

PEACHUM: Gamesters [i.e., gamblers] and Highwaymen are generally very
good to their whores, but they are very Devils to their wives.

So it may be Macheath's story: but it's Peachum's play.

As I've said, the music—sixty-eight separate numbers in the script—is not
original, for Gay pasted his lyrics onto pre-existing folk and popular tunes
that were known as "ballads," thus making Gay's work a **ballad opera**. Of
course, Gay hired an arranger, Johann Christoph Pepusch, to create an overture and score the numbers (for, apparently, strings and oboe). But Gay found
the music itself in collections of the songs sold by street vendors known as
"singing men," who would stroll through a town performing and selling the
latest hit tune.

These songs were printed on broadsheets (usually just the lyrics, though
some sheets offered a G-clef staff of the melody as well), and Gay first thought
to produce *The Beggar's Opera* without an orchestra, letting his actors put
over their numbers exactly as if they were "singing men"—a naturalistic
touch, as Gay's characters are street people in essence. But Gay then saw an
angle in setting up a fake opera with a demure little band, thus ridiculing the
grandiose Handelian works.

And *The Beggar's Opera*'s score is a marvel, rich in variety and absolutely
true to its characters. If one didn't know better, one would assume that the
songs were conceived specifically for this work, just like those for *Bitter
Sweet*, *Lock Up Your Daughters*, *Matilda*: telling us how the characters feel
about life and their place on it.

Thus, Peachum, in 6/8 time marked *Allegro vivace*, ticks off the many
hazards man is heir to in "A Fox May Steal Your Hens, Sir," from "Your wife
may steal your rest, sir" to "A thief your goods and plate." And what of the
worst of all, the lawyer? "He steals your whole estate."

There speaks the merry criminal in his dashing meter, cunning rhymes,
blithe hypocrisy. Gay has fixed him for us; we know him. For extra fun, Gay
delighted in turning naive ditties already known to the public into worldly
ironies, as if drawing even the audience into his web of criminals. Thus, the
show's second vocal, given to Filch, Peachum's assistant in the stolen-goods
shop, was originally "The Bonny Grey-Ey'd Morn," by one Jeremiah Clarke:

> The hearty hind starts from his lazy sleep,
> To follow faithful labours of the day.

In its sweet, high-rising strain, it paints a pedagogical scene, the kind of hymn schoolchildren sing at the start of assembly. But here's Gay's version of the same two lines, in "'Tis Woman That Seduces All Mankind":

> Her very eyes can cheat when most she is kind,
> She tricks us of our money with our hearts.

The Beggar's Opera opened on January 29, 1728, at the Theatre Royal in Lincoln's Inn Fields (which was actually one block south of the park, in Portugal Street, where The Royal College of Surgeons now stands). This was one of London's two "patent" companies, the only ones allowed by law to present spoken drama. The two troupes, founded under Charles II, one in service to His Majesty and the other to his brother, played in various venues till they settled in at Covent Garden and Drury Lane, respectively. In fact, it was the flash success of *The Beggar's Opera* that allowed the Lincoln's Inn manager, John Rich, to build Covent Garden in the first place, the first of several structures at the site.

Rich was a Character. His father, Christopher Rich (who had built the Lincoln's Inn theatre), was exploitative, underpaying his people and threatening them with lawsuits when they rebelled. The junior Rich, acceding to the power at twenty-two when his father died, wasn't rough with his employees, but he was so uneducated that he maintained a calendar of malapropisms that were the delight of theatregoing London, such as demanding a costumer top an actress' head with a "turbot." He got everyone's name wrong, too, not just Millwand and Bradbury but even Smith and West.

But Rich knew theatre. Drury Lane turned *The Beggar's Opera* down, but over at Lincoln's Inn Rich grabbed it, and "It made Gay rich"—to quote another of the most famous remarks in British theatre history—"and it made Rich gay": because everyone who mattered in London went to it, talked of it, played and sang the score. Even Robert Walpole enjoyed it, till someone told him he was in it.

A success like this one provokes imitations, and ballad opera became the genre of the day, with *The Quaker's Opera* (1728) here and *The Village Opera* (1729) there. We should single out Allan Ramsay's very Scots ballad opera *The Gentle Shepherd*, concerning two loving couples and a woman who everyone assumes is a witch, helping the romances along. *The Gentle Shepherd* actually beat *The Beggar's Opera* to the starting gate, as it was published first (in 1725). But it got to the stage *after* Gay's piece (in 1729). According to the eighteenth-century Scots antiquarian George Chalmers, *The Gentle Shepherd* began as separate poems (not plays, precisely), *Patie and Roger* and then *Jenny and Meggy*. "Nothing now remained," Chalmers explains, "but to adopt the intimations which he received from his friends, and to throw his two pastorals [together] into . . . dramatic form, with appropriate songs."

Even if we count *The Gentle Shepherd* as the real First British Musical, it could not rival *The Beggar's Opera*, not least because of Ramsay's dialogue, as murky as the midnight moor:

> ROGER: Tempests may cease to jaw the rowan flood,
> Corbies and tods to grein for lambkins' blood . . .

One can scarcely imagine Londoners relishing this as they did Gay's rowdy miscreants. *The Gentle Shepherd* is a footnote, while *The Beggar's Opera* keeps coming back in increasingly daring musical arrangements. We'll get to the famous 1920 revival at the Lyric Theatre, Hammersmith, in due course. And note that this production, which ran at first for three years, inspired Kurt Weill and Bertolt Brecht to remodel Gay's Newgate pastoral as *Die Dreigroschenoper* (The Threepenny Opera, 1928).

Meanwhile, something odd occurred in the development of ballad opera: the form acquired composers. By the mid-1700s (possibly because there had been such a flood of these pieces that all the good broadsheet melodies had become overused), shows were offering completely new songs. William Shield's *Rosina* (1782) is an example, although the music bore the byline "composed and selected" by Shield (to the words of Frances Brooke), suggesting that at least some of its tunes were borrowed, in the *Beggar's Opera* manner.

Yet the music doesn't sound like ditties hawked in the street; they range too widely for any but legit voices. A look at the romantic lives of country people, *Rosina* wants sopranos and tenors who can handle coloratura—and, lo, Shield's scoring has survived, so it can sound today just as it did in 1782.

It isn't interesting scoring, unfortunately, except in two spots in the overture and in the solo "By Dawn To the Downs We Repair." It's a key piece, for the show's two tenor leads are brothers, one sweet and one a cad, and both love Rosina. But it's the cad who gets the best number, this one. It's supposed to be a song in praise of hunting, but it has a warlike air. "Hark! the volley resounds to the skies!" he sings, fortissimo. "Whilst Echo in thunder replies!" Ha, but then, to thrill the listener, Shield actually gives us that echo, first on horn, then clarinet, and at last the tympani, capping this with a lavish run for the tenor and a fiery cascade up to a ringing high B Flat on "In thunder replies!" He's the bad guy, yet he's exciting; we wish Rosina could go with him instead.

Something else is new here: despite having spoken dialogue, *Rosina* was billed as a **comic opera**—the new term for the early musicals, whether comic or just sentimental. But the taxonomy is vexed, because managers would describe their productions as whatever they thought the public was in the mood for this month.

There were legal considerations as well. The **burletta** was an artificial construct, a "genre" existing only to allow the minor theatres to play, as long as they didn't usurp the patent houses' exclusive right to spoken drama. Add a minimum of five songs to any script, or even merely underscoring, and any playhouse could operate without harassment. (At that, the Theatres Act of 1843 ended the monopoly held by Covent Garden and Drury Lane, though the Lord Chamberlain's office censored the content of all theatrical activity.)

Burletta was anything with music, but **extravaganza** was more precisely derived, as a fantastical show with elaborate scenery and technical effects, dialogue in rhymed couplets, and references to the names and topics of the day. So Cinderella goes to the ball outfitted by a popular Bond Street jeweler.

The presiding genius of extravaganza was James Robinson Planché, a modestly erudite fellow who, though forgotten today, is almost as crucial in the evolution of the British musical as John Gay or even W. S. Gilbert. The son of Huguenot refugees from France, Planché pronounced his surname in the French manner as Plahn–shay. But everybody called him Plank.

Theatre historian Gerald Frow rated him as "the founding father of Victorian extravaganza and burlesque," but Planché was as well the missing link between ballad opera and musical comedy. True, as a lyricist Planché, like so many others, used pre-existing tunes, not only popular airs but also Rossini and Bellini. *Beauty and the Beast* (1841) even borrowed "Oh, Susanna":

> Oh, my Beauty, don't you cry for me,
> I'm going to California to dig gold upon my knee!

Planché loved too-cute-to-fail fairy stories, such as *The Fair One With the Golden Locks* (1843), because then he didn't have to invent a plot and could concentrate on jazzing up the details. Thus, one of the most immortal characters in Gilbert and Sullivan, *The Mikado*'s Pooh-Bah, is really an expansion of Lord Factotum in Planché's *The Sleeping Beauty In the Wood* (1840). Pooh-Bah is pompously corrupt, monopolizing all the chief public offices, from First Lord Of the Treasury to Attorney-General. But consider Planché's original, here complaining in spoken rhymed couplets:

LORD FACTOTUM: As Lord High Chamberlain, I slumber never,
As Lord High Steward, in a stew I'm ever,
As Lord High Constable, I watch all day,
As Lord High Treasurer, I've the deuce to pay . . .

There's more of that, leading up to a brief song using Thomas Arne's setting of Shakespeare's "Where the Bee Sucks" as "Who Would Be a Great Grand Lord High [all the blame on him must lie]."

Planché worked in most of the available theatrical forms, because theatres and theatregoers alike did not discriminate among genres. If it played on a stage, it was theatre. Thus, the modest *Rosina* was premiered at Covent Garden—but so was Carl Maria von Weber's gargantuan *Oberon* (1826), billed as "a grand romantic and fairy opera." But it was composed with dialogue between the numbers, making it an extravaganza. So we should pause here, not least to save its librettist-lyricist from the universal scorn his work on *Oberon* has earned him.

Everyone agrees that *Oberon*'s music is superb, second only to the composer's *Der Freischütz* and, if I alone say so, much more varied and brilliant. *Der Freischütz*, with its haunted evocations of the German forester's life, its traditions and pieties and midnight madness, is a key Romantic work. But *Oberon* is not only grandiose but flighty and mischievous, drawn from Christoph Martin Wieland's epic poem of medieval love and war. The then available English translation, by William Sotheby, is not easy reading; that tells us how careful Weber's *Oberon* collaborator had to have been—and it's our old friend James Robinson Planché.

In his memoirs Planché reveals how tyrannical the spectators were at any big musical number. "A dramatic situation . . . was . . . inevitably received with cries of 'Cut it short!' from the gallery and obstinate coughing and other signs of impatience from the pit."

They wanted lots of plot and plenty of it—but only in the spoken script, which in *Oberon*'s case was not extravaganza's usual puns and capers but straightforward speech from the mortals and verse for Oberon, the fairy king who puts the sweetheart couple, Huon and Reiza,[2] through a test of fidelity.

The action moves from (as the handbill promised) "Oberon's bower with the vision" to "Grand banquetting chamber of Haroun" to "Perforated cavern on the beach with the ocean—in a storm—a calm-by-sunset-twilight-starlight-and-moonlight," and others such. Obviously, Covent Garden was emphasizing extravaganza's spectacular side, easy to do as Planché's crazy narrative does a lot of mapping around. Critics excoriate him for it, but that's what the London public wanted. Extravaganza is supposed to be extravagant, and *Oberon* is filled with radical characters—the fairies so willful, the villains so heinous, the First Couple so gallant. Reiza's majestic recitative-and-aria, "Ocean! thou mighty monster," with a vocal span of two octaves and change, is one reason why everyone thinks of *Oberon* as an opera.

Planché's era is the first to feature performers of some historical note. We know next to nothing about the actors who opened *The Beggar's Opera*, save that the Polly, Lavinia Fenton, won the town's heart and that of a duke. But *Oberon*'s leads, Mary Ann Paton and John Braham, claim articles in all the singers' dictionaries, and Planché's career was bound up in that of the so-billed Madame Vestris, an actor-manager with a valid mezzo-soprano. (She created the role of *Oberon*'s Second Couple woman, Reiza's servant, Fatima.)

And this brings us to the format most dependent on performing talent, **pantomime**. It is also the one genre of the Old Days that is still in operation—but pantomime then was not at all like pantomime now. For one thing, the panto lasted only an hour (sharing the bill with other titles, from Shakespeare to genteel playlets), did not feature an adaptation of a famous fairy tale, and included genuine mime and a lot of outrageous physical comedy involving red-hot pokers, strings of sausage, and various noisy props. Most important, pantomime remained close to its origins in Italian *commedia dell'arte*, centered on devious Harlequin, his sweetheart Columbine, and foolish old Pantaloon. But Harlequin was the star, as shown by his presence in so many titles: *Harlequin William Tell*, *Harlequin and Good Kynge Arthur*, *Harlequin and Guy Fawkes*, and not forgetting *Harlequin and Poonoowingkeewongflibee deeflibeedeebuskebang, King Of the Cannibal Islands*.

---

[2] She's always called Rezia now, as it's easier to pronounce and hear.

John Rich—the manager who put on *The Beggar's Opera*, we recall—was an actor as well and apparently a matchless Harlequin, playing entirely mute in the traditional *commedia* white and bearing his magic bat, invaluable in getting into and out of trouble. The bat made a loud crack when he smacked it—a signal to the stagehands below the deck to run the trap and bring up a new character. The Harlequinade part of panto ran at a furious tempo, as Harlequin leaped into the face of a clock and vanished while a child, in his costume, scampered out as Harlequin Jr. Or as the Demon King whirled around, casting his spells while the rest of the cast ran madly about. Or as a false façade was flipped to change a castle into a sorcerer's garden in seconds.

Incongruity was pantomime's style. Historian A. E. Wilson summons up the picture of "the Demon King who, after consigning the Principal Girl to the dungeon . . . sang with great feeling and tenderness 'When the Angelus Is Ringing.'"

Charles Dickens lovingly mocked this haphazard sort of play-making in *Nicholas Nickleby*, when the hero is recruited into Vincent Crummles' theatrical troupe (not a pantomime outfit, albeit) and, contributing a new script, is told to "introduce a real pump and two washing-tubs" into the action, as Crummles "bought 'em cheap . . . and they'll come in admirably." Then, too, the pony that draws Crummles' carriage has acting in his blood: his mother "ate apple-pie at a circus . . . fired pistols, and went to bed in a nightcap; and, in short, took the low comedy entirely."

In time, characters familiar to today's theatregoers joined the pantomime world—the Principal Boy (a young woman in tights), the Widow Twankey (the hero's mother, a man in drag); the "skin" part (a man in an animal get-up). In the late Victorian era, Augustus Harris' spectacle-pantomimes at Drury Lane dropped the Harlequinade to concentrate on storybook narratives, making a key feature of the Procession, a stately parade of a horde of extras in elaborate costumes.

But Harris was really using pantomime to revise extravaganza, losing panto's essential quality: chaos. Songs give definition to drama, but panto's "drama" was indefinable. And as for the thing we are most concerned about, the quality of the scores, panto's attitude was "Any old thing will do," with the notable exception of the deathless march "Heart Of Oak [are our ships, jolly tars are our men]," freshly written for *Harlequin's Invasion* (1760), at Drury Lane, with words by the famed actor David Garrick and music by the very distinguished William Boyce, one of the progenitors of the modern symphony. Wonderful. But this is unusual, not typical.

The last of these old forms, **burlesque**, is at least easy to define: a spoof of mythology or a literary or dramatic work, all in a lightly risqué air and a narrative structure "soft" enough to accommodate whatever song, dance, or comic event seemed likely to go over. Extremely popular though it was, burlesque was essentially a man's entertainment, too loutish for ladies. In Mike Leigh's film *Topsy-Turvy*, we find W. S. Gilbert finessing a tenor putting on airs during a costume fitting for *The Mikado* with "This is not grand opera in Milan. This is merely low burlesque in a small theatre on the banks of the River Thames."

In fact, Gilbert used almost exactly those words in addressing a soprano rehearsing *HMS Pinafore*—but the point is that Gilbert was deliberately misusing "burlesque" in typical self-deprecating fashion. (And his "small theatre"— the Savoy—was perhaps the most elegant in London.) *The Mikado* is not in the remotest way a burlesque, but before teaming up with Sullivan, Gilbert did write them, because burlesques were the most common form of musical. Opera was Gilbert's favorite target, as with his *Dulcamara; or, The Little Duck and the Great Quack* (1866), a send-up of Donizetti's *L'Elisir D'Amore*, and Gilbert gave even the magisterial *Norma* the treatment, as *The Pretty Druidess; or, The Mother, the Maid and the Mistletoe Bough* (1869). Unfortunately, burlesque, like so many of the works we've looked at so far, applied new lyrics to old tunes, and only when an author was musically inclined could these pick-up scores work. *The Beggar's Opera*, *Rosina*, and *Oberon* are still with us today, but every burlesque was expected to play out its season and vanish forever.

Gilbert was not musically inclined. He claimed he could distinguish only two melodies. "One," he explained, "is 'God Save the Queen' and the other isn't." But when he started writing original one-acts (six in all) for the outfit of actor-manager Thomas German Reed, they used mostly new music (by German Reed himself). And we note with pleasure that the first of these, *No Cards* (1869), was billed as a "musical comedietta," the closest term yet to the genre we're tracking in this book.

Both German Reed and his wife, Priscilla Horton Reed, were in the cast of *No Cards*, performed at German Reed's Royal Gallery Of Illustration (a "moral" title, to euphemize the very notion of theatre, so hedonistic and impious). Priscilla played Mrs. Pennythorne, a young heiress' starchy aunt— and let's admire Gilbert's slyly tilted nomenclature: the aunt's aggressive control of her niece's fortune will prick the guileful fortune-hunter. She really is a pennythorn, at least to a cad. And he would be Thomas' character, Ellis Dee.[3] Luckily, the niece has another suitor, Mr. Churchmouse, younger and nicer than the villainous Dee.

With Sullivan, Gilbert would create a few characters who stand out for philosophizing in a way no one would do in burlesque—*The Yeomen Of the Guard*'s Colonel Fairfax and that medieval policy wonk Princess Ida. But Gilbert really prefers his silly people. Thus, in *No Cards*, both Ellis Dee and Mr. Churchmouse show up disguised as the aunt's long-lost husband. Mr. Churchmouse—and, remember, he's the one we're rooting for—"recalls" details about those nuptials of thirty years before:

CHURCHMOUSE: At St. James' church, Piccadilly—
MRS. PENNYTHORNE: St. George's, Hanover Square.
CHURCHMOUSE: True . . . One lovely July day—
MRS. PENNYTHORNE: January.
CHURCHMOUSE: True, January. It's the same thing.

Now there comes a hiccup of history: on the bill with *No Cards* was *Cox and Box*, three years old by then, a three-character musical farce by F. C. Burnand, based on John Maddison Morton's play *Box and Cox*, with music composed by . . . Arthur Sullivan!

It's destiny, of course—except Gilbert and Sullivan probably didn't meet on this occasion. Anyway, we want to learn how *Cox and Box*'s music sounded, and it suggests the work of a classical composer who tosses off this fribble knowing that he was meant for opera and symphony, yet not condescending to the humble form *in the slightest*. Mr. Cox and Mr. Box unknowingly rent the same room (one works by night, the other by day) but as coincidences pile up, they discover they have much in common. In fact, they're long-lost brothers:

BOX: Have you such a thing as a strawberry mark on your left arm?
COX: No!
BOX: Then it is he!
(They rush into each other's arms.)

---

[3] Note Gilbert's pun on the now bygone Brititsh monetary system of £/s/d for "livre" (the pound), "sol" or "sou" (the shilling), and "denier" (the penny). The French terms, corruptions of Latin originals, came over in the Norman Conquest and the abbreviations were never anglicized.

And Sullivan really gets into the spirit of the thing with genuinely comical music. His admirers scorned his involvement in light entertainment partly because it brought out one of his quirks, unsuitable for a Great Man: he liked almost all his characters, even *The Mikado*'s bloodthirsty Katisha and the maniacal ghost in *Ruddigore*. Only *Patience*'s phony poet Bunthorne seems to have irritated Sullivan, and you hear it in the music.

You hear Sullivan's quirkiness in *Cox and Box*, especially in helpings of recitative, fortissimo chords, and bit of vocal decoration. It's black-market opera. And a duet for the title pair, "The Buttercup," is choice Victorian parlor ballad—because "ballad" had once again evolved in meaning. The day of the broadsheets was over; ballads were now the semi-classical items featured at the home musicale, sometimes sweet and sometimes dramatic but decorous above all.

In fact, "The Buttercup" slipped out of *Cox and Box* to become a popular title on its own (with new words by Margaret A. Sinclair), "The Dicky Bird and the Owl," as the latter bemoans the ceaseless trilling of the former:

> He sings by night, he sings by day,
> Can no one persuade him to stay away?
> He sings his notes from A to Z,
> And an opera star he will be . . .

But note that this music had to be pulled out of *Cox and Box* and be re-lyricked to become widely known—a testament to how well its original setting suited *Cox and Box*. In other words: look how "integrated" Sullivan's first musicals were. That German Reed double bill of *No Cards* and *Cox and Box* brings us out of the helter-skelter of pantomime, burlesque, and extravaganza into the artistically more sophisticated world of character-consistent music theatre. Thus we see both Gilbert and Sullivan separately moving into the modern musical—and taking the British theatre along with them.

So all we need is for something to bring the two together, and it was a burlesque stock company that did it. Gilbert can't have rejoiced in the commission, for he was now directing his shows (as the "stage manager," in the argot of the time), and directing a burlesque troupe is like herding aardvarks. And Sullivan would have known that musicality was the least of a burlesque performer's abilities.

The piece, called *Thespis*, told of an acting company taking over for the gods on Mt. Olympus. It ran for a bit but made no great impression, and the authors parted on good terms. Then something else brought them together: a manager's vision of how British music theatre might establish itself with works of imagination, wit, and style. This man saw in Gilbert and Sullivan the team to realize that vision.

And now it begins.

2

Gilbert and Sullivan

Our Loving Frivolity

The manager who created the concept of "Gilbert and Sullivan" (hereafter G & S) was Richard D'Oyly Carte,[1] who was presenting Offenbach's *La Périchole* at the Royalty Theatre in Dean Street in 1875. Though Paris had already seen Offenbach's expansion of the show from two into a richer three acts, Carte was staging the shorter original. But London audiences liked long evenings, especially triple bills, so the farce *Cryptoconchoidsyphonostomata; or, While It's To Be Had,* opened the program and, following the Offenbach, something else was needed to close it. Carte commissioned *Trial By Jury*, G & S's only one-act and a miniature opera, through-sung from start to finish.

This led to the famous series of shows, now all with spoken dialogue, that changed the course of the Anglophone musical—but Carte had tasked himself weightily, as he now faced years of the most delicate diplomacy, keeping the act together when Gilbert got too prickly or Sullivan felt unappreciated. Further, Carte recruited G & S performers into the D'Oyly Carte Opera Company, to tour internationally in the G & S canon for over one hundred years. It became a family business, managed after Carte by his son Rupert and then by Rupert's daughter Bridget before disbanding in 1982, albeit with sporadic initiatives thereafter.

The most immediate effect of Carte's G & S program combined the appeal of superb craftsmanship with that of fresh material, replacing the derivative nature of extravaganza and burlesque. True, Gilbert often drew on short pieces previously published, especially his *Bab Ballads* (after his childhood nickname). In fact, much of *Trial By Jury's* libretto had already appeared in *Fun* magazine, verbatim. But the music was original.

This is a vital point, as the works of Jacques Offenbach, first staged in England in 1857, became so popular that, from 1868 to 1870, French companies led by

---

[1] Though he was generally known thus, Carte alone was his surname. D'Oyly was a family name from a French ancestor.

Offenbach's pet star Hortense Schneider gave London seasons of *La Grande-Duchesse de Gérolstein*, *La Belle Hélène*, *Orphée aux Enfers*, and *Barbe-Bleue*, often with José Dupuis, her regular partner in Paris. These opéras bouffes ("musical farces") set forth as the musical's first virtue a bespoke score, tailored to fit each story and its unique characters. Similarly, in G & S, the audience was not put through the zillionth repetition of the march from Handel's *Rinaldo* (known as "Let Us Take the Road" in *The Beggar's Opera*) that had turned up in everything ever since. No Planché title was complete without it.

G & S were well aware of what Offenbach was achieving. Gilbert actually put into English the libretto of Offenbach's *Les Brigands*, and Sullivan, a constant visitor in Paris, had access to the bouffes in their own domain. So some of Offenbach's style was absorbed in G & S.

For one thing, they took over Offenbach's extended act finale, in which plot and music interact intensely. It had been a staple of music theatre since Mozart's day, but not common in British "light opera"—yet another term that seeks to define but only creates confusion.

Then, too, G & S adopted Offenbach's lead comic, usually an older male more actor than singer. This became the "patter" role in G & S—Ko-Ko, for example, in *The Mikado*. Further, Sullivan utilized an Offenbach specialty in the ritornello that opens and closes a song (and separates the verses) but is never vocalized. The fluttery intro to *The Mikado*'s "Three Little Maids From School" is a famous instance; one couldn't imagine the music without it, as it establishes that air of guiltless merriment intrinsic to musical comedy.

Sullivan was so quick to make this usage his own that it turns up in his second musical, *The Contrabandista* (1867), in "From Rock To Rock." The entrance number of the lead comic, a Mr. Grigg, this bizarre little piece is all fuddled up with fears and regrets. *Cox and Box*'s F. C. Burnand wrote the words here as well, and his Mr. Grigg longs to return home "with my spouse, and my cows, and my li–i–tle pigs, and rear my lot of Li–i–tle Griggs," capping his hysteria with loony "Ha-ha-ha"s. It's a wild number, and Sullivan knew it needed wild music. So when his ritornello bounds in like something out of Offenbach's shows, it roots *The Contrabandista* in what Offenbach himself called "le genre primitif et gai": the musical so elemental in its joy it feels like Eden before the discovery of sin.

But Offenbach is more than carefree: Offenbach is zany, something G & S never quite got to. Among countless examples we might adduce the Bolero from Offenbach's *Le Pont Des Soupirs* (The Bridge Of Sighs), in which a mock-love duet explodes in a rhythmic rave-up of rabid coloratura and percussive effects from hiding courtiers that sounds like a mad cuckoo clock.

There is nothing like that in G & S, which is never more than impish. In their *Ruddigore*, the formerly deranged Mad Margaret and Sir Despard the wicked baronet turn up in the second act as stately, black-clad Methodists (known at the time for a puritanical worldview). Yet Margaret backslides. Like an S & M couple with a "safe word" to tame the sex when it gets edgy, this pair has a cure when Margaret starts wilding up again. "Basingstoke!" he cries, and she subsides with "Basingstoke it is!"

Comparably, all of G & S is Basingstoked, preferring simple drollery to Offenbach's gai primitif. Now let's consult a chart of the G & S output, to get our bearings:

I. THE LOST TITLE
Thespis; or, The Gods Grown Old (1871)
This aforementioned piece, partway between burlesque and extravaganza, survives only in its script, one song, a chorus later used in *The Pirates Of Penzance*, and some ballet music.

II. THE ACTIVE CANON
Trial By Jury (1875)
Also aforementioned, the one-act opera, on a woman's suit for breach of promise. D'Oyly Carte used it (and Sullivan and Burnand's *Cox and Box*) as curtain-raisers for the shorter full-length works.

The Sorcerer (1877)
Centering on a love potion and typical of Gilbert's fanciful side, which vexed Sullivan, who longed for more naturalistic stories with an emotional core.

HMS Pinafore; or, The Lass That Loved a Sailor (1878)
Romance is the plot driver, but class is the content, as the lass' father is the sailor's captain, and the First Lord Of the Admiralty got his position through politics. Patriotic but scathing.

The Pirates Of Penzance; or, The Slave Of Duty (1879)
The entire show is based on one of Gilbert's characteristic paradoxes: an apprentice pirate is free of his obligations on his twenty-first birthday, but he was born in a leap year on February 29, and thus won't be on his own till 1940. "It seems so long," his sweetheart sighs.

Patience; or, Bunthorne's Bride (1881)

Rival poets outdo each other in preciousness. During the run, Carte opened the Savoy Theatre and moved *Patience* out of that fire trap the "Opera Comique", a short distance across the Strand. These are now "Savoy operas" and those who perform, write about, or love them are "Savoyards."

Iolanthe; or, The Peer and the Peri (1882)

A culture war that turns political, between Fairies (i.e., nonconformists) and the House of Lords (the ruling class).

Princess Ida; or, Castle Adamant (1884)

Spoofing feminism. A reworking of Gilbert's burlesque *The Princess* (itself spoofing Tennyson), with new lyrics but retaining the old script's blank verse. With *The Sorcerer* the least popular of the canon.

The Mikado; or, The Town Of Titipu (1885)

A "Japanese" England, with a plot so complex that much of it has occurred before the curtain goes up, a strange failure of dramaturgy necessitating expository songs that are difficult to follow. It's still the biggest smash till *Oliver!*.

Ruddigore; or, The Witch's Curse (1887)

A spoof of fantasy melodrama, and so poorly received that Carte dropped it from the company repertory till 1920.

The Yeomen Of the Guard; or, The Merryman and His Maid (1888)

At last, something for Sullivan: a naturalistic and even rather arty work, avoiding Gilbert's characteristic absurdities. The time is the sixteenth century, the place is the Tower Of London, and the action is haunted by the headsman. Solemn and operatic.

The Gondoliers; or, The King Of Barataria (1889)

To Venice (and imaginary Barataria), yet the subject is, as so often, the English caste system. A huge success, the show marked a suspension of G & S when Gilbert got mad at Carte over the trio's financial responsibilities and Sullivan sided with Carte.

III. THE SELDOM PERFORMED FINAL PAIR

Utopia Limited; or, The Flowers Of Progress (1893)

A tropical island apes British ways. One-third of the score is wonderful, but a second third is no more than acceptable and the last third is poor.

The Grand Duke; or, The Statutory Duel (1896)

Ruritanian espionage. A bore, and the end of the partnership.

Trial By Jury isn't just an opera, but an opera spoof, so, at the action's climax, Sullivan builds "A Nice Dilemma We Have Here" into an ensemble in the style of Bellini; numerous writers have compared it to *La Sonnambula*'s "D'un pensiero e d'un accento" (By thought and word).[2] This sly use of pastiche is endemic to G & S. Every score has at least one number from Somewhere Else, be it a "fa la la" madrigal or a bit of Handelian Baroque—"in" jokes that Sullivan delighted in. Comparably, he punctuated *Trial*'s opening music with *les trois coups* (the "three blows" that traditionally signaled the rise of the curtain in French theatre) on the tympani.

Gilbert's jokes as such lay in his stage business, perpetuated by the D'Oyly Carte company into the modern era. On a personal note: the D'Oyly bill of *Trial By Jury* and *HMS Pinafore* was one of my first theatre visits as a lad, when the troupe encamped in the Shubert Theatre in New York in 1955 for its longest local visit ever, lasting seven weeks. It was a repertory-intensive postwar reacquaintance; they even brought *Princess Ida*. And I vividly recall how, in *Trial*, when the chorus of bridesmaids entered, the appreciative judge gave a note to the Usher to pass to the First Bridesmaid. She read it, smiled, and parked it in her bodice. But then, when the Plaintiff entered, the newly besmitten Judge got the Usher to retrieve the note from the First Bridesmaid and give it to the Plaintiff. Who read it, smiled, and parked it in her bodice, to the First Bridesmaid's fury.

This is Gilbert in effect directing from the grave, as also in the bored judge at one point reading a newspaper and, near the end, receiving his set of golf clubs, eager to ditch the court and obtain recreation. Gilbert was not a coach of actors; he expected his principals to know their business and only edited them when he felt their interpretations confounded his intentions. What Gilbert concentrated on were the overall stage pictures, the behavior of the

---

[2] Some have discerned instead a link to the Sextet from Donizetti's *Lucia Di Lammermoor*, but in structure and melody the *Trial* scene and the *Sextet* have nothing in common.

chorus, the placing of physical jests. Like many in England, he had a toy theatre, with which he would plan exactly how each scene would look from moment to moment—the physics of the show, so to say.

Savoyard commentators find *The Sorcerer*, G & S's full-length "comic opera," old-fashioned for its day, with its many recitatives and stock characters, from its Miles Gloriosus of a hero to its village grandees, stately on the surface but throbbing with secret passions underneath.

However, *The Sorcerer* is actually about something, and that is a somewhat new idea for light opera. Here is the military hero, Alexis of the Grenadier Guards, evangelizing on his theory that marriage must conquer the "artificial barriers of rank, wealth, education, age," and so on:

ALEXIS: I have preached in workhouses, beershops, and lunatic asylums, and I have been received with enthusiasm. I have addressed navvies [working-class men] on the advantages . . . if they married wealthy ladies of rank, and not a navvy dissented.

Impatient to see his program fulfilled, Alexis hires the sorcerer of the title to drug the entire village with a love potion. This creates social chaos and even causes Alexis' fiancée, Aline, helplessly to desert him for the local vicar. And then—of course!—Alexis turns against the whole exercise. He wants to do unto others, not be done to himself.

But the sorcerer himself is the key participant, with an establishing patter song, "My Name Is John Wellington Wells," that celebrates the most grisly requests (as in "If you'd melt a rich uncle in wax . . .") in sheer jollity. Is this a tradesman or a ghoul?

Yet the character really landed, and its originator, George Grossmith, went on to introduce almost all the G & S patter roles. In fact, G & S seemed to realize they had created their first great eccentric—the forerunner of such outstanding comics as Leslie Henson and Lupino Lane—and thus expanded his stage time in an 1884 revival.

Back in 1877, the second act opened in sunlight with the brand-new couples larking about the stage in celebrating Alexis' democratic project:

> Love is the source of all joy to humanity,
> Money, position, and rank are a vanity . . .

But the new second-act opening takes place earlier in the story, when the village is still comatose from the effect of the potion. It is midnight—a sorcerer's time—and Wells, bearing a lantern, leads Alexis and Aline in to inspect the sleeping town. But note that the magician has arranged for the local ruling class to be trundled home to bed "respectably." And in wording that has more meaning today than in their own time, Alexis commends Wells' "delicate appreciation"—so rare, he thinks, "in persons of your station."

The issue of social rank, running intermittently through the canon (even through the saga of the British musical altogether) is elemental in the next G & S title. "*The Sorcerer* was a popular comic opera," writes G & S critic Gayden Wren. But *Pinafore* "was a popular craze." Another Savoyard, Leslie Baily, tells us, "Music shops sold ten thousand copies of the piano score in one day."

HMS Pinafore does have flaws, at least in the central storyline, in which the captain's daughter loves a common sailor. It turns out that captain and sailor were switched as infants. So when they take their rightful—their socially appropriate—places in the Navy, the heroine will now marry a man old enough to be her father! Still we are in Gilbert's world of—as it was called— "topsy-turvydom." As with Lewis Carroll's Wonderland, you can start with the peculiar as long as your characters pursue its consequences logically. It isn't topsy-turvy to them, so it ceases to be for us. Unlike early extravaganza, the G & S shows are grounded: they have a confidence in their own silliness.

Consider, for example, *Pinafore*'s famous exchange between the Captain and his crew in his first number. He's "never, never sick at sea," he declares. His men question this: "What, never?" He responds with "No, never!" But they insist: "What, *never*?," and Sullivan lets a sly imitation of a raised eyebrow on the bassoon prod the Captain into surrender with "Hardly ever!" The bit became so familiar that writers toy with it yet today.

Even the two sweethearts get into this lovable twaddle, as when he bursts into a flowery speech about "antithetical elements," "the Cimmerian darkness of tangible despair," and "a living ganglion of irreconcilable antagonisms." At which she confides in us:

JOSEPHINE: (aside) His simple eloquence goes to my heart.

Pinafore is the matrix of all the rest of G & S, for instance, segregating the male and female choristers—as brutish dragoons vs. poetry devotees in *Patience*, or bridesmaids vs. rakehells in *Ruddigore*. In *Pinafore*, it's the sailors on one hand and the First Lord of the. Admiralty's "sisters and his cousins and his aunts" on the other, and Sullivan gets one of his trademark double-choruses out of the girls' entrance, playing their "Gaily Tripping" against the boys' "We Sail the Ocean Blue." Later, the two groups unite to support the love plot as the authors race to the resolution when—another G & S routine—most of principals pair off, in topsy-turvy marriage.

The Pirates Of Penzance innovated with fussy coloratura decoration in the heroine's waltz song, "Poor Wandering One," but otherwise affirmed *Pinafore*'s approach, even re-using the "What, never?" business (though this was dropped early on). But *Patience*, the canon's fourth full-length piece, is something different: a spoof of the "aesthetic" movement led by Algernon Swinburne, James McNeil Whistler, and others who popularized a love of the exotic. The rule was: if more than twenty people liked something, it had no value. Only the singular—such as one perfect lily in a vase of the most delicate blue *tinta*—could thrill the enlightened soul.

Few aspired to follow the new movement, but everybody talked about it, making *Patience* a Zeitgeist musical. It presented two rivals vying for the love of dairymaid (the title role), "a Fleshly Poet" and "an Idyllic Poet." The former, a certain Reginald Bunthorne, drives the plot—and, lo, George Grossmith's Bunthorne was clearly made up as Swinburne, with the original's monocle and little white splotch in the middle of his shaggy mop of dark hair. Moreover, Gilbert's bibliographer Townley Searle unearthed the draft of *Patience* that was sent to the Lord Chamberlain to allow the work for performance, and there Bunthorne's name is Algernon.

So it's Swinburne! Yet *Patience* is always thought of as the Oscar Wilde musical, especially as Bunthorne has a line about defying "the philistines" to attain high status "if you walk down Piccadilly with a poppy or a lily in your mediaeval hand." That strikes the Wildean note, surely.

But Wilde was a charmer and a wit of great dimension, while Bunthorne is as irritable as Henry Higgins and as selfish as Eva Perón. Consider: Ellen Terry played Lady Macbeth in a production spare and dark except for her Lady, painted by John Singer Sargent in a robe of billowing sleeves of blue and green such as to excite envy in a butterfly. Of it, Wilde remarked that this Lady "patronises local industries for her husband's clothes and the servants' liveries. But she [does] all her own shopping in Byzantium."

We hear no such cultured irony from Bunthorne; his "poetry" is excruciating. Surely a Wilde avatar would match the model's brilliance. But then three Dragoon officers don aesthetic costume and moosh around imitating Bunthorne, giving the story a gay twist: and of course Wilde was gay, virtually the founder of the line. And consider this tidbit, when Bunthorne threatens to curse his rival if he doesn't immediately get out of the aesthete business:

GROSVENOR: (throwing himself at Bunthorne's knees, and clinging to him)
   Oh, reflect, reflect! You had a mother once.
BUNTHORNE: Never!
GROSVENOR: Then you had an aunt!

The stage direction reads, "Bunthorne affected," but it is customary for D'Oyly Carte Bunthornes to go completely to pieces at this—and even in those days "aunt" had connotations. P. G. Wodehouse's Bertie Wooster, a no more than latent heterosexual if ever there was one, was virtually a professional nephew.

Patience ran about a year and a half, mostly in a theatre (Carte's new Savoy) half again as large as *Pinafore*'s Opera Comique. Of the canon, only *The Mikado*, three shows later, enjoyed a longer first run. But then, *Patience* was the first cultivated G & S show, complimenting the audience on its taste and breeding, for the musical as a form was in the process of reinventing itself as the property of the educated middle class.

Thus, the patter song of *Patience*'s Col. Calverley of the band of Dragoons is filled with the *nomyenklatura* of Britain, from Lord Nelson, historian Macauley, playwright Boucicault, novelists Fielding, Defoe, and Thackeray to a character in *David Copperfield* and Madame Tussaud, among many others. There are erudite references as well, so when Bunthorne auctions himself off in the first-act finale, the chorus women lead him onstage singing in terms to enchant a Classics master:

> Let the merry cymbals sound,
> Gaily pipe Pandaean pleasure,
> With a Daphnephoric bound . . .

"Pandaean" of course pertains to the god of the rural life, and the Daphnephoria was an ancient Greek procession centered around a comely youth, popularized some five years before *Patience* in Frederic Leighton's eponymous painting, a respectably fanciful canvas that the bien-pensants would have known of. As critic William Archer put it, Gilbert "restored the literary self-respect of the English stage."

With *Iolanthe*, Sullivan's genius bursts into Carte's "popular" genre. Thus, the overture—a rare one that Sullivan wrote himself rather than a medley by his music director—starts with an Andante of a brooding theme in the lower instruments answered by the high winds in a kind of woodland cry: Sullivan is ushering us into fairyland. The show's scoring is inventive all the way through, so when the hero, Strephon, enters with "Good Morrow," the music suggests the shrilling of a shepherd's pipe across the lambkins' meadow. Strephon's rivals for his shepherdess, in the House Of Peers, have their own sound, in "Loudly Let the Trumpet Bray!," as they stamp over the English terrain as if they owned the place.

Iolanthe is music with a geography; the fairies are light as air and the mortals unpleasantly substantial. So, in the first scene, when the Fairy Queen brings Iolanthe back from exile for having co-habited with a mortal, Gilbert's words are simple:

> FAIRY QUEEN: Rise! Rise, thou are pardon'd!
> IOLANTHE: Pardon'd!
> FAIRIES: *Pardon'd!*

but Sullivan responds ecstatically. He moves from the tonic to the dominant seventh and back—just that little. Yet the setting is so right and strong and tender that we fall in love with the entire work before half the cast has appeared.

Thus Sullivan pulled Gilbert out of burlesque and extravaganza into music theatre of emotional power. True, *The Mikado* seems almost entirely an airhead of a show. It even lacks a clear-cut protagonist, the figure who, by definition of the ancient Greek stage, drives the plot. G & S never give us a Phantom Of the Opera, a Matilda: showrunners in the purest sense. Take *Evita*: Che confides in us and Perón has political power, but once Eva gets to her tempestuous Wanting Song, "Buenos Aires," we're attracted to this immoral beast, because the one who needs is the one who owns the music.

Nevertheless, *The Mikado* is musically sophisticated, in large and small ways. Small: when the Mikado mentions "Bach, interwoven with Spohr and Beethoven" in "My Object All Sublime," Sullivan sneaks in a scampy quotation of the first twelve notes of the "Great" Fugue in g minor (BMV 542 in the Bach Works Catalogue). Large: Sullivan biographer Arthur Jacobs traced multiple uses of an ur-theme and its variations throughout *The Mikado*'s score. It's really two themes—the first bit of the "Miya Sama" march and the falling theme of the "Miya Sama" vocal.

Of course, *The Mikado* is the canon's masterpiece, and no doubt the audience taking its places for the next G & S premiere readied itself for yet another wonder show. And that's when they had their miserable flop.

Ruddygore, as it was originally (but briefly) spelled, was the second G & S spoof, this time of an old Victorian staple of the neighborhood playhouse, Gothic melodrama. This genre was called "transpontine," meaning "across the bridge" and thus on the opposite—that is, the south—side of the Thames, catering to a public that enjoyed the good old shows that the West End had largely retired.

It was Gilbert's idea to build the show around a family curse: each Baronet of Ruddigore must commit at least one crime a day or suffer an agonizing death. Robin, the current scion (the Grossmith part), hiding in plain sight, has let this grisly inheritance fall on his younger brother while Robin woos Rose Maybud. Unmasked, a Gilbertian paradox saves him: to refuse to commit crimes is suicide, but suicide *is* a crime. So the curse is lifted and everyone pairs off in Savoyard style.

This narrative left plenty of room for transpontine hanky-panky. Besides the curse and the traditional "bad baronet," a cross between a matinee idol and a cad in the Heathcliff manner, there was the haunted castle; Mad Margaret, crazed by a failed romance; the kidnaping of a young maiden (though in this case she's a tough old bird); the entrance of an especially spooky character through a trap door in the stage; and the Jolly Jack Tar, another traditional figure, beloved of melodrama writers because he came with a prefabricated vocabulary of nautical similes.

But why did G & S fail to please, right in the middle of this unprecedentedly successful series? The trouble started after the intermission, in the haunted castle, where Robin pursued a storyline that grew increasingly contrived. The portraits of his ancestors came to life to plague him, each in a completely different and elaborate outfit, from a bishop and a kilted Scot to an admiral and a Cavalier in ringlets and plumed headgear. It was the most sumptuous visual in all G & S, an hommage to the "processions" in Drury Lane pantomime, very much a part of the theatre scene at the time.

Still, the second act moved so slowly that the audience became restless and the gallery booed at the curtain. Hastily revised, *Ruddigore* lasted 288 performances, so it must have paid off. But Gilbert always referred to it as his one Savoy failure because of its disappointed reception.

By the time of *The Yeomen Of the Guard*, Sullivan's ambivalence about working in popular rather than classical forms was overwhelming him. He was England's great hope in the realm of serious music, and he needed Gilbert to give him a humanistic story, whereas Gilbert was happy only when inventing goofy monstrosities—for instance a "lozenge" plot, in which the ingestion of one causes social havoc, in the *Sorcerer* manner.

It's not terribly unlike what happens some seventy years later in *Salad Days* (wherein a magic piano makes people dance). But enough of these fantasies! Sullivan more or less cried. Let us have yearnings, rivalries, the peril of villainy and the safety of love. "I have lost the liking for writing comic opera," Sullivan wrote Gilbert. These were all "Gilbert's pieces, with music added by me."

The problem was that Sullivan was a romantic and Gilbert a satirist. Yet *The Yeomen Of the Guard* is the most romantic work in G & S, and the comedian's character even ends up sadly. The stage directions say he "falls insensible," but many Savoyards believe he dies of a broken heart.

Set on the greensward of the Tower Of London during the sixteenth century, *Yeomen* offers a wide variety of principals intersecting in very believable dances of love and death. Colonel Fairfax (the tenor) is to be beheaded for witchcraft on the denunciation of an evil cousin hoping for a legacy. To foil him, Fairfax decides to create an heir by marrying . . . well, anyone. For a sum. Blindfolded.

And that would be Elsie Maynard (the sweet soprano), half of a strolling-player couple, though her partner, Jack Point (the comedian, attired in the jester's motley), loves Elsie himself.

Yet another maid (the saucy mezzo) loves Fairfax, and the Tower's hideous "Head Jailer and Assistant Tormentor" (baritone) loves *her*, while the Tower's grim housekeeper (contralto) has designs on a Yeoman officer (bass). That much is simply a tumble of attractions—but the officer engineers a scheme to allow Fairfax to escape. It's not a cute and bumbly musical-comedy scheme: those involved will lose their lives if discovered.

The authors truly extended their art in this work. For instance, the first-act finale spends ten minutes on pageantry with the beefeaters, tales of heroics, and a flirty kissing game. Suddenly, on a single beat, Sullivan abandons C Major for c minor, the glowering of the lower strings, and the tolling of a bell: funeral music for the condemned man.

"The pris'ner comes to meet his doom," the chorus intones, backing away to leave room for the agents of execution. "The block, the headsman, and the tomb." Of course, *we* know that the condemned man—Fairfax—has escaped already; disguised, he has been singing merrily throughout the finale thus far. So of course his cell is empty and now the music turns panicky as all race off to find him. Gilbert's original blocking left only three on stage: Fairfax, Elsie (who has fainted in his arms), and—rhapsody dwindling into horror—the headsman, the icon of the story though he hasn't a single line.

Some of *Yeomen*'s score touches on the customary G & S points—the comedian's patter number ("Oh! A Private Buffoon Is a Light-Hearted Loon"), the glee quartet ("Strange Adventure!"), in which the orchestra plays the ritornello at the start and finish, letting the voices sing a capella in between. But much else is brand-new, first of all a Leitmotiv of princely splendor devoted to the Tower itself, heard at assembly points throughout the piece. The show's "hit tune," so to speak, Elsie and Jack's street entertainment "I Have a Song To Sing, O!," is sly antiquing, a sort of "Twelve Days Of Christmas" in a lovingly severe E Flat Major that veers back and forth between tonic and dominant over an E Flat pedal, in magnificent simplicity.

More: the overture, like that to *Iolanthe* Sullivan's own work, is a high-tech sonata-allegro movement incorporating six themes from the score (along with a few new ones) with extraordinary intersectionality. *The Yeomen Of the Guard* is so ingeniously musical that *The Gondoliers* (the last title in the canon) is a bit of a letdown, lacking *Yeomen*'s singular characters and other-worldly atmosphere.

And then came the famous "carpet" quarrel that provoked the aforementioned split among the three partners over who should pay for a new rug in the Savoy lobby. No one knew how to hold a grudge like Gilbert; when Sullivan invited him to the opening of his *Ivanhoe* (1891)—grand opera at last!—Gilbert declined ("insolently," Sullivan thought) to come.

G & S attempted a comeback with those last two unsatisfying titles, then separated conclusively to work with other partners on more comic opera. As well, G & S associates came into the light: Sullivan's music director Alfred Cellier composed *Dorothy* (1886), which outran *The Mikado* but is now so obscure that even aficionados couldn't identify its big ballad ("Queen Of My Heart") or its subject matter (it's almost the same tale as that of Friedrich von Flotow's *Martha*). Poor Cellier even agreed to set the lozenge (now a potion) plot with which Gilbert kept pestering Sullivan; it appeared as *The Mountebanks* (1892).

More prominent and even somewhat immortal was Edward German, who took over the composition of *The Emerald Isle* (1901) when Sullivan died, collaborating then with that work's librettist-lyricist, Basil Hood, on *Merrie England* (1902). Here's a work with an overtly Savoyard flavor, and it was introduced at the Savoy by G & S stylists, including Henry Lytton, who was to inherit the Grossmith roles for a generation.

Set in Elizabethan times near Windsor town and then in the nearby forest, *Merrie England* put Elizabeth I herself on stage, along with Robert Devereaux, Sir Walter Raleigh, and rather too many principals for the audience to care about, such as the local May Queen (she has no other name), who is extremely unpleasant.

But then, so is Elizabeth, anticipating the error of Benjamin Britten's coronation opera *Gloriana* (1953) in picturing the monarch as petty and vindictive. In a distasteful turn during *Merrie England*'s first-act finale, German's Elizabeth condemns to death at the stake a poor soul, Jill-All-Alone, whose only crime is to be different, the usual reason innocents were burned alive in bygone times.

Thus, when Sadler's Wells Opera revived *Merrie England*, in 1960, it had to revise the book. Hood's lyrics, at least, are clever enough, as in a song for Walter Wilkins, a Shakespearean actor (and note the slithery Gilbertian enjambment):

> As a patriotic Briton I have ponder'd on and written
> A jolly sailor song about the sea,
> With a hornpipe (tho' perchance one
> Be incongruous), I dance one,
> Whatever kind of character I be.

It is the music that has kept *Merrie England* alive. German's other well-known title, *Tom Jones* (1907), after Fielding's novel, is comparably appealing in its score, now in the post–G & S Edwardian style, and it benefited from the casting of a matinee idol, Hayden Coffin, as young Tom.

Still, German's works don't age as . . . well, youthfully . . . as G & S. Writing in *Opera* magazine of the Sadler's Wells *Merrie England*, William Mann likened it to "a decrepit, terribly old-fashioned shop assistant who ought to retire [but who] pleases a lot of the customers. . . . And with a whiskey or two, and a new suit, he shows up quite well at the Christmas party."

3

Toy Town

The Edwardian Musical

We've had ballad opera, pantomime, burlesque, and comic opera, but now at last we get **musical comedy**. The man who invented it was George Edwardes, famed as the manager of the Gaiety Theatre, so the dawn of musical comedy became known as the Gaiety Era, roughly the 1890s to about 1915.

Breaking away from the school developed by Richard D'Oyly Carte under professors Gilbert and Sullivan, Edwardes set forth a new model: carefree fun in modern-dress settings with life-affirming songs of quaint delight rather than strictly story-and-character scores, and emphasizing star personalities who might overshadow the shows themselves.

Or so the legend runs. However: one, the term "musical comedy" was first used in America, in the billing of *Cinderella At School* (1881); two, the influence of the "Guv'nor" (as Edwardes was called) spread well beyond the Gaiety; and three, musical comedy did not displace the more technically musicalized comic opera. The two forms progressed together.

What really happened was that burlesque ran out of juice and needed to turn into something else. All the usual topics, from Shakespeare to Donizetti, had been spoofed to death. Besides, G & S had recruited an audience of middle-class married couples who would have found burlesque's low comedy and girls in tights unsuitable. At that, burlesque's expert practitioners, such as Fred Leslie and Nellie Farren, were aging out or dead.

"A new invention was urgently called for," says theatre historian Ernest Short. Yet Edwardes' first such production, *In Town* (1892), did not *quite* introduce a new genre. It starred burlesque comic Arthur Roberts as a genial bon vivant disclosing the pop-cultural advantages of contemporary London, and this was a novelty. But the play's structure ran loose, in the burlesque manner. Another theatre historian, W. Macqueen-Pope, calls *In Town* "something between" burlesque and musical comedy—that is, the old form and the new. It wasn't even a Gaiety show per se, moving there only after opening at the Prince Of Wales.

And now comes a bit of confusion, as there were two Gaiety Theatres, the new built while the old was being demolished. John Hollingshead managed the first one, which rose up in 1868 on the site of today's One Aldwych Hotel, the bulk of the older structure aligning with little Wellington Street, leaving the Gaiety's entrance looking like that of a disused counting house. But at least it was in the Strand; Hollingshead thought it essential for his playhouse to assert a presence in the high street. And he seems to have led burlesque into a final Golden Age, featuring evening-long titles (traditional burlesque lasted only an hour) and brand-new scores.

In fact, it was Hollingshead who brought Gilbert and Sullivan together for the aforementioned *Thespis*—but *Thespis* was really a burlesque, with a cast of burlesque stalwarts. It was Old Musical; George Edwardes was the New. So of course he had to build that second Gaiety Theatre, in 1903, this one physically dominating the Strand just where the newly constructed Aldwych sprouted out of it, the Gaiety's façade gazing westward toward the rest of the theatre world as if affirming command.

Meanwhile, Edwardes had been managing his revolution. That "first musical comedy," *In Town*, was a hit, lasting some thirty-five weeks. Next, *A Gaiety Girl* (1893) was a smash at 413 performances, and this one actually had a plot: a captain woos the titular heroine, who is then (falsely) accused of stealing jewelry, soon to be a favorite narrative speed bump in English-speaking musical comedy on both sides of the Atlantic.

So we're clearly moving toward a model for the modern story musical, and librettist Owen Hall (working with composer Sidney Jones and lyricist Harry Greenbank) deserves much of the credit. Theatre legend tells us that Hall, destined to write the books for two of the most successful of the Edwardian shows, *The Geisha* and *Florodora*, ran into his majesty Edwardes in a railway carriage, and, introducing himself by his real name as James Davis, he asserted that if he couldn't write a better show than *In Town* the devil could take him.

He must have said more than that, because Edwardes heard in Davis' pitch the wit of a born writer and commissioned him to create the script to what would become *A Gaiety Girl*. Typically for British theatre writers of the day, Davis chose a user name, Owen Hall. It's a pun. Apparently, Davis was slow to pay his bills and would find himself . . . yes, "owin' all."

Like *In Town*, *A Gaiety Girl* opened at the Prince Of Wales (and then moved to Daly's), so it was left to the third in the series to bring the New Musical home to the Gaiety Theatre. This was *The Shop Girl* (1894), with music by Ivan Caryll and book and lyrics by H. J. W. Dam (and a few numbers by Lionel Monckton and Adrian Ross). History! And note the beginning of an obsession, as gaiety tales revolved around not a comic (as *Patience* does) but a sprightly and coquettish young woman.

This figure wasn't in the story. She *was* the story: *The Circus Girl*, *The Cherry Girl*, *The Pearl Girl*, *The Sunshine Girl*, *A Country Girl* (a prominent singer in disguise), *The Girl From Utah* (fleeing marriage to an ogreish Mormon), *The Quaker Girl* (now greatly subdued in severe black with white bonnet and apron), or, for a breather, *The Belle Of Mayfair* and *Lady Madcap*.

The Shop Girl's girl was a missing heiress, which is all we need to know, as this huge hit (at 546 performances) won its favor by delving into the "smart" London of snappy dialogue and dressy young bons vivants, known as "knuts" (the *k* is silent) or "Johnnies." The outstanding knut got his big break in *The Shop Girl*, albeit in a subsidiary role, as one Bertie Boyd: George Grossmith Jr. Edmund Payne—universally referred to as "Teddy"—was the show's designated jester, but Grossmith made such an impression that some writers see Bertie Boyd as the inspiration for P. G. Wodehouse's Bertie Wooster.

The son of the G & S Grossmith who created comic leads at the Savoy, young Grossmith—or G. G., as he was known—enjoyed an ID number that helped to habilitate Edwardes' format, a kind of theme tune for the New Musical. Grossmith wrote the words, to the music of Lionel Monckton, and the song was "Beautiful, Bountiful, Bertie," a gleeful caper piece in springy $\frac{6}{8}$ time:

> I joined a junior pothouse[1]
> And drop in when I am by.
> I don't possess much brains
> But I have got the latest tie . . .

"Beautiful, Bountiful Bertie" was a position piece in the very spirit of musical comedy: sportive and saucy and above all London contemporary, all about what the informed set was up to at that very minute. Typically, G. G. was costumed not only to guide the Bertie Woosters in the audience on trending fashion but to initiate them. Macqueen-Pope tells us that G. G. sought to popularize the Panama hat, unsuccessfully.

---

[1] The *Oxford English Dictionary* defines this ancient word as "An ale-house; a small, unpretentious, or low public-house." By Grossmith's day, young bloods used the term ironically to mean any drinking establishment, even, as here, a private club.

The Grossmiths were a talented clan. Besides performing, Grossmith Sr. co-authored (with his brother Weedon) *The Diary Of a Nobody*, a deliberately glum satire that has retained classic status for well over a hundred years, and G. G., a writer and manager as well as performer, joined George Edwardes' stable of recurring authors. These included composers Lionel Monckton, Ivan Caryll, and Howard Talbot; and librettist-lyricist Adrian Ross: the top of the profession.

Indeed, Caryll, though a Belgian, became the very voice of the Edwardes musical, not least as the main composer of that all-important title *The Shop Girl*, along with such other important shows as *A Runaway Girl* (1898); *The Messenger Boy* (1900); *The Toreador* (1901), the last show to play the Gaiety before its demolition; *The Orchid*, which provided Noël Coward with his standard audition piece when he was a wee lad just starting out; *The Duchess Of Dantzic* (1903); *The Spring Chicken* (1905); *The Girls Of Gottenberg* (1907); and *Our Miss Gibbs* (1909), which we're about to consider in detail. By 1911, Caryll had made a career move and relocated to Broadway.

Even so, Caryll's London output exemplifies the compositional level of the Edwardian musical, marking a comedown from the model that Arthur Sullivan had left his colleagues. There are materialistic changes, such as the loss of traditional English part-singing, as in "fa la la" glees. However, the real problem was emotional, for Edwardes liked his art light, unpsychologized. Do any of these later shows give us a character number like unto Elsie's "Through Tear and Long-drawn Sigh" in *The Yeomen Of the Guard*, so guiltily compassionate over the condemned man she has just married for a fee? Musical comedy cultivated charm, not emotional nuances.

At least Edwardes' other main base, Daly's Theatre, just off the north-eastern edge of Leicester Square, favored comic opera, of a denser musical texture than musical comedy. "The keynote at the Gaiety," says Macqueen-Pope, "was comedy; at Daly's it was sentiment." In other words, the Gaiety offered the New Musical, while Daly's somewhat honored the Old. It would be helpful if every work in Gaiety style billed itself as a "musical comedy" and every work in Daly's style as a "musical play" (the new term for comic opera). But managers are reckless with their terminology, and, just for instance, Leslie Stuart's *Florodora* (1899)—which played neither Gaiety nor Daly's but the Lyric, still in use on Shaftesbury Avenue—is the most densely musical of the early Edwardian titles yet called itself a "musical comedy."

One element we should note about all of these entertainments is the blatant exposition with which each one started. Consider the first minutes of *Florodora*, set in the Philippines. Curtain up, and we get a langourous women's chorus ("Flowers A-blooming So Gay"), followed immediately by the entrance of the "Spanish Girls," for a burst of pep. The music builds to quite a climax, giving us a foretaste of how expansive a composer Stuart was. As the audience applauds, Leandro, the overseer of boss Gilfain's flower farms, bustles in with:

LEANDRO: You are very troublesome, you girls. Just the very day that Mr. Gilfain's arriving from his trip to England, you're all late. . . . The world is waiting for this season's supply of Florodora, our great perfume. We must see that they get it.

Good, we were wondering. Nothing gets as antique as fast as the book of a conventional musical, but it was musical comedy proper that really trifled with dramatic realism. Ernest Short tells of the day after some show's successful premiere, when comedian Seymour Hicks said, "Now we've got good notices from the critics, let's call a rehearsal and cut out the plot."

We should consider the Daly's style in general using as our model *The Geisha: A Story Of a Tea House* (1896), one of the era's more enduring titles, with a book by that roguish Owen Hall and lyrics by Harry Greenbank to Sidney Jones' music. The Japanese setting attests to a cycle of exotic shows following *The Mikado*: Edward Solomon's *The Nautch Girl* (1891), laid in India; Sullivan's *The Rose Of Persia* (1899), written with Basil Hood; another Sidney Jones' title, this one Chinese, *San Toy* (1899), which starred most of the principals of *The Geisha*; *A Chinese Honeymoon* (1901), about finding a suitable bride for the Emperor and the first musical to run over 1,000 performances; *The White Chrysanthemum* (1905), back in Japan; and there were others.

One advantage of these very foreign objects was the opportunity to dress the stage in a rash palette of color that would have overwhelmed stories set amid daily life at home. Further, both composer and lyricist could help themselves to intriguing atmospheric effects, from the pentatonic scale to quaint verbal gymnastics, as with this snippet of the second-act opening of Monckton and Talbot's co-composed *The Mousmé: The Maids Of Japan* (1911). Throughout, the music stabs at the sixth of the scale (A, in C Major), lending the song a certain tang:

Very fine tea house, this,
Very good trade they do,
Very much sought-for home of bliss,
Very nice tea girls, too!

Now for *The Geisha* itself. The storyline is simple, using a Japanese First Couple and English Second Couple for romance, an interfering Japanese potentate for plot suspense, and the fussbudget tea house owner, Wun–Hi, who speaks in a pidgen English that would have the Grievance Committee repairing to the fainting couches today.

The cast was Daly's Standard, with Marie Tempest as the head geisha, O Mimosa San, and Hayden Coffin and Letty Lind as the Britons. The Japanese villain—actually, he's not all that bad, and he takes his defeat sportingly—was Rutland Barrington (who in fact succeeded to the role during the long run), an expert in pompous overlords after his bigger-than-life Pooh-Bah in *The Mikado*. Barrington may have lacked the last word in vocal polish, but Tempest and Coffin were genuine singing stars, and the Wun-Hi, Huntley Wright, was clever enough to enliven a role that is silly but never really funny.[2]

Still, it was the music that mattered, and *The Geisha* sings most attractively—even consistently despite an assortment of interpolations. One dramaturgical problem vexes the score, however: Hayden Coffin should be O Mimosa San's sweetheart simply because he looked and sounded like the hero of everything he was in.

Yet she was First Couple and he Second. This may be why he spent some of the action engaged to Letty Lind, Daly's resident "kick up her heels" soubrette. It's as if the authors weren't sure what to do with the main love plot. Even more confusing, William Philp, O Mimosa San's fiancé, scarcely sang at all, so he never properly challenged Coffin as a romantic lead.

Still, *The Geisha* is a rich and varied score that, counting the numbers added during the 760-performance run, runs to thirty-six separate instances of what we now think of as operetta material, from the military comraderie to the romantic effusions to the ensembles in which everyone gets excited about something.

---

[2] As for why a Chinese man is running a tea house in Japan, this was presumably because a comic Chinese stereotype had already been established, whereas there was no matrix for a Japanese version. Not even in *The Mikado*? No: *The Mikado* is set in Japan but the characters are all effectively English.

But now let us leave Daly's and head for the snazzier art of the Gaiety, as in *Our Miss Gibbs* (1909). It took five men to write it, typically for the era but an absurd byline jam for yet another "shop girl wins a lord" plot. It was almost a Gaiety franchise; these shows simply brought together "types," leaving it to the players to provide individual spark. Prim yet roguish Mary was a type, and so was *Our Miss Gibbs'* lead comic Edmund Payne (universally known as "Teddy") as Mary's cousin. Unfortunately very short and odd-looking, Payne was born to be the butt of jokes—but he capitalized on it, enlivening shows with his bizarre get-ups and emphasizing a natural lisp. Unlike some comics, Payne was adept in song and dance; one might say he was really born to play in musical comedy.

He was famous for his methodical planning of each new part. *Our Miss Gibbs'* subplot centered around the usual petty-crime caper, with which Payne got innocently involved, so there was a lot of "business" to plan out as the misunderstandings accumulate. Still, Payne was obsessed with getting his entrance just right: and that meant the clothes. Mary and her cousin are from the north and Payne was greatly offended at the costumer's inability to fathom what "going down to London" means to a Yorkshireman's dress code.

Macqueen-Pope tells the story: Payne rejected one suit after another till Edwardes, "a stickler for detail," sent Payne northward to pick out something locally authentic from the haberdasher's—and ready-made, please, not bespoke. Buy what a Yorkshireman buys.

Payne returned in triumph with an ensemble of perfectly ramshackle flash. *This*, he might have said, is how the compleat thespian greets his public, and it cost Edwardes less than three pounds, though adding in the discarded suits, Edwardes ended up paying "about fifty-five pounds" in all, a tremendous sum in the old money.

George Grossmith was in *Our Miss Gibbs*, too, as ever epitomizing the "knut," though in this version he's a sort of dillettante criminal. Building on *The Shop Girl's* "Beautiful, Bountiful Bertie," G. G. introduced a second "Bertie" number in prancing 6/8 time, this one by Cuthbert Clarke and R. C. Tharp, "Bertie the Bounder." He's not a cad, mind you—he hops instead of walking:

> I said, "Bertie boy, why do you bound?
> What have you found
> Wrong with the ground?

The song had nothing to do with *Our Miss Gibbs*' plot. But then the show's core numbers didn't give G. G. a main chance; sometimes you have to make your own fun. So he dropped in yet a second irrelevant piece, the huge American hit "Yip-I-Addy-I-Ay," a kind of foolhardy waltz (by John H. Flynn and Will D. Cobb). G. G. was very much attuned to the music coming across the Atlantic to England, and "Yip-I-Addy" was as American as it gets, brash and youthful and full of freedom. Broadway singing star Blanche Ring more or less owned the song in the US, but comparing her recording with G. G.'s, we hear him get more out of it, trumpeting with Dionysian glee and sliding up to the "Yip" on a long *e* vowel to glory in the fun you have when you're in a musical:

> Sing of joy, sing of bliss,
> Home was never like this.
> Eeeeee*yip-I-Addy-I-Ay!*

Thus Grossmith took stage in *Our Miss Gibbs*, and he really did need the boost, because—as he joked at the time, albeit in euphemistic wording—his heroine co-star got all the best songs because she was sleeping with the boss.

She would be Gertie Millar as Mary Gibbs, arguably the greatest musical star of the Edwardian age, pretty and winsome with a daffy soprano voice. She wasn't known for love songs, however, but rather for "cute" numbers— "Neville Was a Devil," "Toy Town," "Bedtime At the Zoo," "Pretty Baby" (an interpolation from America, possibly on G. G.'s advice), "[I'm] The Fool [Fool, Fool] Of the Family." Every Gertie Millar show had to include at least one Exhibition Cute Piece, and *Our Miss Gibbs* had "Moonstruck," written, words and music, by Lionel Monckton, for he was the boss Millar was sleeping with: her husband.

Millar sang "Moonstruck" in a nighttime scene wearing a navy-blue Pierrot outfit stippled with miniature moons, backed up by the girls in their own Pierrots of an unobtrusive light blue (to avoid pulling focus). This number, too, had nothing to do with *Our Miss Gibbs*' storyline—but one of the flaws in early musical comedy is its reliance on the structure of classic three-act farce, with the exposition in Act One, development in Act Two (always the liveliest part of the show), and resolution in Act Three, which therefore tends to lack content. Musical comedy, usually in two acts, runs both exposition and development in its Act One, leaving too little plot for Act Two.

So Edwardian musicals often filled out that last act with a beaux arts ball, Parisian cabaret, or anywhere suitable for a variety show, allowing the cast to run through a set of party pieces. *Our Miss Gibbs* didn't go that far, but "Moonstruck" was presented as an isolated specialty. Preceded by a chorus ("Moon-Fairies") and dance, it brought Millar on for a verse in the key of a minor for that air of mystery:

> Moon, Moon, mischief-making Moon!
> What are you doing there?

Then the refrain jumps into A Major for a frolicsome, syncopated melody that must have had the Gaiety public's heads nodding in rhythm:

> I'm such a silly when the moon comes out;
> I hardly seem to know what I'm about . . .

Modern ears may hear (on Millar's recording of the number) rather too much squealing in Millar's vocal, but in 1909 the number appealed greatly, all but crowding the show itself. "Moonstruck" was a Big Hit in a way that nothing in the G & S generation had been—but this was an age of Big Hits. Biggest of all was the *Florodora* Sextet, "Tell Me, Pretty Maiden." Sung by six male clerks and six female friends of the show's heroine, the piece was as famous for its staging as for its music: the twelve performers, each gender in uniform fancy dress, strolled on from opposite sides of the stage, their heads bobbing in time to an insouciant vamp, then pairing off for a courtship number that intriguingly glides from melody to melody without repeating any of them.

And note that *Florodora* made no attempt to tie the Sextet into the plot. These twelve singers had been established, but only in a minor way. Why were they suddenly entranced with one another? "I must love someone," the girls sang; "Then why not me?," the boys answered. It's as good a reason as any.

The fiction writer Saki (H. H. Munro) had fun mocking the Big Hit in a short story of 1914 called "Cousin Teresa," in which a ne'er-do-well "feverishly engrossed in . . . [a] medley of elaborate futilities" at last comes up with a winner in a Dog Number, to wit:

> Cousin Teresa takes out Caesar,
> Fido, Jock, and the big borzoi . . .

With the bass drum banging away on the last two syllables, the singer playing Cousin Teresa draws a set of wheeled wooden dogs across the stage, each crossing presented in a variation: they all wear coats, then a knut leads them (Saki spells it phonetically as "Nut"), and so on.

The scene is inserted into the latest revue and enjoys a sensation, even among intellectuals. "A revered lady," Saki tells us, with "pretensions to oracular utterance" claims that "One cannot understand the message all at once." Saki is ridiculing the musical's commercialism—but he has caught as well its wonderful foolishness. So it is very sad to report that our author, a gay man and a war hero, was killed on the battlefield because some idiot lit a cigarette, exposing his outfit to German sniper fire.

Nevertheless, this mordant satirist has isolated a new development in the British musical: the cultivation of self-contained "fun" numbers. And be it said that Lionel Monckton's most popular songs were usually of the type: "The Sly Cigarette"; "The Boy Guessed Right"; "Maisie [is a daisy]," with its irresistible refrain of "And they all cry 'Whoops' when Maisie's coming near"; "Two Little Sausages," on a heterosexual couple of them who fall in love; "Try Again, Johnnie," mocking a London lad having trouble landing rural girls.

There's a hint in this of the music hall, that unpretentious variety show a world apart from the musical, though both John Hollingshead and Augustus Harris (in his Drury Lane pantomimes) hired music-hall talents at times. Even: comedian Arthur Roberts interpolated a music-hall number made famous by Vesta Victoria, "Daddy Wouldn't Buy Me a Bow-Wow," into one of our very first New Musicals, *In Town*.

The music hall's essential quality was its working-class worldview, reveling in proletarian situations in bad grammar and amoral merriment. Further, many music-hall singers were barely singers at all. They "put over" a number rather than enhanced it. Above all, they were Characters. "I'm Henery the Eighth, I am" was the start of a typical refrain, associated with Harry Champion (who artfully dropped the song's *H*), because his wife has been married eight times, invariably to men named Henry.[3] Or: my gentleman friend took up with me mum and—here's the title—"Now I Have To Call Him Father."

Music-hall stars weren't people in a story, like Macheath or Yum-Yum: they came complete with their own story. Perhaps the most typical artist "on the

---

[3] The number was revived in the vinyl era by a number of singers, but Herman's Hermits made the best-known single in 1965, the ditty's original galumphing 6/8 modernized into 4/4.

halls" was Marie Lloyd, whose raw vocalism and risqué jests tell us how far afield the music hall was from George Edwardes' West End. The musical was prim; the music hall was wild. You wouldn't have been shocked to learn that a music-hall star or two had had to sleep rough, while Gaiety girls all had mothers.

Marie Lloyd was no Gaiety girl, as we hear in her recording of "Buy Me Some Almond Rock":

> I shall say to a young man gay,
> If he treads upon my frock,
> "Randy pandy, sugardy candy,
> Buy me some almond rock!"

"Almond Rock," the name of a popular sweet, was Cockney rhyming slang for "cock."

But music hall had its cultured side. Florrie Forde's specialty "Oh! Oh! Antonio," about an Italian girl searching for her missing boy friend, quotes Johann Strauss' "Artist's Life" as the singer utters the title words, and, more broadly, after some big West End theatres elevated the once-raucous format, opera was heard. Pietro Mascagni conducted his one-act *Cavalleria Rusticana* twice daily at the Hippodrome with a handpicked Italian cast, a chorus of fifty, and an orchestra of sixty-five. Ruggero Leoncavallo, also at the Hippodrome, led his similarly short *I Zingari*, and the theatre's herald ran his photograph captioned "THE GREAT MAESTRO," on a bill with "Irish Comedians," Williams & Warden, and the Stein Esther Trio, "Comedy Acrobats."

Music-hall stars could reach national prominence, as Marie Lloyd did, but West End people regarded that territory as professionally outré. Yet there is a quasi-music hall moment in the masterpiece of the Edwardian musical, *The Arcadians* (1909). Its huge ensemble cast includes a racing jockey whose shtick is claiming to be "merry and bright" though he's a doleful loser with the warmth of a snow crab. In short: a Character, exactly what the music-hall stars were. In "My Motter" (i.e., My Motto), he sings of his supposed joy in life to a lugubrious tune that sounds nothing like the rest of the show's score. It's Eeyore singing, "Oh, What a Beautiful Mornin'." To add to the irony, the original player, Alfred Lester, "accompanied" himself on a lyre and tried a few cockamamie dance steps. And note that he was costumed as a Greek shepherd.

That's because *The Arcadians* starts in a primeval fairyland (Arcadia, where no one tells a lie) and then travels to a very up-to-date fairyland (fashionable London, where everyone is so "civilized" that phoniness is embedded in the social contract). Lester's jockey is caught between two worlds, pure and adulterated at once.

The Arcadians' book, by Mark Ambient, A. M. Thompson, and Robert Courtneidge (who also produced the show, at the old Shaftesbury Theatre)[4], is lively enough, but the show's score is superb. Co-composed by the ubiquitous Lionel Monckton and Howard Talbot to Arthur Wimperis' lyrics, the music is rapturous in the first act (in Arcadia) then shifts to popular song in Acts Two and Three (in London). In other words, the piece starts in the Daly's comic-opera mode, then darts off into Gaiety musical comedy.

Thus, the first-act finale, a soaring choral scene that would not have shamed Arthur Sullivan, gives way after the first intermission to such events as the jaunty "Back Your Fancy," on the art of gambling; or "Charming Weather," as a couple tries to flirt while trapped (by eavesdroppers) into making vapid small talk; or the breathless "All Down Piccadily," the confessions of the most popular beau in town, forever outrunning female admirers.

The show's premise is highly original: the English aviator James Smith crash-lands in Arcadia, is thrown into the Truth Pond, and emerges rejuvenated as one Simplicitas to squire two Arcadian maidens on a mission to reform "a land peopled by savages":

EVERYONE: Savages?
SOMBRA, AN ARCADIAN SHEPHERDESS: Yes. They call them—the English.

Smith gives us a hint of how sophisticated (meaning "dishonest") manners are in London, with a touch of Gilbertian wit:

SMITH: You don't know what jealousy is?
SOMBRA: No.
SMITH: Well—it's the friendship one woman has for another.

In the end, the mission fails: London loves its social structures too much to abandon them for truth.

---

[4] Not the current so-named house on the edge of Bloomsbury, but an older theatre much farther west, halfway to Piccadilly.

A smash hit at 809 performances, *The Arcadians* was state-of-the-art rather than avant-garde, employing the old "tableau curtains" at the end of the first two acts: the house curtain would fall, then rise again once or twice to show the company posed in visual summations of the action—gazing aloft, for example, to follow the flight of Simplicitas and the two Arcadians as they wing their way through the sky to wicked London.

Even so, the original cast opened a door into the next era. The typical Edwardian show depended on performers established in the previous generation; a few actually created roles for G & S. But some of *The Arcadians'* leads were just getting started. Harry Welchman and Phyllis Dare played the prominent London sweethearts Jack and Eileen, he the typical Lochinvar and she made an Irish lass simply to accommodate a roguish waltz, "The Girl With a Brogue." They were headed for big careers, Welchman most often in imported operettas, from Leo Fall's *Der Liebe Augustin* (*Princess Caprice* in London) to *The Desert Song*. Phyllis Dare, famous for having a big sister in the business, Zena Dare, managed to last long enough to appear (with Zena) in Ivor Novello's final show, *King's Rhapsody*.

Comparably, the Sombra, Florence Smithson, was in only her fourth year in West End theatres. Known as "The Welsh Nightingale," she boasted a very high soprano, useful in differentiating her from the more conventional singing of Phyllis Dare and thus contributing to *The Arcadians'* almost Manichaean view of two intersecting worlds, one light and one dark.

James Smith (comic Dan Rolyat), representing the dark to Sombra's light, would be the show's protagonist if it weren't so fascinated by all its characters. There are no supporting players in this ensemble, and we keep wondering who really drives the plot. But the score is filled with establishing numbers that appear to "star" everybody by turns, and the book glides from this character to that so coquettishly that it's like a map without place names.

One youngster actually started a major career here. She was producer Courtneidge's sixteen-year-old daughter, who took over as Eileen during *The Arcadians'* long run. Once she revealed that she was more effective as a comic than a sweetheart, Cicely Courtneidge became one of the biggest stars in Britain, so essential to its show business that she was still getting top billing in London's staging of the American *High Spirits* over fifty years after *The Arcadians*.

4

Charleston Mad

The 1910s and 1920s

Revue became the rage in the 1910s. The London Hippodrome specialized in big variety shows, and *Joy-Land!* (1915) was typical, each number calling up gala visuals and gigantic ensembles. In the 1920s, Charles B. Cochran would reinvent revue as small but arty: sophisticated in not only its material but its fizzy performing talent. In the 1910s, however, size mattered.

Apparently, an American flavor did, too. Thus, French tenor George Carvey sang (in slightly impenetrable English) "I Love the Girl In Ninon," telling of his penchant for women in lingerie, be it velveteen or crinoline—"In fact, I really lo–ove them a–ll!" This led to a parade of showgirls in contradistinctively complete ensembles from hat to shoes to accessories. Carvey himself was in white tie and tails, and the whole number was exactly what Florenz Ziegfeld was already doing in the US in his *Follies* revues.

Then, too, there was a Homesick Number called "California"; a military march entitled "Our Own Dear Flag" that sounds like something George M. Cohan would write; and of course there had to be "When You Hear That [simple] Raggy Refrain," because the sound of London in 1915 was ragtime.

Obviously, *Joy-Land!*'s authors must have been American—but they weren't. The Hippodrome's idea man, Albert de Courville, collaborated with the intriguingly named Wal Pink on sketches and lyrics, and the music was by Herman Darewski, an émigré from Minsk in what is now Belarus. But they were all respecting the Hippodrome's new American styles based on its earlier hits, *Hullo, Rag-time!* (1912) and *Hullo, Tango!* (1913), which *were* largely the work of Americans. (Though we note with surprise that the former's sketches were written by James M. Barrie.)

Further, *Joy-Land!* featured an American lead singer, Shirley Kellogg, de Courville's wife.[1] Fielding a light soprano, Kellogg was unlike the

---

[1] An amusing backstage tale finds Kellogg entertaining *Joy-Land!*'s children in her dressing room during the break between matinee and evening. The kids appeared in "The Tulip Song," a Dutch

belters primarily associated with ragtime in America, such as Ethel Levey, George M. Cohan's ex-wife, who was in both *Hullo* shows and also two Irving Berlin musicals imported from Broadway, *Watch Your Step* (1915) and *Stop! Look! Listen!* (retitled *Follow the Crowd*, 1916). Even more authentically, Berlin himself appeared in *Hullo, Rag-time!* as a guest singer halfway through its year-long run, at a fee of £20,000, all but unimaginable when even leading players could make less than £200 a week.

True, Berlin was the monarch of ragtime. But the most celebrated visitors were the Astaires, brother Fred and sister Adele, in three Gershwin shows.[2] Lionized in commercial plugs for shampoo, skin care, and cough drops, and taken up by the Best People, the Astaires turned charm into something fleet and winning. They were more than charming: joyous. A generation before them, George Edwardes sent Gaiety and Daly's chorus girls to see *The Belle Of New York*—playing London with most of its original New York cast— so the Edwardes people could acquire American "pep," and here were the Astaires reviving that playful flash of the New World. In their second and third Gershwins, *Lady, Be Good!* (1926) and *Funny Face* (1928), the Astaires' popularity epitomized a second American Revolution. Musical comedies and operettas alike colonized the playhouses; Drury Lane became an American outpost.

It wasn't for the pep alone. William B. Friedlander and Con Conrad's *Mercenary Mary* (1925) boasted a racy storyline (it was based on a sex farce called *What's Your Wife Doing?*) and jaded New Yorkers merely shrugged. Yet it was a smash in London, just risqué enough to be a guilty pleasure. London changed the score a bit, but "Charleston Mad" was retained from New York as an authentic Yankee rhythm number. As for Mary, she was mercenary only because men are. "You must always take it from them," the title song warned, "or take it from me, they'll take it from you."

---

number, and while they were visiting Kellogg, the house phone rang. One girl automatically picked up, but it was the stage manager, and she panicked.

"What do I tell him?" she asked Kellogg.

"Tell him something nice."

Returning to the receiver, the little one said, "Miss Kellogg says she loves you."

[2] The first of them, *For Goodness Sake*, rebilled for London as *Stop Flirting* (1923), was actually partly Gershwin and partly Gershwin imitation by others.

It was the "gold digger" figure, against which we can set the British ideal in the heroine of *Lady Mary* (1928), a British show, albeit with music by the Hungarian Albert Sirmay and the American Phil Charig. *This* Mary isn't charleston mad. Her big solo, "Calling Me Home," told of the Briton's homesick longings when in foreign climes. Simple yet distinctive, it has the air of a tender anthem, loving rather than prideful. "For there's a small grey island," the refrain begins, "far over the sea," and, hearing it, one realizes that however much British and American musicals may borrow from each other, at this time in their histories they maintain very separate domains, the one essentially idyllic and the other aggressive. Or: legato vs. staccato.

Still, the furor for that grabby American sound, stimulated by local dance bands adopting the American style, led producers to hire American songwriters. Comedian-turned-manager Laddie Cliff even got a few British composers to pose as "Hal Brody"—Cliff's idea, apparently, of an unmistakably American name—for *Lady Luck* (1927), *So This Is Love* (1928), and *Love Lies* (1929), though Cliff used also composer Billy Mayerl, who was much jazzier than "Hal Brody" and thoroughly English to boot.

Authenticity demanded songwriters of real standing. After enjoying a great success with Jerome Kern's Ziegfeld show *Sally* (1921), the managers of the Winter Garden in Drury Lane, J. A. E. Malone and our old friend George Grossmith Jr., wanted another Kern for their permanent company. The obvious choice would have been Kern's *Good Morning, Dearie*, the top musical of Broadway's 1921–22 season, with a Big Hit, "Ka-lu-a." But when G. G. read the script, he realized that, despite the winsome title, *Good Morning, Dearie* was too American for London.

The main problem was the villain of the piece, a gangster named Chesty Costello who not only threatens the two sweethearts but has a nasty tussle with the Boy. Now, the British musical had its share of crooks—operetta allowed for dreadful characters, as we're about to learn. But in the Winter Garden's stock-in-trade, musical comedy, lawbreakers were comic as a rule.

True, in Paul Rubens' *To-Night's the Night* (1915) first staged in New York in 1914 and then put on back home by Grossmith and his then partner Edward Laurillard (at the Gaiety), there was a number called "Murders." In it, the singer (Leslie Henson in New York, though G. G. appropriated it for himself in London) recounts the grisly homicides he has racked up: of an incompetent laundress, a barrel-organ player, even the singer's naggy mother-in-law.

("She'd never been contented, and I thought it time she went.") He concludes with a spoken postlude: "Take me away, constable, I am quite ready." However, the number is a party piece, not a character song, so out of story that the New York program didn't list it.

Good Morning, Dearie's villain, on the other hand, is the real thing; the British public would have rebelled at such a monster in a fun show. Worse, *Dearie* had no role for G. G. So he suggested that Kern simply compose the songs for a piece to be written by G. G. and P. G. Wodehouse to British specifications, with some place or other found for the indispensable "Ka-lu-a."

The new show was *The Cabaret Girl* (1922), the tale of a nightclub entertainer in love with a high-born lad, just as in one of the old Gaiety musicals. Dorothy Dickson and Geoffrey Gwyther were the sweethearts, and G. G. and Leslie Henson formed a double act as eccentric music publishers. Their merry bickering got a number of its own in "Mr. Gravvins-Mr. Gripps," a deliberate knockoff of a *Ziegfeld Follies* ditty, "Mister Gallagher and Mister Shean." An inside joke for theatre buffs, the new number's style coincided with that of a typical British patter song, so the audience didn't need to know anything about Ziegfeld or his *Follies*.

Kern had more to do on *The Cabaret Girl* than simply make music, for it was imperative that the show give valid opportunities to the Winter Garden favorites, especially Henson, Vera Lennox, and Heather Thatcher. G. G. and Wodehouse wrote roles around the players' personalities, providing a juicy scene in which local grandees are unavailable for a country garden party and Lennox and Thatcher merrily deputize as grand ladies while Henson appears as the vicar. So of course the real vicar shows up as well. Uh-oh:

THE REAL VICAR: Ah, a fellow member of the cloth. . . . Have you a cure [i.e.,
    the charge of a parish] in the neighborhood?
HENSON: A cure? Why, is something the matter with it?

Lennox and Thatcher were in a few ensembles, but Lennox got most of an early chorus number about the London theatre scene, "You Want the Best Seats":

> We've Eastern dramas where they dress
> In strings of beads and less . . .

while Thatcher joined G. G. and Henson in "Nerves," and they were all in on the bouncy nonsense number "Whoop-De-Oodle-Do." It wasn't great Kern, but at one point the jazzy "Shimmy With Me" (for the girls) was mated in double-chorus style with the soothing "Journey's End" (for the boys), a lovely touch.

After *The Cabaret Girl*, G. G. tried the same thing again with George and Ira Gershwin, in *Primrose* (1924). George worked mainly with the English Desmond Carter but also with brother Ira, and the result—as with all these London shows with "American" music—was too insular to be exported to Broadway.

The *Primrose* songs can be divided into sweet (for the First Couple, Margery Hicklin and opera baritone Percy Heming, usually busy with Wagner's Amfortas and the like); comic for Leslie Henson, including an out-of-story duet for him and Claude Hulbert, "[Isn't it horrible what they did to] Mary, Queen Of Scots"; and jazzy for Heather Thatcher, as the gold digger who gets the usual couples-confusion plot moving.

In all, the best numbers were Thatcher's: "Boy Wanted" (later used in the Tommy Tune-Twiggy Broadway pastiche *My One and Only*); "Naughty Baby," rife with syncopation (also used in a pastiche, *Crazy For You*); and "I Make Hay When the Moon Shines," echoing Gertie Millar's "Moonstruck" in *Our Miss Gibbs*.

"Hay" is a gem. A hedonist's anthem of such contagious revelry that the chorus cannot resist whistling along with the last refrain, it was wasted on Thatcher, who like Millar would talk through the notes and sound terribly thin when she actually sang them. It was a defining generic feature. In operetta, the Big Sing was the first virtue. In musical comedy, personality outranked all else.

Even less musical than Thatcher was Sylvia Hawkes, whose audition for *Primrose* gave rise to a classic tale. Remember W. S. Gilbert saying he knew only two songs, that one was "God Save the Queen" and the other wasn't? Well, Sylvia Hawkes knew only "God Save the Queen" (which by 1924 had of course become "God Save the King"), and that's what Sylvia sang—all of it, while the patriotic G. G. and his staff stood at attention. After the first verse, they started to sit again, but Hawkes plowed on. There are three standard verses (the second beginning "O Lord Our God arise" and the third "Thy choicest gifts in store"), but a certain William Edward Hickson added on four extra strophes in the early nineteenth century. There are yet other alternatives: and Sylvia sang them all. Guy Bolton and P. G. Wodehouse popularized the tale in

Bring on the Girls!, noting that G. G. had to stand for the entire rendition: "No one dared to call a halt. The national anthem is sacrosanct—especially if you're an actor-manager clinging to the hope of a belated knighthood."[3]

Rodgers and Hart also tried going native, in *Lido Lady* (1926), one of countless shows for the husband-and-wife team of Jack Hulbert and Cicely Courtneidge, and a Charles Cochran revue, *One Dam Thing After Another* (1927), a title rather advanced for British taste. Most folks were so unwilling to utter "the word"—in *HMS Pinafore*, Captain Corcoran catches utmost heck for saying "Damme"—that one and all referred to "the new Cochran show" or "that London Pavillion revue."

Perhaps Cochran was in a racy mood. He did collect a good cast—Sonnie Hale, Melville Cooper, Max Wall, onstage pianist Edythe Baker, and especially a very young Jessie Matthews. Baker led the chorus kids in the jazzy "I Need Some Cooling Off" ("Hot coffee!" they cried, between couplets), exactly why Cochran had hired American songwriters in the first place. But the show's title song, sung by Matthews dressed as a baby, was a shock. It deals, humorously, with premarital sex and even . . . no, let's let Hart tell us himself: "Uncle John makes much piggyback and such," Baby laments. And that uncle dares slap "what a decent chap wouldn't even touch!"

Perhaps because it was so edgy, *One Dam Thing* seemed doomed at first. Then—in another classic tale—the Prince of Wales stepped in. Cochran loved to give parties—everyone come, musicians will play, stars will sing— and the Prince heard *One Dam Thing*'s "My Heart Stood Still" and loved it. Later, at a dance, he asked the band for it. They didn't know the piece, but he hummed it and bit by bit the players picked it up.

The story made national headlines. One that Rodgers remembered to include in his memoirs was THE SONG THE PRINCE LIKED, and as no one at the time knew what a reckless Nazi shithead His Royal Highness would turn out to be, everyone immediately had to book tickets to Cochran's revue to hear "the Prince's song," and the West End had another of those Big Hits.

It's interesting that so many foreign songwriters were eager to work in London while having to adapt to the style of a London show; they didn't do this elsewhere, such as Paris or Berlin—and it wasn't because of the language barrier. London had long been Europe's theatre capital, with a prestige

---

[3] G. G. never got one, but Sylvia Hawkes not only joined the cast of *Primrose* but married into the aristocracy. She was a real beauty; everyone wanted to wed her. Her five husbands included two lords, two American movie stars (one of whom was the main one, Clark Gable), and one Georgian noble, a refugee from Communism, who raced cars and horses.

founded by Shakespeare. Too, London was an opportunity center, for the passing of the Edwardians, from Lionel Monckton to Paul Rubens, left a gap that composers from elsewhere could fill.

Thus, the Russian Vernon Duke, fleeing the Soviets, spent time in Britain trying to launch a songwriting career to supplement his classical output. But Duke's esoteric craftsmanship was perhaps too ingenious. In *The Yellow Mask* (1928), a musical thriller with a script by Edgar Wallace (a specialist in the mystery field), "The Bacon and the Egg," is musically direct—and lyricist Desmond Carter can turn a phrase. The bacon is enraptured: the egg's "beauty made him thrill" and, after one look at *him*, "her fluttering yolk stood still."

Nice. But then, in *Open Your Eyes!* (1929), whose first production closed out of town, in "Too, Too Divine" (to lyrics by Collie Knox), Duke's harmony is so experimental that its published key, E Flat Major, is a euphemism.

Vernon Duke's opposite is Franz Schubert, pure melody in diatonic settings. Schubert died in 1828, but that didn't stop a new German operetta on his life, love, and music from touring the West in various versions. London's was *Lilac Time* (1922), a sensation of its day at 626 performances (and revivals in 1925, 1927, 1928, 1930, 1932, 1933, 1936, and 1949) because most of the music was drawn from Schubert's very singable dance strains. (The famous G Major theme from the Unfinished Symphony was used only by the orchestra, in dramatic punctuation.)

As Schubert, Courtice Pounds actually looked like the composer, and—as critics always said of him—he acted even better than he sang. His best friend was Percy Heming (the opera baritone we know from Gershwin's *Primrose*), who steals the heart of Schubert's love, Clara Butterworth. And note that Heming does this through the power of his singing, even of one of Schubert's own songs, "Ungeduld" ("Impatience"), here as "I Want To Carve Your Name On Every Tree," with its insistent cry of "Yours is my heart!"

It was this outpouring of melody that made *Lilac Time* a British classic despite its Continental origin. At the time, the piano and sheet music interests created an infrastructure for the dissemination of theatre scores, and most musicals published a "selection" of six or seven of their best tunes. But it's worth noting that only *Lilac Time* had to bring out two separate selections: there was too much good music for just one.

What, now, of the Gaiety and Daly shows? The latter was in a stronger position, as operetta doesn't have to reflect shifts in pop music the way musical comedy does. And here a Daly's classic appears: *The Maid Of the Mountains*

(1917). As so often in this era of the history, many names crowd the by-line: book by Frederick Lonsdale, score mainly by Harold Fraser-Simson and Harry Graham with important interpolations by James W. Tate with lyricists F. Clifford Harris and "Valentine" (Archibald Pechey, primarily a crime novelist). But the result was a tremendous success at 1,352 performances. And as there were something like 250 legit theatres in provincial Great Britain—at least six, for example, in Liverpool alone—a London hit could glide through the rest of the land for years, sometimes in multiple units.

Much of *The Maid's* success depended on its vivacious leading lady, José Collins. Operetta heroines are generally either haughty ladies or tigresses with street cred, and Collins was the latter type, but lovably, with a thrilling top register. As Teresa, allied in vague ways with a bandit gang in the imaginary south European land of Santo, Collins held center stage throughout the evening, defying the local governor (Mark Lester), protecting the bandit chief, Baldassare (Arthur Wontner) while flirting with his subaltern Beppo (Thorpe Bates), and embodying the very basis of post-comic opera operetta in her establishing number, the swinging waltz "My Life Is Love." True, it has a touch of Arthur Sullivan's classical craftsmanship in the pizzicato strings in the song's trio[4] section. Even so, it is a world away from G & S, even from *Florodora* and *The Geisha*.

The Maid's score does have a problem in its failure to fulfill Teresa's emotional yearnings. If her life is love, why does the duet "A Paradise For Two" tilt toward a Teresa-Beppo romance when the script ultimately sends Teresa into the arms of Baldassare, who is completely unlovable and doesn't even have a song or duet of his own?[5] Actually, we know why: José Collins thought it made more sense that way. But it doesn't, and we're left worrying about what happens with Beppo.

The Maid, too, has a Big Hit, Teresa's "Love Will Find a Way," another waltz—and an amusing tale hangs on it. Fraser-Simson was starving for melody for this central spot in which Teresa makes her great defiance in favor of the outlaw gang. She even sings, "There's honour among thieves." Take that, General!

---

[4] The trio (originally the middle section of a symphony's minuet or scherzo movement) is my own term for the episode in theatre music that comes between a number's first and second refrains. For example, in *Oliver!*'s "As Long As He Needs Me," the first refrain starts the vocal with the title words and the trio slips in on "He doesn't say the things he should," leading to the second refrain.

[5] We sometimes read that Baldassare is a non-singing role, but while he does talk his part in "Dividing the Spoil," the vocal score clearly requires him to sing at certain points.

But the Tune, the Tune. Thinking of a Big Hit of ten years earlier, pro-ducer Robert Evett asked Simson, "Can't you just write the *Merry Widow* waltz?"

Simson replied, "I'm afraid someone else did that already."

"Well, couldn't you write it again a little disguised? It's certain to take."

Evett hums the first notes, and Simson, who knows it well—who didn't?—fingers the keys in Evett's office. Perhaps Oscar Asche, the show's director, is there as well, listening in. Simson tries doubling the pitches of the Lehár, creating a new first phrase out of the old one, and Simson tops it off with a little flourish dipping down chromatically to the supertonic resolving on the dominant.

"Yes!" Asche cries. "But what more now?"

We can picture the movie version of the scene, as Evett and Asche draw close while Simson continues using the repeated pitches on every phrase, even in the release—then the camera cuts to José Collins on stage on opening night, singing "Love Will Find a Way" to the public's cheers, snapping her fingers at the General and his stooges—it's in the script—then exiting only to return to blow an ironic kiss at the governor (in other words aiming it at the audience), thus building the applause to cue in the encore.

Teresa's numbers hold the score together; she's the character who needs the music. "Come joy or pain," she cries at the end of "My Life Is Love" jumping down from a startling high B Flat, "love will remain." She's the only one in the story who believes in something; all the others are fools or brigands. The two leading fools, Tonio and that governor, can't even get into a good fight without turning it into a duet with encore shtick, "[There'll be] Dirty Work [at the crossroads tonight!]." After the vocal and the inevitable dance come the silly bits of "business"—slapping faces, presenting cards, waving swords, miming opening a bottle and toasting—all to musical sound effects, including a final nuclear crash of the glass.

Collins had sung Johann Strauss and Lehár (both in New York), and after *The Maid Of the Mountains* she would introduce the British public to Jacobi's *Sybil*, Oscar Straus' *The Last Waltz*, and another tigress heroine in Lehár's *Frasquita*. But first Evett wanted a follow-up to *The Maid*, and this was *A Southern Maid* (tour 1918; London 1920), the noun in the title signaling that Collins was "back in her role."

With the same composer, Harold Fraser-Simson, and *The Maid*'s main lyricist, Harry Graham, now co-writing the script (with Adrian Ross) and

The Maid's governor, Mark Lester, *A Southern Maid* was reasonably faithful to its predecessor. Again, Collins, here called Dolores, was tempestuous; her establishing number, "Love's Cigarette," was what Carmen would sing if Carmen starred in musicals. And, again, there was a bandit gang whose chief was involved with Collins. Also again, the setting was somewhere in Latinland, here the made-up isle of Santiago. And, yet again, Simson used a matrix for the big waltz tune, "Dark Grows the Sky," its closing minor and dominant $\frac{7}{3}$ chords pure Lehár.

Still, many details were innovative. Teresa dressed off the rack, but Dolores was a fashion plate, appearing at one point in a hat that looked like a giant bejeweled pin cushion. And this time Collins loved a good guy, a baronet but a real scrapper. Menaced by the bandit chief, the hero threatens to take a stroll down "the middle of the street," utterly fearless. "And if I see anything ugly, I shall shoot at sight . . . and I always kill."

A Southern Maid was a modest success, but a very different sort of show was going to beat *The Maid* with a long-run record that stood till *Salad Days*, some forty years later. This was *Chu Chin Chow* (1916), a visual spectacle that adhered to neither Gaiety nor Daly's style with a rich, suspenseful plot filled with principals vying for riches, freedom, or love. The composer was Frederic Norton, but its true author was Oscar Asche. We already know him from his work directing José Collins, but he was much more: writer, Shakespearean actor, and manager.[6]

Asche wrote *Chu Chin Chow*'s book and lyrics and also played the title role . . . in a way. In fact, Chu Chin Chow, a Chinese merchant visiting Bagdad, never appears, having been killed by Oscar Asche's *real* character, yet another bandit chief, Abu Hasan, the sadistic leader of the forty thieves. For, yes, *Chu Chin Chow* retells the Ali Baba story, a favorite subject of Victorian theatre.

Just so we're all on the same page: in the original tale, Ali Baba sneaks into a cave of stolen treasure whose door opens at the call of "Open Sesame." Ali's crumb-bum of a brother is trapped in the cave, and the thieves cut him into four pieces as a warning to others, but the Babas get a tailor to sew him together for burial. The robbers use the tailor to track down the Babas, and the chief poses as the merchant, bringing with him oil jars in which his men hide, ready to leap out at a signal and cut everyone down. However, a clever slave

---

[6] Just to confuse us, "manager" remained the term in Britain but became "producer" in the US. At the same time, "stage manager" became "producer" in Britain but "director" in the US. Eventually, the two cultures came together to an extent, so *The Phantom Of the Opera* was "presented" by Cameron Mackintosh and "directed" by Harold Prince.

pours boiling oil into the jars and stabs the chief during a banquet, gaining both her freedom and Ali's son (and heir to the treasure cave) as her husband.

It sounds like a spoken play rather than a musical, but Asche made some important changes. First, he broke the slave girl into two separate characters, one a sweetheart (to sing romantic numbers with Ali Baba's son) and the other to drive the plot. Second, Asche built up the villain's role, from a generic brigand of minor consequence to the unique, the forbidding, the unearthly . . . *Abu Hasan!* Third, Ali Baba became a traditional comic role for Courtice Pounds, our future *Lilac Time* Schubert, thus to maintain musical-comedy feeling amid all the dire Eastern intrigue of scimitar and magic words. Further, Asche cast his own wife, Lily Brayton, as the plot-driving slave, Zahrat. It didn't break the fourth wall, but it did tease it a bit, for now Mr. and Mrs. Asche were playing life-or-death co-conspirators, secret enemies, and (against Zahrat's will, it would seem) lovers.

So the Asches made a fascinating duo as they circled around each other while the rest of the cast sang ballads ("Cleopatra's Nile," "Corraline"), atmosphere numbers ("Here Be Oysters Stewed In Honey"), character songs ("Temperamental Am I," "I Built a Fairy Palace In the Sky"), and so on, in a very long score. The bandits got a strangely merry march, "We Are the Robbers of the Woods," Asche took stage with the operatically declamatory "I Am Chu Chin Chow," and there was even a new concept in romance—maturity—in "Any Time's Kissing Time." To rephrase Shakespeare, here was a musical fitted.

Shows set in the fabled East were not unusual, especially when scripted in "West End Oriental" (Abu Hasan, at a banquet: Who is this father of mirth and girth, O host of hosts?). But some of the songs really were innovative in their subject matter—"Behold," for the master of a slave auction; "I Shiver and Shake with Fear" when Ali discovers the robbers' cave; or his advice to his son on the advantage of the Junoesque woman: "When a pullet is plump [she's tender]."

Oddly, the best-known number is the dullest one, "The Cobbler's Song." Baritones both pro and amateur acculturated the piece and made it as omnipresent as *Cats'* "Memory," as it sits gracefully in mid-range. That it's turgid and contentless didn't matter; everybody wanted to sing it, and it became the *Chu Chin Chow* song, more so than the genuinely lovely ballads.

Chu Chin Chow's flash success (which supported a phenomenal 2,235 performances) encouraged Asche to celebrate by adding new scenes and songs. The showgirls' costumes became more elaborate yet more revealing—a sunburst headdress, say, over a bikini top; or a skirt of a thousand crazy curlicues matching a bodice of brazen clarity. This prompted a stern reproach from the Lord Chamberlain. Even the animal cast underwent a change, when the camel missed its footing and suffered a fatal injury.

Feeling most secure with the exotic, Asche went on to a *Cairo*, Oscar Straus' *Cleopatra* (with Evelyn Laye), then revisited the East in *Kong*, a kind of *Chu Chin Chow* with pirates. Audience support was waning; *Kong* lasted only 20 performances. Still, it had been a gala cycle, and it all came about simply because Asche's golf game got rained out and he decided to stay in and write an Ali Baba musical.

After these colorful pursuits in wild places, it feels almost Disneyesque to revisit *The Beggar's Opera*, in Nigel Playfair's famous 1920 revival at the Lyric, Hammersmith. Frederic Austin, who played Peachum, arranged the music, using as his models both the original Pepusch settings and a later edition by Thomas Arne, scoring for strings (with spare use of the viola d'amore and viola da gamba), flute, oboe, and harpsichord. As Austin explains in his introduction to the vocal score, he did some fresh composing himself "where reasons of stage action have made it necessary," and his version became *Final Beggar's Opera* till Benjamin Britten's very free rendering of 1948.

In *Showman Looks On*, Charles Cochran gave special credit to Playfair's designer, Claud Lovat Fraser, who "brought something new and delightful to his scenery with a permanent set, Palladian in style." The look of the piece was studiously archaic, all wigs and buckled shoes—and Macheath wore the red coat used in 1728, a trademark of the piece ever since.

Still, Playfair's cast was on the stately operatic side, and as actors they didn't quite animate characters who live on the very edge of life, risking deportation or hanging at any moment. Critic James Agate (soon to reign at the *Sunday Times* for twenty-four years) found the actors (except the Filch, Alfred Heather) offered too much "gallantry and romance." The whores who betray Macheath were "qualified to mate with an earl" and "you would have unhesitatingly invited [these characters] to sup at your own house."

Far more "class naturalism" could be found at *The Bing Boys Are Here* (1916),[7] neither Gaiety nor Daly's in style but rather a West End show in music-hall manner. George Grossmith Jr. and Fred Thompson wrote the script and Nat D. Ayer and Clifford Grey the songs. Historians treat the work

---

[7] There were sequels with varying casts: *The Bing Girls Are There* (1917); *The Other Bing Boys* (a Jewish version); and *The Bing Boys On Broadway* (1918).

as a revue, but it was in fact a book show, in which two roughhewn provincial brothers, Lucifer (George Robey) and Oliver (Alfred Lester), visit London, trailed by Emma, the family cook (Violet Loraine), sweet on Lucifer. The revue aspect inheres in wacky episodes strung together at random—a visit to the zoo, Emma's emergence as a showbiz star and then as the wife of the Duke of Dullwater.

Though it would play successfully in America, *The Bing Boys Are Here* was the most British of shows in its local references (even if Ayer had originated in the US). Indeed, the show's Big Hit became one of Britain's immortal songs, "If You Were the Only Girl In the World [and I were the only boy]," a duet for Lucifer and Emma favored by Britain's fighting forces in World War I. (We even find it in the film *The Bridge On the River Kwai*, as Japanese-held POWs feature it in a variety show, with two men, one in drag, singing the number.) Oddly, it has an ABACA structure, which suggests sophistication though the lyrics are aimed at mass appeal:

> I would say such wonderful things to you,
> There would be such wonderful things to do . . .

Still, *The Bing Boys'* best song was "Another Little Drink," performed by the three stars with the zany primitivism that was the music hall's identifying quality. So each verse of the piece starts to tell a story only to pivot to "And another little drink wouldn't do us any harm!" As we hear on a contemporary disc, Robey, Lester, and Loraine get increasingly playful, "ad libbing" spoken bits and gaming with the vocal lines, Loraine especially embellishing her part in her creamy pop contralto. There were verses about imaginary people but also the Prime Minister, H. H. Asquith; no doubt during the long run other prominent names were guyed.

The trio even ragged on one another. So, while the orchestra repeated its affably coarse rum-ti-tum vamp, we got some dialogue:

ALFRED: Me again?
VIOLET: Yes, go on.

and he sings:

> Oh, there was a little man, and he went into revue,
> George Robey was his name, and he knew a thing or two.

GEORGE: (speaking) Be careful what you say!

ALFRED: He tickled all the girls till they shouted in alarm—

GEORGE: Did he?

ALL THREE: And another little drink wouldn't do us any harm!

And they ultimately cap the whole turn with a

Rai tickedy–um tai . . . tai tai!

Certain shows couldn't help but present such unpretentious characters, so different from the socially tidy folk of the George Edwardes era. Consider for instance *The Better 'Ole* (1917), a musical of the Great War, based on Bruce Bairnsfather's cartoons on the military adventures of Old Bill, a soldier with a trademark walrus mustache. He came to glory in a famous drawing depicting him and another fighter in a bomb crater in no-man's land amid whizzing bullets, puffs of explosives, and a house flying in the air. Says Bill to his comrade, "Well, if yer knows of a better 'ole, go to it!"

Old Bill's escapades were so popular that it was inevitable that he make it to the stage—but in a musical? With songs composed by Herman Darewski (of the aforementioned *Joy-Land!* that same year) and Bairnsfather co-writing the script? And with the elegant Shakespearean Arthur Bourchier as Old Bill? Even with a chorus of French girls to dress the stage, we're still talking about trench warfare and even espionage, when Bill foils a German plot but is falsely incriminated.

All ends well, and the show ran over 800 performances. But far more typical of the song shows of the day was the comedy-centered musical focused on middle-class civilian life, often adapted from an old farce, hewing closely to the original plot and, for novelty, changing the characters' names. Thus, a reigning comedian of the 1910s could in effect revive an antique, brushing it up with songs and adding in a young couple for sweetheart numbers.

Two such events, both huge hits, were created for W. H. Berry for two-year runs each at the Adelphi: *The Boy* (1917), a last hurrah for Monckton and Talbot, and *Who's Hooper?* (1919), by Talbot, co-composing now with Ivor Novello. Fred Thompson wrote the scripts (after Arthur Wing Pinero), and all these authors had the problem that it takes real ingenuity to get a farce to "sing," as the relentless plot activity makes it physical rather than emotional.

Still, Berry apparently made them work. In *The Boy* he was a magistrate enduring a very Bad Day. (The "boy" of the title was his step-son, a young man who his mother pretends is a child, for a Ponce de Leon effect on her age.) Then, in *Who's Hooper?*, Berry, an amnesiac, was mistaken for a law-breaker. It's basically one long chase with pauses now and again for mostly unnecessary music, though Berry did have a viable "West End" singing voice and an amusing habit of ad libbing spoken bits during the songs and hitting deliberately off-pitch high notes.

These songs weren't memorable, but they functioned capably in the nar-rative. In *Who's Hooper?*, Berry enjoyed a waltz duet with Cicely Debenham, as a young woman Berry gets temporarily involved with, "Wonderful Love," cued in by a flirting scene with an au courant joke tucked into it. Buffs of an-tique cultural trivia get ready:

DEBENHAM: Have you ever been in love, Valentine?
BERRY: I've read about it. I read *Three Weeks* in three days, and it took me three months to recover![8]

On her own, backed up by the chorus, Debenham got the "American" number (by Novello), "The Wedding Jazz," with a portentous orchestral intro and an allusion to the indicated bit of *Lohengrin* before the refrain cuts loose with a syncopated rampage. It's enjoyable enough, but irrelevant—a common state of songs written for these comedy musicals.

On the other hand, what we might call the "sweetheart" musical-comedy style depended on an above all tuneful score. *Betty In Mayfair* (1925) is typ-ical: country-bred Betty and her twin sister, Kitty, are told one of them will be given a season in London. In their establishing waltz, "Two Hearts," the sisters sing "Two heroines—which of them wins?" But they are loving rather than competitive, and in fact Betty, who gets the social honor, finds herself attired in period dress to please a chap who likes his women Old Style, as if ready to go on in Nigel Playfair's genteeled *Beggar's Opera* revival.

Then Betty rebels, along with her coterie: at a fancy ball, all the girls drop their operatic Victorian gowns to stand forth as trim-lined Young Moderns.

---

[8] *Three Weeks* (1907) was Elinor Glyn's scandalous novel that cleverly drew on the social taboos of the day from sex to murder, becoming the bestseller no one could admit to reading.

This is 1925, sir! And the staging was persuasive, casting lookalikes Evelyn Laye and Mary Leigh as the twins, to set them on stage in matching dark bobbed hairdos. Still, *Betty In Mayfair* banked its appeal on Harold Fraser-Simson and Harry Graham's score, quite tuneful and devoted to the twins, who get plenty of chances to show off their sopranos with lots of rubato and portamento. The comedy musicals played games with their songs; the sweetheart shows sang them.

Still, these are musical *comedies*, after all, and there was one rather piquant number, "The Countryside," in which Kitty (Leigh) shows a beau (Jack Hobbs) around the family grounds. Hobbs was on hand to play the Bertie Wooster stereotype that George Grossmith Jr. had invented, here to marvel at the trees and greenery and . . . whatever those other things are. (Daisies; there's a comparable moment in Andrew Lloyd Webber's *By Jeeves*.) "The Countryside" turns on a charming gadget: every strophe ends with Kitty's exclamation of "Rather!" Thus, she notes all the fruit trees about; harvesters "needn't look much farther." Her beau "might find a peach within [his] reach." Oh, really? "Might I?":

KITTY: *Rather*!

Evelyn Laye, then twenty-five and already a principal in some dozen musicals, including leading a 1923 *Merry Widow* revival, was becoming London's go-to operetta heroine, though she had a limited top.[9] She was a sharp actress as well, and so well-liked that she could postpone her farewell tour till she was in her nineties. More important, hers was the first "movie" generation of West End stars, and while she did fail to crack the Hollywood musical successfully, we can sample her and her colleagues in their films.

Jessie Matthews was one such, arrestingly intertwined with Laye in that Laye's first husband, Sonnie Hale, left Laye for Matthews, which made everything in British show biz rather complicated for a while. But the biggest star of this generation was Jack Buchanan, a Scot who modernized George Grossmith's knut into a more self-assured figure, above all a suave rather than eccentric dancer. Buchanan's abundant laugh may have irritated some; others might resent the use of the knut to ridicule the upper-middle-class

---

[9] When Laye played the heroine of London's *The New Moon* (1929), all her numbers had to be transposed down, to let Laye sail up to B Flats where New York's Evelyn Herbert sang high Cs.

Englishman as a dope. Guy Bolton thought the stereotype as essential to a musical-comedy script as the stolen jewels in Act Two.

Nevertheless, Buchanan elevated the figure to matinee-idol status, and after playing the hero in *Faust On Toast* (1921), a disastrous attempt to revive Victorian burlesque (the title rhymed, by the way), Buchanan turned manager and took control of his shows, such as *Battling Butler* (1922), as a fake boxer; *Boodle* (1925), as a fake circus clown; and *That's a Good Girl* (1928), always choreographing his own dances (with perennial partner Elsie Randolph) and demanding jazzy "American" arrangements to accompany them.

That's a Good Girl seems to be the best of the lot, as Randolph played a detective hunting Buchanan, a far cry, finally, from the dainty ways of the Edwardian shop-girl heroine. The score was assembled from spare parts and mainly American in co-composers Phil Charig and Joseph Meyer and co-lyricist Ira Gershwin. Ira thought *That's a Good Girl* "a lively, peppy [piece] that's full of laughs," though he resented librettist-lyricist Douglas Furber's revision of Ira's lyrics—"not for the better, either." The prize number, the Meyer-Charig-Furber "Fancy Our Meeting," rather sums up the bittersweet appeal of the Buchanan-Randolph pairing, a slow ballad with a tonic minor augmented $\frac{7}{4}$ chord in the second measure, a doozy of a noise. The show's most popular tune, it tells us that Buchanan really knew how to raise the originality level of his musicals, and his women fans' cries of "We love you, Jack" during the calls (along with his oh so casual stage persona) obscure the abilities of a very capable producer, utterly in tune with the state of the art.

We can cap this chapter with what has become the most vital British musical of this era, *Mister Cinders* (1929). It is a classic in schools and regional groups because it's easy to stage and cast—yet how strange the start, for *Mr. Cinders* was an accident of twisted origins. Comic Leslie Henson seems to have thought it up: a re-gendered *Cinderella* for him and Violet Loraine (whom we recall from *The Bing Boys Are Here*) as Jim and Jill, the Cinderella boy and his combination of fairy godmother and Prince[ss] Charming. Clifford Grey and Greatrex Newman were the wordsmiths, but there was no composer. However, Grey had been working a lot in Hollywood and on Broadway, and he was in possession of a little batch of numbers by composer Richard Myers.

Then came the first twist: Henson was offered the comic lead in the London staging of *Funny Face*, another Gershwin show with the Astaires. Having had good luck in American shows in London or London shows with American participation—*Sally*, *The Cabaret Girl*, *Primrose*, *Tell Me More*,

Kid Boots—Henson found *Funny Face* irresistible and bailed on *The Kid* (as *Mister Cinders* was first entitled).

The second twist was Violet Loraine's marriage, as she had wed one of those Lords With a Castle In the North, and, much as she yearned to perform again, her in-laws took a Presbyterian view of the stage, and she canceled. The show was off.

Until producer Julian Wylie became interested, along with composer Vivian Ellis, whose blithely sardonic autobiography presents Wylie as a mad schemer with "the roar of a dying bull in the arena." Wylie was the sort of showman who inserted a railway scene into *The Kid* simply so he could treat the public to a train roaring across the stage. But at the Edinburgh opening the train came in backward, another twist.

In all, *The Kid* played out of town for four months, undergoing myriad changes—a new producer, new directors and choreographers, new principals, songs such as "Paradise Bound" and the whistly "By Myself With You" cut and new songs added, the racy "Jill" re-lyricked as a throwaway First Number, "Tennis," and the title changed to the one we know. Yet when *Mister Cinders* opened, at the Adelphi, the twists were finished and the audience loved everything in it.

And with so many twenties shows getting by on no more than a tuneful score or an appreciable comic, *Mister Cinders* was a novelty in its clever use of the Cinderella trope. Set in modern times, the tale saw Jim as the slavey with the traditional "ugly" (here, selfish) step[brothers] and the imperious stepmother. Jim meets Jill, who sends him to, yes, a ball and sees him through the ordeal of being accused of yet another musical-comedy jewel theft till the glass slipper (here, a bowler hat) fits him: and Jim shall have Jill.

Ellis tells us how lucky the production was to get Bobby Howes and Binnie Hale for the leads. Slight and a bit elfin, Howes suited the awkward Jim who wins because we like him; in *The Blue Train* (1927), a Robert Stolz operetta written with Britons, Howes set his ID as the guy who can't get a break. Duetting on "You'll Miss My Dancing" with Cicely Debenham, Howes was dismissed for his clownish footwork. "I shall miss you," he sang, while she snapped back with "But you never miss my feet!"

And that was Jim: winsome yet a loser without the support of the ingenue. Thus, Binnie Hale completed him. The sister of Sonnie Hale, Binnie was versatile enough to field comedy and romance in one package, so the show's key number, "Spread a Little Happiness," was hers: a tender anthem about seeing the glass as half-full, a central tenet of musical comedy in general.

Jim's best number was "On the Amazon," sung when he attends the ball disguised as a South American explorer. He awes the chorus girls with the terrors of the jungle. Here's the lead-in dialogue:

ONE GIRL: I suppose there are lots of terribly ferocious animals in the Amazon?
JIM: Oh, there must be. (Suddenly remembering that he's supposed to be the expert in such matters:) I mean, there *are* be. Yet, you wouldn't believe it unless you saw them. And when you saw them . . . you wouldn't believe it!

There follows an insidious chromatic vamp, and Jim's vocal—as he really knows nothing of jungle fauna—uses big words in place of the scary animals—"agnostics," "catacombs," "metronomes." The "hypodermics howl," he sings, to the girls' cries of horror, and "the prophylactics prowl."

Mister Cinders was an international hit, retitled *Jim and Jill* in various languages. Then it went into a Sleeping Princess hiatus till, in 1982, Sting sang "Spread a Little Happiness" as an ironic coda to the movie *Brimstone & Treacle*. As a weirdo who latches onto a family, eventually molesting their disabled daughter, Sting turned the song on its head, glass half-empty. Then, piling irony upon Pelion, the video of his hit single of the number presented him as a cleric leading soup-kitchen ladies in a genial dance, a YouTube essential (not least for Sting's eerie facial expression when he turns toward us at the end).

So "Spread a Little Happiness" was now a Big Hit, and the little King's Head tavern–theatre raised *Mister* (now as *Mr.*) *Cinders* up again on its little piano-accompanied stage, with Ewan McGregor's uncle Denis Lawson as Jim. Having scored a major success in a scaled-down revival of *Pal Joey* opposite Siân Phillips, Lawson was now a go-to for little resuscitations, though he gave a more intense Jim than Bobby Howes had done—a sign of how acting in musicals had changed since 1929. Howes' "On the Amazon" was smooth while Lawson's was fruity and louche, with a devious dance break that almost repositioned "Amazon" as the show's central number.

The 1929 script and score suffered little revision, save for bitty tweaks along the way. (The spoken "Amazon" intro, for example, was delivered almost exactly as quoted above.) Still, as the star, Lawson got the solo of "Spread a Little Happiness." (The Jill sang it in a reprise at the end of Act One.) So popular was the King's Head staging that it moved to the Fortune Theatre, just around the corner from Drury Lane. Lawson led a partly new cast and now there were orchestrations and even a new Ellis number, "Please, Mr. Cinders."[10] So the Sleeping Princess awoke as a classic.

We should note, however, that when it was new, the show's main contribution was to unveil the talent of Vivian Ellis, a remarkably versatile composer who will be filling our ears as these pages turn.

---

[10] Some sources claim the song had been set for and cut from the 1929 original, but the Fortune cast album clearly denotes it as "specially written for this production."

5

And Then a Violin Began To Play

Ivor Novello

Welsh, born (in 1893) Davies and named David Ivor—the Novello came from his musician mother's professional name—he was both stage-struck and musical, and he bound the two into the art by which he is best known, acting in his own operettas. His reputation as a matinee idol and movie star (even scenarist, as author of the dialogue in MGM's *Tarzan the Ape Man*, the start of the Johnny Weissmuller series) has faded. But his seven Big Sing musicals, from 1935 to 1949, stand among the British theatre's most imposing body of work.

They are partly terrible and partly wonderful, vexed by boisterous storytelling yet protected by Novello's extraordinary gifts in melody and harmony. True, these were slow to reveal themselves. He burst into renown for the World War I anthem "Till the Boys Come Home" (to the lyrics of Lena Guilbert Ford), quickly republished as "Keep the Home Fires Burning" and thus known today. It's an effective yet rudimentary piece, giving no hint of what he had in him.

Perhaps experience nurtured an individualist streak, but when he began to write West End shows (we've already seen him contributing to José Collins' *A Southern Maid* and co-composing *Who's Hooper?*), Novello toyed with a chameleon-like ability to tilt his sound toward any style he fancied. So he wasn't Ivor Novello yet. When he and the so-billed Jerome D. Kern shared writing the music to *Theodore & Co.* (1916), a comedy-musical smash about a girl pretending to be her double to get out of a difficulty, some of Novello's songs sound like Kern's.

The latter has the best number, in an aggressive waltz, "Three Hundred and Sixty-Five Days"—but Novello composed the bulk of the score, and he did create (with lyricist Clifford Grey) the evening's Leslie Henson craziness specialty, "My Friend John." Here the melody and harmony are even more primitive than in "Keep the Home Fires Burning," and Grey's words obsess over the pattern of "Whatever I do, it's a certainty, my friend John does the same as me." In fact, they marry the same girl—simultaneously.

It's the coronation of monotony, yet Henson made it a sensation in spite of itself. At least we can relish, in another number, "The Candy Girls," Novello's playful quotation of Mendelssohn's *Midsummer Night's Dream* Wedding March in the last A of the refrain, on the words "Oh! How I want to marry all the little candy girls!"

By the 1920s, Novello was usually the sole composer of his shows, especially in the revues of André Charlot, a Parisian who put on "smart" revues—small-scaled and depending on subtle talents—from the 1910s into the 1930s. In Charlot's *Puppets!* (1924), to the generally vapid lyrics of Dion Titheradge, Novello is clearly experimenting with unusual chording and even mischievous "wrong" notes in the melody. "Same Old Moon," a ballad, takes off on a verse in—most unusually—$\frac{6}{8}$ and runs the first phrase of the refrain from the third of the scale down to an augmented fourth, a flavorsome and all but historically startling sound for 1924. And this isn't a one-off: another song in *Puppets!*, "[She's not content with only me] She Needs Another Now," toys with "American" syncopation in nearly every bar of the refrain.

Of all Novello's work in this early period, the outstanding title is "And Her Mother Came Too!," from another Charlot revue, *A To Z* (1921), which my readers may recall from Jeremy Northam's rendering in the "stuffy house party" film *Gosford Park*.[1] Jack Buchanan introduced the song in *A To Z* in the gloomy-wistful tone he saved for ballads, for "And Her Mother Came Too!" is a lament. Like "My Friend John," it ends in a twist, but it's quite amusing all the way along, Titheradge outdoing himself in a sharp dramatic premise: no matter where Buchanan goes—to the club, to a restaurant, to Ciro's to try the shimmy—his sweetheart's mother crabs his act. At last, while golfing, the old dame loses consciousness. But note the pun:

> She fainted just off the tee,
> My darling whispered to me—
> "Jack, dear, at last we are free!"
> But her mother came to!

---

[1] In fact, Northam is playing Novello, who was, yes, handsome and obliging in the Northam manner. However, Novello seldom if ever left the security of show-biz precincts to dare the iron resistance of the manorial class, with its asinine bias against theatre people. At that, dragon lady Maggie Smith, playing cards during Northam's impromptu concert, passes remarks about how much she loathes having him around.

It's really Novello who makes the number special, because the music, so poised and suave, gives the words a life of their own, starting with a supertonic ninth chord that lends the refrain the sigh of gentlemanly resignation. This chord is a pianist's inspiration, the kind of thing the fingers naturally relax in when noodling around to find a tune; just looking at the sheet music, one sees Novello happening on the chord with a smile, for it's the very voice of a social class trapped by its own etiquette. So beautifully turned that it's akin to an art song, "And Her Mother Came Too!" is the only show tune Novello composed before his late series of operettas that is still heard today.

But we have at last reached those operettas, and a story hangs upon them, improbable yet authentic. "The setting was the [pet thespian hangout] Ivy restaurant," says our old friend W. Macqueen-Pope, "the table just facing the door, with the broad pillar at the back." Novello was lunching with H. M. Tennent, then running Drury Lane when it was failing commercially, and, out of nowhere, Novello told Tennent he had an idea for the next Drury Lane spectacle.

Mind you, Novello wrote plays to this point, not musical librettos, and he was known for more or less trim offerings, not the vast pageants Drury Lane's public expected. Moreover, Novello actually *didn't* have an idea for the next one: he simply started inventing a plot. But then, everything came easily to him; he virtually ran his career on first drafts, and he had no trouble livestreaming (so to say) to Tennent a dire melodrama full of quirks of fate, romantic interludes, big ballets, and even a disaster act-finale only Drury Lane could stage: a shipwreck, with the screams of the doomed, the upturning of the prow, and—

"When can I have it on paper?" Tennent asked, according to Macqueen-Pope. If the Lane's governing board accepts it, the house is Novello's to play with, shipwreck and all.

Of course, when he had to write up his treatment, Novello didn't remember all the details and had to reinvent them. Then, too, perhaps now he was guided by images of specific players for the principals, to sculpt his show around them—Mary Ellis, Broadway's original Rose-Marie (though resident in England since 1930), as heroine Militza Hajos; or the black American singer Elisabeth Welch, for an all but nonexistent role, to sing two numbers in her velveteen alto; and any generic tenor, who ultimately turned out to be Trefor Jones, doughy-looking but a splendid match for Ellis in the surging romantic melodies Novello must already have had in his head; and Novello himself, even if he was no longer able to get through a song with security.

The whole thing was falling into place beautifully, yet Novello always said that what persuaded the theatre's board was the title: *Glamorous Night*. It just sounded like a sure-thing Drury Lane hit.

So *Glamorous Night* initiated the genre of musical by which Novello is known today, virtually unrevivable as wholes yet musically imperishable. And note Novello's unique set of tasks: he wrote the scripts, composed the songs (mostly to Christopher Hassall's lyrics) played the leads, and generally supervised the entire production without actually directing.

As the Novello operettas are hard to tell apart, let us set out another chart. Note that there is invariably a lead soprano and that Novello plays the hero in all but one title:

Glamorous Night (1935)

The one with the shipwreck and the gypsy wedding. Ivor Novello (hereafter IN) as a television inventor—an ultra-modern touch in a very old-fashioned, melodrama-like program—who loses Mary Ellis to the King of Krasnia. Alas my darling we must part: Ellis says, "Happiness is always too much to ask," reprises the title song, and sweeps out of IN's life. Curtain.

Careless Rapture (1936)

The one with a carnival on Hampstead Heath on a bank holiday (featuring a working carousel) and a busy street in China during the Feast Of the Moon: peasants, grandees, priests, tourists, all menaced by ominous thunderclaps till the whole place is torn up by an earthquake. IN as his brother's rival for the soprano (this time Dorothy Dickson) and, hidden by makeup, in disguise as a Chinese bandit chief. IN actually sang for once, albeit in a comic bit, and also took part in the "Miracle Of Nichaow" ballet wearing very little. Macqueen-Pope: "To tell the plot . . . is not possible in cold blood."

Crest Of the Wave (1937)

The one with the train crash: rotating scenery of a landscape behind a passenger car, creating the illusion of a train hurtling along the track. Then: noise! Smoke! The Screams Of the Damned! Also a procession of ghosts in a country mansion singing the patriotic "Rose Of England." IN in a genuinely dual role this time, as a duke and a bad guy. Soprano: Dorothy Dickson.

The Dancing Years (1939)

Much less feverish than the first three, with IN as a part-Jewish composer in Austria from 1911 to 1938. Mary Ellis as an operetta star, with another laden line, to IN: "You know what they'll say of you? He made the whole world dance." Chorus enters, stage is bathed in blue light, everyone waltzes. Curtain.

Arc De Triomphe (1943)

The one that IN wasn't in. A look at a generation in the life of a French opera singer (Mary Ellis), it's the sole work in this list that is lost, except for about half the songs.

Perchance To Dream (1945)

The one with three generations of lovers, the first two unhappy and the last happy. IN's most story-conscious score (to his own lyrics), with unique numbers, unlike the one-size-fits-all passion ballads of previous shows. In particular, "We'll Gather Lilacs" emerges as IN's most potent song, intensely haunting in women's wartime yearning for a reunion with their husbands.

King's Rhapsody (1949)

The intrigues of European royals, in IN's least plot-crazy operetta, with the air of a comedy of manners. IN as an exiled prince involved with princess from elsewhere Vanessa Lee. They marry, but politics intrudes and, once more, alas my darling we must part. The show ends just after the spectacular coronation of IN's young son. On an empty stage, IN slips out of the shadows to pick up a rose that Lee has dropped—for him?—and kneels in prayer at the cathedral altar. IN died during the run and was replaced by Jack Buchanan. Curtain.

These seven titles suffer from long books and short scores inflated by reprises. Worse, they're heavy in ballads even as few of them offer any character individuality. One could trade them out of one show into another, because they're all about romance, romance in the vaguest possible terms— "Love Made the Song," Why Is There Ever Good-Bye?," "Haven Of Your Of My Heart," "Man Of My Heart," "Fly Home, Little Heart," "Waking Or Sleeping [my thoughts are of you]," "[Fling wide] The Gates Of Paradise."

Novello would lay out the tunes, then Christopher Hassall would come up with the words, but no matter how the song was to be used, Hassall seldom had a plot situation to tie his poetry to. So we don't get site-specific lines such as "You've got to pick a pocket or two" (in *Oliver!*), "They're waiting for my Twankey" (in *Trelawny*), "You Jews produce messiahs by the sackful" (in *Jesus Christ Superstar*). Instead, songs are blithely generic—the military or patriotic number ("Uniforms," "Pick Of the Navy"), the New Dance Sensation ("The Glo-Glo," "The Manchuko"), the carefree fox trot ("[You're] Easy To Live With").

Worse yet, Novello loved play-within-the-play scenes, either in rehearsal or performance, extended episodes that had nothing to do with the story at hand. Someone finds sheet music on a piano. Someone's taking a vocal lesson. So the Novello stock company (he loyally kept using the same performers; contralto Olive Gilbert was in all seven shows) could sing about anything or, more often, nothing.

Yet Novello himself, though he played heroes in six of these titles, did not generally sing. Imagine *The Boy Friend* without "I Could Be Happy With You" and "A Room In Bloomsbury." In youth, Novello had been vocalist enough to take part in an eisteddfod; now he was a romantic lead with no voice for romance. Of course, Novello's women leads sing quite passionately of love, for he understood that amorous hunger is operetta's soul. Yet these various noblewomen and opera stars and operetta personalities are singing to a man who is "there" only in the dialogues.

Still, the songs, as such, are stupendous. No other operetta composer outdoes Novello for sheer soaring grandeur, which is why the rest of it didn't matter. These shows had terrific impact when they were new, partly because he is now exploiting chromatic harmony and major seventh chords, and in much more expansive phrases than before. Put simply, he's now writing Big. And *Glamorous Night* even has a few integrated numbers.

Thus, Mary Ellis sang "When the Gypsy Played" because she *is* a gypsy, and the music is a wild Hungarian rhapsody, with the traditional slow *lassan* ("Weave your spell, soft melody of gypsy strings") and the fleet *friska* ("Wild and free as the cold gypsy hills"), then for novelty, a tango section ("Trees in ev'ry leaf began to sing"). Novello called for a solo violin—the showbiz lingua franca of Romany—and Hassall's lyrics are heady (if vague), letting us concentrate on the sensual pleasure of the singer and the music.

Even Elisabeth Welch's two numbers are useful, despite her being nothing more than an insert in the story. She's a stowaway on board the ship that

Novello and Ellis are traveling on, and that's all the credential she needs to deliver "Far Away In Shanty Town," a nostalgic reverie with the feeling of a black spiritual. Then, alone "in one" while, behind the curtain, stagehands readied the set for the second-act-finale ship explosion, she added "The Girl I Knew," an autobiographical "credo" number.

Why does the ship explode? For the most Novello of reasons: Mary Ellis is the mistress of the King of Krasnia, so revolutionaries target her for assassination. Somehow or other—the usual Novello explanation for each next event—Novello and Ellis find their way to a gypsy encampment, where they marry in an elaborate choral scene including some savagely discordant vocal writing and leading at last to the glorious "March Of the Gypsies" (to the music of "When the Gypsy Played," with the Drury Lane brass pealing out like the rage of God).

It's not only Ruritanian but preposterous, though Novello's defenders point out that only two of the operettas, the first (this one) and last (*King's Rhapsody*, set in "Murania" and dealing also with "Norseland") are set in fantasy countries. Further, the audience might have noticed the coincidences piling up in the narrative but for Novello's wonderful music whirling everything around.

Then, too, there was the sheer prestige of The Lane, which really meant something back then. In the second most famous Novello story, King George V and Queen Mary saw the show a few months before the king's death. Meeting Novello at a garden party not long after, the King chided the playwright for ending the musical sadly: "You made the Queen cry." But the most famous Novello story ends more sadly yet, because H. M. Tennent had booked The Lane's annual pantomime before he knew how *Glamorous Night* would go over, and the production had to be taken off while still doing tremendous business.

Novello was beside himself with frustration, but The Lane's pantos were technically complex; many contracts would have been signed long in advance with the creative personnel. Then there was the carping about Mary Ellis' successor, Dorothy Dickson, as the Novello Soprano, on *Careless Rapture* and *Crest Of the Wave*. For, too, Dickson was American (though thoroughly Anglicized) and belonged to the world of musical comedy. Was she worthy of The Lane, London's most historic playhouse? Didn't The Lane suffer a dire flop with an American show, Kern and Hammerstein's *Three Sisters*, filled with musical-comedy riffraff, from Stanley Holloway to (the also American!) Charlotte Greenwood?

However, Dickson proved equal to the challenge of high-toned operetta, and Novello was now at his height, for his fourth (and last) Drury Lane title, *The Dancing Years,* was his biggest success—the only one to get a West End revival (in 1968), with June Bronhill and David Knight. Mary Ellis was back, along with many of the Ivor Novello Light Opera Society players, and for the first time Novello brought the real world into his art: Nazi race mania is part of the plot, and two Wehrmacht officers appeared in the last scene. Rudi Kleber (the Novello role) gives Ellis a son, in secret, for she has married a prince, and of course the script brings the boy on stage to meet—unknowingly—his father.

So *The Dancing Years'* plot twists were the ones that amused your grandparents, and the repartee was imitation Noël Coward: on the matter of taking an Italian lover, Ellis said, "One must have an Italian, it's like the meazles." But there were imaginative touches as well, as in two scenes in dance and mime, both entitled "A Masque Of Vienna." Unrelated to the plot, they presented "types" of Viennese—army officers, a cabby, a toy vendor, young girls and their governess in the first set; the earlier principals now on hard times (the main officer has become a chauffeur), along with a group of beggars trying out the charleston in the second set.

One might call these arty propositions "flamboyant" or "precious" or, looking past the euphemisms, "gay," because Novello was. Further, the King's criticism notwithstanding, his operettas continued to end sadly; five of the seven deal with thwarted love, and what, in Novello's era, could be gayer (even if Novello had a lifelong partner, the actor Robert Andrews)?

In the world of creativity, gays are often the most inventive people in the room. They are also defiers of tradition, and Novello aroused great suspicion in the theatre community by insisting on Leontine Sagan as his director on all four of the Lane shows. It was the first time a woman directed there—a Central European woman at that, used to screaming at and reviling actors in rehearsals, which violated British etiquette. But Sagan had trained with Max Reinhardt, so masterly in his use of crowds, and Novello's operettas were heavily populated. He didn't want capable producing: he wanted magic, all the more so because the dialogue portions were so dryly composed. These works really are bizarre concoctions, immensely successful and famous when new and now just famous in a blithely has-been way, like a veteran actor who enlivens a party when the other guests had thought he was dead.

Leaving The Lane, Novello went freelance, first with a failure, *Arc De Triomphe.* Perhaps thinking he'd better pull a rabbit out of his hat with an alteration of format, Novello had another vast hit with *Perchance To Dream*, with its three sets of lovers from the Regency period to Novello's present day, all three couples played by Novello and Roma Beaumont. By far Novello's best work, *Perchance To Dream* avoids the bizarre escapades of the earlier shows and even, somewhat, the performance pieces to concentrate on character and situation songs. Interestingly, he wrote his own lyrics this time, pursuing a single theme (and in scenery that almost never changed from the front hall of the country house Huntersmoon): the thwarted love of Graham and Melinda in 1818 that is thwarted again for Valentine and Melanie in 1843 at last resolves happily for Bay and Melody in 1945.

Other players also doubled or tripled, with the usual Novello troupe of Olive Gilbert; Muriel Barron; Dunstan Hart; the faithful Robert Andrews, known to all as Bobbie; and, new to the lists, professional old crab Margaret Rutherford. She had the best lines:

LADY CHARLOTTE: Any man worthy of the name has a mistress, until he marries—then he has several.

Amid the typical Novello plot twists there is an abiding aperçu, from Hamlet's worry, in his "To Be Or Not To Be," that death might lead to a meditative state, a kind of solitary confinement of the mind, endlessly going over one's disappointments:

>   ... To die, to sleep;
>   To sleep: perchance to dream: ay, there's the rub;
>   For in that sleep of death what dreams may come ...

If we dream, we become ghosts, dead but not gone, less haunting than haunted. Thus, in a reversion to the old anything-goes Novello, Act One's Graham is a highwayman who returns to Huntersmoon gravely wounded. We can imagine the audience's worry that the act might end with the beloved star's death. As the lights start to fade and Melinda looks on in despair, Graham delivers a key line, anticipating the show's (happy) ending:

NOVELLO: Look for me, my sweet—as I shall look for you—always—always.

And he dies as the curtain closes down Act One.

That would have been some intermission at the premiere: *Novello dies?* Always alert to an opportunity, he then left the second generation of lovers, in Act Two, preparing to run off together adulterously and thus face social ruin. "No more Windsor [Castle and visits with the Royals]," Valentine warns Melanie. But love sweeps all before it in shows like these, even if we die for it. So Valentine actually quotes Graham's last line to Melinda (in the previous act, cited just above) about looking for her. But how does Valentine know those words?

And what happened to the elopement plan? We find out in *Perchance To Dream*'s final act: Melanie killed herself before they could get away. But now all is well between the Novello characters and the Roma Beaumont characters, as the third couple redeems all the sadness:

MELODY: So much has happened here—real tragedies.
 It's a happy house now, it must give them peace.
BAY: You mean that the present is healing the wounds of the past?
MELODY: Yes, that's it.

They leave, and the ghosts appear while, backstage, Novello and Beaumont frantically get back into their Act One Graham and Melinda costumes. Music. Chorus of ghosts. Then the two stars re-appeared as if meeting for the first time ever, redeemed for a dreamless sleep, the end of worry and all. And there the curtain fell.

The reason this score is so good, I repeat, is Novello's sudden wish to bond it with the action. When Olive Gilbert's majestic contralto was heard in the usual Olive Gilbert Specialty, it was "Highwayman Love," a driving waltz that points up Graham's extracurricular hobby. So the song is, for once, about the show, a thrilling piece especially when Gilbert reached the end of the second verse and the men's chorus instantly piled into a repeat of the refrain. This was not an arranger's work, but Novello's: the Welsh know music.

There was one problem in this, for Roma Beaumont, the Melinda-Melanie-Melody, played the central romance with Novello's Graham-Valentine-Bay yet had relatively little to sing, because her voice was unsteady. A secondary principal, Muriel Barron, in effect substituted for Beaumont, who was left with the minuet-like "When I Curtsied To the King" and the New Dance Sensation, "The Glo-Glo," upbeat enough for Beaumont to glide through without incident—and she was at least a capable dancer.

Still, it's odd to find Muriel Barron getting the choice ballads, the aching "Love Is My Reason" and "A Woman's Heart." Isn't it already strange enough that Novello's many romantic heroes never sing? And consider "The Victorian Wedding," *Perchance To Dream*'s romantic production number, all thrilled up with bridesmaids, guests, the vicar, and all the principals including Margaret Rutherford. Surely we will hear Novello's opposite caroling of her nuptial joy—but, again, Beaumont wasn't up to it, so Barron has to be the bride, with a rapturous solo beginning "My heart's afire and filled with desire"—and the music leaps off the words with a fierce splendor. Isn't this why Novello's problematic format ruled the theatrical scene? The flaws were as nothing next to the intensity of the music.

Barron had as well, in duet with Olive Gilbert, "We'll Gather Lilacs," Novello's greatest song and a wartime anthem (again, of women awaiting their men's return) to match his "Keep the Home Fires Burning." Unlike the Novello passion ballads with their deceptive harmonies, "Lilacs" is pure melody, Schubertian in its wistful grandeur and obviously of great appeal to the public in *Perchance To Dream*'s 1945. Its last line, "When you are home once more," could be the most intimate lyric of the era.

At 1,022 performance, the show put Novello back on high, and his last completed operetta, *King's Rhapsody*, returned him with great success to the boulevard-comedy royal intrigue of elites high-hatting each other. While appearing in it, he unveiled *Gay's the Word* (1951), an exit from his operettas as a musical-comedy backstager built around Cicely Courtneidge, as actor manager Gay Daventry. Alan Melville wrote the lyrics; he and Novello devised an opening chorus spoofing Novello's style, as unmistakably "Ruritanian" guardsmen lament that they no longer enjoy "nights . . . considered glamorous," because "Since *Oklahoma!*, we've been in a coma."

Novello's dialogue was really terrible here, though thinking of Courtneidge's energetic sarcasm, one can believe she landed every scene:

A PRODUCTION ASSISTANT: How are we going to pay for all these dresses?
GAY: The same way as we pay for everything else.
ASSISTANT: But we haven't.
GAY: Exactly, that's what I mean.

Composing down as befits musical comedy, Novello nevertheless turned out a tuneful score, though critics have overpraised Courtneidge's Act One finale specialty, "Vitality," on the essential quality of all the great stars—and

Courtneidge names them, from Gertie Millar to "José Collins as the 'Maid.' " It's one of those fake nostalgia numbers, bordering on emotional blackmail as if intimidating the audience into having to keen over a series of icons. (It even cites sisters Zena and Phyllis Dare, appearing for the first time together with Novello in *King's Rhapsody*, a few hundred yards downstream from *Gay's the Word*'s Savile Theatre at the Palace.) With the chorus building the number into a Big One, Courtneidge fakes exhaustion, collapses into a chair, and then leaps up at the last second to shout, "Vitality!" to end the act.

Courtneidge's own vitality, and the music, and Novello's name were enough to make *Gay's the Word* a hit. But now Novello was losing his own vitality at only fifty-eight, and he had a number of small attacks. Olive Gilbert, who lived almost next to him upstairs at the Strand Theatre, got a late-night phone call from Bobbie Andrews, and came at once with a flask of brandy. The doctor came, too, but there was nothing to be done, and Novello, feebly answering the doctor's questions, pronounced his own epitaph: "I'm afraid I've had it."

6

Dancing With a Ghost

The 1930s and 1940s

Thus far, we have seen the invention of the musical (in ballad opera); the development of a strong musical foundation (in the G & S era); the separation of the musical's elemental power into the mostly amusing shows (such as *The Bing Boys Are Here*) and, alternatively, the mostly lyrical ones (such as *The Maid Of the Mountains*). Each next era marks an advance on the previous era.

Until now—for the years between the 1920s and the 1950s are disappointingly conservative. In the US, despite the economic collapse that all but banned experimentation, there were a few notable breakaways, as in the enhanced musical integration of Jerome Kern's *The Cat and the Fiddle* and *Music In the Air* (both seen in London at the time) and the social-inquiry shows *Johnny Johnson* and *The Cradle Will Rock*, too American to travel just then (though they made it to the UK later on).

Comparably, the British musical lacks ambition at this time. Excepting the operettas of Ivor Novello (in the previous chapter), those of Noël Coward (in the one after this), and *Me and My Girl*, now celebrated because of a smash revival, only the aficionado could readily cite many thirties or forties West End titles. *The Mikado*, *Florodora*, and *Chu Chin Chow* are conjuring names. But there follows a gap not broken till *The Boy Friend*, *Salad Days*, *Oliver!*.

One problem was the paucity of Jewish writers, as this ethnic group is notable for imaginative expertise in musical theatre, one of many reasons why the American brand is so protean. By comparison, Nazi race psychosis all but destroyed the German stage musical in the 1930s; things got so dire that the Jewish composer Eduard Künneke had to be quietly assigned official Aryan status just to keep the form singing.

Most disappointing is the passéiste choreography, while the American musical was letting dance evolve most originally. One reason was the American penchant for binding elite with popular art, drafting people from the ballet world to rejuvenate the traditional show-biz "combinations" with the physics of modern dance. Another reason was the influence of the twenties black musicals: Broadway's critics always mentioned how novel black dancing was, and one may be sure that theatre people frequented the shows, looking for inspiration. By contrast, Britain's Pathé newsreels (seen today on YouTube) record how ordinary ensemble dancing of the thirties British musical really was (though the solo dance stars such as Jack Buchanan and Elsie Randolph could be quite adventurous).

It's worth noting that Charles B. Cochran—Britain's biggest producer of musicals between George Edwardes and Cameron Mackintosh—hired American choreographers for his most aspiring shows of the early 1930s, *Ever Green* (1930) and *Nymph Errant* (1933). Cochran commissioned Americans for the scores as well, though as with similar outings discussed in the chapter on the 1920s, the shows as wholes were so British in style that they never got a major mounting in New York.

Cochran has joined us several times already for his "smart" twenties revues, but he put on many a book show, at that in spendthrift opulence. Not only was *Ever Green* a spectacle—Cochran even rebuilt its theatre, the Adelphi, in art deco fashion, the fourth playhouse at its address, like so many others of the old days right on the Strand.

Like all great producers, Cochran was a talent spotter. So was André Charlot, Cochran's rival in the revue—but Cochran lured Jessie Matthews away from Charlot, as we saw in *One Dam Thing After Another* and now in *Ever Green,* a spectacular book musical that introduced Britain to the recent German invention of the revolving stage. Rodgers and Hart wrote the score and, more interesting, two black Americans, Buddy Bradley and Billy Pierce, handled the dances.

Ever Green was a sensation, though it sold only 254 performances, because Cochran loved putting shows together but grew impatient after they opened and sometimes took a piece off to free the theatre for the next one.

A sensation, yes. Yet the book, by Benn W. Levy, is insane: Matthews becomes a stage star by pretending to be her grandmother. "A clever blend of musical comedy and revue," said the *London Daily Mirror,* aligning with all the other critics—another way of noting that the score leaned heavily on "on-stage" numbers having nothing to do with the plot. But it looked great and it sounded great, making the usual musical-comedy stop in Paris (and Spain as well) and singing with that crispy American syncopation and crazy harmony. One ballad, "Dear! Dear!," slips slithery chromatic harmony in between the vocal phrases, and the release of "Harlemania" has the effect of *Salad Days'* magic piano: if you hear it, you must dance. The Big Hit was "Dancing On the Ceiling," in which Matthews and Sonnie Hale executed their pas de deux on an upside-down set, moving around a chandelier that, Richard Rodgers thought, looked like "an incandescent metal tree."

Nymph Errant, also at the Adelphi, featured a score by Cole Porter—the ideal songwriter, Cochran must have thought, for a work that passes risqué into outright bawdiness. Romney Brent's book, from James Laver's novel, told of a finishing-school maiden exhorted by her headmistress to "experiment"—which turns out to be an international search for the perfect lay. The narrative proved unfortunately episodic, though the heroine's four school friends each turned up somewhere along the way, lending the evening a shallow unity.

More troublesome was Porter's score, which left most of the situation numbers to the ensemble, as in a quartet to open a scene *sur la plage*, "Neauville-Sur-Mer"; a tarantella for Italian servants, "They're Always Entertaining"; and, in Turkey, "Ruins," from a gang of tourists. The rest of the music—the character songs that should focus on the principals—was mainly cabaret specialties sung by a succession of minor players, because there was only one principal, the heroine. So the ear was relentlessly distracted by glorified extras who entered, pulled focus, and left. The songs were fine, but they had no reason for being—"The Cocotte"; "Georgia Sand"; "Plumbing"; "Si Vous Aimez les Poitrines," on the stage of the Folies Bergère; "Solomon," for American Elisabeth Welch, who made it the sensation of the show and went on trademarking it for some sixty years.[1]

The heroine had one superb number, "The Physician," cut from an earlier Porter show. The lament of a woman whose doctor is captivated by her looks but emotionally unavailable, it revels in gaudy rhyme: "larynx" and "pharynx"; "double hurdle" and "pelvic girdle"; "He thought a lot o' my medulla oblongata." However, the piece was originally written for the veteran Marie Cahill, playing a Society gadabout in *The New Yorkers*: it needs a mature woman used to paying heavy doctor bills to get a man's attention while her husband is out roostering. It doesn't suit *Nymph Errant*'s finishing-school girl, and, worse, it is crowbarred into the script on bald pretext. ("In school,

---

[1] Welch told Porter biographer William McBrien that Porter himself explained the song's bizarre melisma whenever the name Solomon is mentioned thus: once, in Turkey, Porter was having coffee with the sultan and could hear his concubines ululating in their apartments. Intrigued, Porter noted down the pitches that were to give the song its Eastern tinta, as the first syllable of *Solo*mon takes over a dozen notes to traverse.

two years ago, I had measles," she says, in the Turkish harem scene that hosts also "Solomon," and off we go.)

Ironically, the score is a fine suite of songs in itself—Porter's favorite among his own, in fact. But it's not a good score for a book show, as it emphasizes the disconnected plot. The men in the heroine's life come and go as the sets keep changing; *Nymph Errant* is the West End's *opera senza amore*. At least Cochran let Doris Zinkeisen spend lavishly in designing the decor. And, last and most, he built this show around the single greatest star the British musical ever produced—Gertrude Lawrence, crazy, dazzling, and unique.

Nymph Errant was the one time Lawrence's home country gave her an important story musical; aside from her straight plays, Lawrence's essential music theatre was all American, from *Oh, Kay!* (which she did take to London) to *Lady In the Dark* to *The King and I*. Unlike such stars as Jack Buchanan or Julie Andrews, Lawrence is indefinable. Her soprano was unsteady, she was what they call a "dance faker," and she occasionally uttered lines in a kind of sing-song. Still, Noël Coward wrote plays for her because no one else could match her for sheer presence. "Every night," in *Private Lives*, he told his godson Sheridan Morley, "I would look across the balcony [set] at Gertie in her white Molyneux dress and she would simply take my breath away."

She was a theatre animal rather than a technician, and she completely lacked impulse control, which made her mercurial—so you couldn't take your eyes off her because you sensed she was capable of anything. "The stage was . . . jumping with excitement," Agnes de Mille said of Lawrence, at *Nymph Errant*'s Manchester tryout premiere. "Acting shimmered. Gertie moves like a fish through shadows."

It was a big night generally. Le tout London had come up to get the first look, and such was the interest in a Cochran-Porter-Lawrence show with possibly scandalous subject matter that American NBC sent a radio team to broadcast a "special" on the event back in the states.

Then *Nymph Errant* opened in London, and despite all its Cochran style, Porter wit, and Lawrence sorcery, it got deflating notices. "A pantomime for intellectuals" was one take—in other words, a kind of sophisticated kiddy show. "In sentiment," ran another report, "it is as parched as a pea," because the lack of a romantic throughline made the show as emotionally unavailable as that physician. What was expected to be the hit of the year, even of the decade, ran only 154 performances.

Yet it remained famous because of Lawrence, who had only nineteen years of life left by then. The word "legendary" should be limited to people like Gilgamesh and King Arthur, but if ever a modern-day thespian was legendary, it was Lawrence. The tradition of lowering the lights of Broadway in memoriam—back when it was reserved for the elite and not made into a participation trophy—started when Lawrence died. And one of my earliest memories was of my mother's getting me out of bed on the night of her death as a television channel was about to run a kinescope of Lawrence singing "Getting To Know You," as it would have been my last chance to see her in her element.

Second to Lawrence at this time was Jack Buchanan, still in the kinds of roles we saw him playing two chapters ago. But they were good musical-comedy parts: direct, sporty, carefree. Even reassuring—you always knew what Buchanan was about, whereas the protean Lawrence was the girl who doesn't dance with the man who brought her. Here's Noël Coward again, with host Edgar Lustgarten on BBC Radio in 1957: "What fascinates me is when a beautiful, talented actress can come on the stage [and make] your blood curdle with excitement and pleasure yet . . . make such a cracking pig of herself over where her dressing room is or some such triviality." Lawrence's instability was what exhilarated her performances, while Buchanan, the perfect gentleman, seemed so on stage, even in his dancing, as when he would suddenly freeze in mid-step with a smile at his partner: just fooling, my dear. In a way, Lawrence's shows were wondrous problems; Buchanan's were sweet solutions.

Still taking a superintendant role in production, Buchanan appeared in such stage shows as *Stand Up and Sing* (1931), *The Flying Trapeze* (1935), and *This'll Make You Whistle* (1936), then concentrated on movie musicals. Of his West End titles, *Mr. Whittington* (1934) was the most interesting, as a modern version of the Victorian burlesques that helped take the musical from ballad opera to the Gaiety shows. Buchanan played a present-day Dick Whittington (supported by his ever-faithful dancing mate, Elsie Randolph) who conquers adversity to acquire a fortune and the Girl. Oddly, *Mr. Whittington* borrowed the plot structure of Rodgers and Hart's Broadway hit *Peggy-Ann*, seen in London in 1927: the title-role protagonist spends most of the evening in a surrealistic dream made of essentially disconnected episodes. As always, the score was tailored to Buchanan. His "Weep No More, My Baby" (smuggled in from Broadway's *Murder At the Vanities*) created a personalized moment for the star's fans.

The comedy musical became less popular, as the jesters made the now eminently respectable music hall their venue of choice. Nevertheless, W. C. Sellar and R. J. Yeatman's *1066 And All That* was turned into a musical revue with a short and rudimentary score. Really, how would songs fit into this whimsical spoof of history books, grandly characterizing this or that event as "memorable" or "not memorable" and declaring such and such "A Good Thing"? Sample jest: Henry VIII played a game with his ministers, who were "blindfolded and knelt down with their heads on a block of wood; they then guessed whom the King would marry next."

As it was, composer Alfred Reynolds and librettist-lyricist Reginald Arkell[2] emphasized sketches over songs, simply trifling with the doings of British history rather than adapting Sellar and Yeatman specifically. So Canute and the tide turned up in a beach scene, as a bathing beauty sang, "I'm the good friend of King Canute," followed by "How do you like my bathing suit?" Later, Nelson, Napoléon, and Wellington got into "The Same Old Hat," arguing over how to wear those old military chapeaux that look like upside-down soup tureens.

But there was an outstanding comedy musical in *Me and My Girl* (1937), famous then and phenomenal later, when the 1984 revival monstered its way from London and New York to Mexico City and Tokyo (by the all-women Takarazuka company). The original production centered on Lupino Lane, of a notable theatre dynasty (the actress and director Ida Lupino was his niece), specializing in insouciant Cockney characters. His Bill Snibson was the protagonist of *Twenty To One* (1935), a piece with just a few songs and fleet enough to fit in two shows a night. Figuring that Snibson was too rich a character to waste on a single show, Lane announced *Me and My Girl* as a sequel, though nothing connected the new piece with the old one.

In fact, there was shocking news: Snibson was the scion of a fancy family! To assume the title, he must alter his personal style from bloke to lord and also renounce his lady love (Teddie St. Denis). So the fun stems from Bill's struggles with the ways of the bosses (including a wrestling match with a re-gally red ermine-lined cape) and the romance teeters on whether he will give up his girl for the gala Lady Jacquie (Betty Frankiss), a British knockoff of the American gold digger type. Filling the narrative out with an imperious

---

[2] Arkell claims a singular credit as author of the book for the only English-language musical Kurt Weill composed before he went to America: *A Kingdom For a Cow* (1937), a revision of an unfinished German work, *Der Kuhhandel*. *Kingdom* lasted only two weeks, at the Savoy; the lyrics were by Desmond Carter.

dragon of a duchess (Mignon O'Doherty) and a sympathetic mentor of a lord (George Graves), Lane had a neat parable about class: to rise in station, must one first lose his individuality?

Another two-shows-nightly attraction, *Me and My Girl* was the work of composer Noel Gay, with L. Arthur Rose and Douglas Furber on book and lyrics, though as producer-director Lupino Lane could be called the show's auteur. And his message, in the end, is that the Bill Snibsons of the world are too much a natural force to lose their individuality. It's the noblesse who lose out, because their every act is a chore. Where's the fun in life? True, they're the materially well off and they get a lot of kowtow. But noblesse *oblige*.

Further, the show had a secret weapon outlining this, in the first-act finale, when Snibson's people meet the bosses right there in the baronial mansion that Bill is to inherit: "The Lambeth Walk." One of the Biggest Hits in the British musical's history, this number uses an ebullient melody and some cocky syncopation to express an idyll of working-class life in the transpontine neighborhood of Lambeth. "Everything free and easy,"[3] it tells us, "do as you darn well pleasey." It's a false idyll, of course, oblivious of the Dickensian outrage of the workhouse, child slavery, debtors' prisons. But thirties musicals were one-and-a-half generation ahead of naturalistic depictions of life on the mean streets, as we'll presently see.

No, for now a *Me and My Girl* can give us only the fantasy, not least when a very aged codger with a cane responded to the thrill of this Lambeth Walk by going gaga over Teddie St. Denis and had to be pulled away by (so it appeared) his reproachful daughter. Immediately after, the assembled toffs picked up the dance themselves, striking a discord with little Lane in his somehow uppity little mustache and St. Denis in her cheesy finery. After a bit, the two traded hats, she taking his derby and he donning her flowery whatsit, and it was all . . . jolly. A live radio broadcast of a matinee made *Me and My Girl* a national treasure, and there was even a television relay.[4]

During *Me and My Girl*'s original run of 1,646 performances, Lane starred in a film version (called *The Lambeth Walk*, because the dance steps and song

---

[3] Thus published, though on stage Lane would say "Everything bright and breezy."

[4] In an internet series entitled *Screen Plays*, John Wyver explores BBC Television's little-recalled experiment in filming West End productions, using cameras set up to capture both full-stage and semi-close-up shots. Limited to the late 1930s, the project took in three musicals: *Magyar Melody*, a *Desert Song* revival, and *Me and My Girl*. Caught nineteen months into the run, in the spring of 1939, the telecast was such a hit it was repeated, but the war ended television service, and when it resumed, in 1945, West End managers banded together to discourage giving away the store with further such transmissions.

had become more famous than the show itself), then put on several revivals. Came now an apotheosis, in 1985, when Mike Ockrent put together a revisal, working with Stephen Fry on a new script. They followed the 1937 storyline, sneaking in one racy joke:

POSH MADAME: (introducing a debutante to Bill) Do you know my daughter May?
BILL: No, but thanks for the tip.

In fact, it's an old gag, dating back at least to Cole Porter's *Fifty Million Frenchmen*, which had never got to London before, closing during its 1931 Glasgow tryout.

Naturally, Ockrent had to expand the stingy 1937 score. As it happened, Gay and Furber had already done so, much earlier, to make the show agreeable to regional amateur groups. Then a few other Gay pieces were added as well, some with his own lyrics. These included a key number, "Leaning On a Lamppost," a George Formby number from the film *Feather Your Nest*. The sight of Bill Snibson in his ermine cape, leaning on that lamppost, formed the key art in the show's posters and was built into the second act's big number. So it is odd to screen its appearance in *Feather Your Nest*, as there is no lamppost in sight: Formby is simply performing in a studio, playing his banjo and accompanied by a pianist. He sings it as "Leaning On *the* Lamppost," the original title, and from his vacuous delivery, it's clear that he hasn't the slightest idea what the lamppost is doing in the song—but we'll get to the curious talent of George Formby a bit later on.

Ockrent's *Me and My Girl* deserved its great success. His cast, apart from Robert Lindsay's casually appealing Bill Snibson, was no more than acceptable, but the "new" score pleased even when a song took a detour out of the plot simply to make merry. True, by 1985, the best musicals had abandoned these makeweights. A show like *Wild Grows the Heather* (1956) slipped "He's Got the Whole World In His Hands" into a piece based on farouche James M. Barrie highland fluff; and even the experimental *Stop the World I Want To Get Off* (1960) seduced the pop charts with the incongruous "Gonna Build a Mountain." Yet a high bar was set by the 1970s, and musicals needed some generic or structural reason if a number or two strayed off the reservation.

Me and My Girl's reason was archeological: it was a revival of not just an old work but an old style, with the scene-setting opening chorus, the "Isn't it time for a cheer-up ditty?" attitude, the song-plugging reprises. "The

Lambeth Walk" itself enjoyed endless self-indulgent repetitions before the first-act curtain, and "The Sun Has Got His Hat On" had no purpose beyond rousing the public after the intermission.

Further, Lindsay broke the fourth wall in "Love Makes the World Go Round," giving his line of the release in an Al Jolson "Mammy!" voice, while mentor Frank Thornton responded with a Noël Coward imitation, clipped and disdainful. Then, too, a duet for Thornton and duchess Ursula Smith, "If Only You Had Cared For Me," dared to revive the Jurassic Era $\frac{6}{8}$ rhythm, though this was easy to miss, as the two talked rather than sang their parts. To top it all, "Song of Hareford," a dynastic march, recalled the "ancestor portraits coming to life" sequence in Gilbert and Sullivan's *Ruddigore*.

All this retro was startling in 1985, but Ockrent's production made it seem fresh from the mint. The opening number, "A Weekend At Hareford," is a great example, for on the cast album it's no more than a tolerable place-setter. Ockrent, however (with his choreographer, Gillian Gregory, and set designer, Martin Johns), filled it with kinetic detail using stage technology so advanced it questioned whether this really was, precisely, a "revival."

The curtain rose on a freeze-frame of grandees perched in and atop a roof-less motorcar. As they sang of the excitement of getting away from the dreary affairs of the city, they got into position for a chauffeured ride, bobbing up and down as the car took off. (Of course, it was the backdrop that moved, in the same old theatrical trick Ivor Novello used for the speeding train in *Crest Of the Wave*.)

Throughout, the passengers maintained the illusion of traveling—bouncing in their seats, rising and sitting again, avidly "conversing." All along, they were singing with the fastidious articulation British actors in musicals employ to characterize the upper set, thus warning us that the show will be about class as much as romance. After all, these merry people are, in another part of the forest, Bill Snibson's antagonists.

With the ride's end signaled by the rise of a scrim, the car was physically dismantled even as the luggage was taken away, and now the backdrop rose into the flies, opening up the stage for a view of Hareford's front door. Servants bustled about as the mansion's gate separated into halves. Top staff came out to greet the guests even as the song took on the air of a lovably dotty march.

Ockrent wasn't done yet: the house façade now turned on a revolve as side-pieces were lowered left and right, creating a completely new set of the interior as the guests poured in through the front door. (We had missed their exit in all the activity, so this seemed to be another trick of the eye; the audience would clap.) As a last little extra, three legal types tossed their bowlers to waiting footmen, and the number then sped on to its conclusion.

Robert Lindsay's indispensable protagonist led the company when New York finally saw the show, and the rest of the casting was stronger than in London, Maryann Plunkett's "my girl" a more interesting singer than London's Emma Thompson. Then, too, the domineering duchess reached ultimate completion in New York's Jane Connell, the ranking expert in such parts. Interestingly, though America got a replica of the London staging, there still were tweaks. Another Gay number, "Hold My Hand," was added for Bill and his girl to remind the audience that the story is as much theirs as his, and the two oldsters' clopping $\frac{6}{8}$ duet was dropped during the tryout; that much antiquing Americans couldn't absorb.

In a way, Noel Gay typifies the musical's sedentary nature in this era, its lack of ambition. Gay was a good tunesmith—but Gay's shows were all comedy musicals, the form least concerned with an artistic score. Sonnie Hale and Jessie Matthews, fresh from *Ever Green*, were in Gay's *Hold My Hand* (1931), but mainly to give Stanley Lupino (of the family) rest periods. Gay's *Love Laughs—!* (1935), made on Laddie Cliff, was perhaps the eight thousandth show with a stolen-jewels plot. Gay's *The Love Racket* (1943) offered comic Arthur Askey, meek and be-spectacled, with a zany whimsy; but it was more of the same. Even Gay's *Meet Me Victoria* (1944) was just another Lupino family outing, despite the intriguing title, referring to the railroad station next to Lupino Lane's business address, the Victoria Palace Theatre.

Other than Coward and Novello, one songwriter was willing to try unusual outlets for his talent: Vivian Ellis, classically trained and thus often ingenious in how he put his music together. His interpolation into the Novello score for the Hulbert-Courtneidge revue *The House That Jack* [Hulbert] *Built* (1929), "My Heart Is Saying," starts its A strain with straightforward quarter notes then instantly slithers into chromatic-jazz sixteenth notes, as if baiting the dance bands to take it up.

Wary of headliners and their self-centered demands, Ellis nevertheless took on a Sophie Tucker vehicle, *Follow a Star* (1930). When Ellis played his score (written with Douglas Furber) for Tucker, she announced, "Tomorrow we must see about *my* songs"—because, like all unique performers, America's "red hot mama" demanded material made on her. She didn't sing what-have-yous. She sang Sophie Tucker numbers.

"I knew," says Ellis in his memoirs, most ironically, "that I was going to *love* her." He felt the same about her house composer, Ted Shapiro, and lyricist, Jack Yellen, but he had to work with them. Worse, *Follow a Star* was very loosely structured precisely to let Sophie sing whatever she wanted, with a Dixie number here and an intimate confession there—but, gritting his teeth, Ellis wrote them: the rousing "That's Where the South Begins" and the comical "I Never Can Think Of the Words."

And he did learn something about songwriting. "That old buzzard is after something," he noted: to "tear the hearts out of her fans." So, he says, he "borrowed a book of Hebrew tunes" to bone up for creating "If Your Kisses Can't Hold the Man You Love [then your tears won't bring him back]." It's uncanny how well Ellis caught the American torch sound (to Jack Yellen's lyric), lachrymose yet strangely determined, feminist despite despair. It was so right for Tucker that she had no choice but to conclude the show with it: nothing could follow that number.

Ellis is known for story musicals, but he did one major (and very successful) Cochran revue, *Streamline* (1934). With lyrics by A. P. Herbert and Ronald Jeans, Ellis produced what revue required, the up-tune "You Turned Your Head," the ballad "Kiss Me, Dear," and the lament of the eternal nanny, "Other People's Babies, Norah Howard's touching report from a community seldom heard from—"mother to dozens and nobody's wife."

Streamline's pièce de résistance was an extended takeoff on Gilbert and Sullivan, *Perseverance* (a play, obviously, on *Patience*). Like every musician in the land, Ellis had had the Savoyard style in his ear since childhood, and Herbert[5] worked up a faultlessly stylish pastiche. The premise: one of a pair of twins will succeed to a title—but which?—as the chorus women follow the plot with cries "Oh, rapture!" and "Oh, disappointment!" and everyone gets in on the tra-las. There was a patter song, an a cappella glee in four-part harmony, and, after one of the brothers said, "But see, here comes an elderly female who may be able to untangle us," a Little Buttercup figure revealed her role in the mystery.

It was all quite zany, not least when "Take a Dainty Paradox" (mating *The Gondoliers'* "Take a Pair Of Sparkling Eyes" with Gilbert's love of puzzles) went on to "Dress it like a chocolate box." The critics thought *Perseverance* a treat, but the first-nighters took it in, Ellis later recalled, "in almost complete silence." Worse, Florence Desmond, Esmond Knight, and the others

---

[5] *Streamline* co-author Ronald Jeans did not contribute to *Perseverance*.

must have started overplaying to force the laughs, for Cochran biographer James Harding reports that on a later visit Cochran thought *Perseverance* had devolved from "a burlesque of Gilbert and Sullivan" into "a rather bad burlesque of an amateur operatic society."

Ellis wrote lyrics as well as music, in three shows in 1938, The *Fleet's Lit Up*, *Under Your Hat*, and *Running Riot*. One of Ellis' favorite singers, Frances Day, had a luscious ballad in *The Fleet's Lit Up*, "South Wind," haunting in its pivoting from tonic to subdominant sixth chords and use of sixths and major sevenths in its vocal line. It was staged hauntingly, too, with a follow-up dance, but the show's producer, George Black, cut it during the tryout. "I hate art," he told Ellis.[6]

After war service, Ellis renewed his old alliance with A. P. Herbert and Charles Cochran, on the fantastical tale of a shopgirl running for Parliament who leads a fight against closing the nation's pubs. Herbert called it *Big Ben* (1946), and Cochran, thinking its romantic-satiric air needed a classical master, asked William Walton to compose. Walton said no and Ellis got the job, unveiling his own romantic-satiric "light opera" style.

But *Big Ben* did not succeed—and it isn't first-class Vivian Ellis, either. It did end wonderfully, though. After being locked in Big Ben's tower under a banning by Parliament, the heroine emerged to join the entire cast, lined along the apron to gaze upstage at a huge replica of Big Ben's clockface. To the tune of "London Town," a thrilling anthem that Ellis constructed as a passacaglia, with a ground bass banging out Big Ben's chimes while the melody proceeded above it, the company touched a patriotic nerve in war-ravaged 1946, at peace yet burdened with many of the deprivations of homefront culture.

Cochran's next Ellis-Herbert title, *Tough At the Top* (1949), was another "combination" musical, a Ruritanian romance with a political subtext, as if Clement Atlee had written an operetta. Casting was difficult, as the Boy was a prizefighter and the Girl a runaway princess, types a bit exotic for the West End talent pool. So Cochran went a-marketing, to find his two leads in New York in late 1948, where Maria D'Attili was in a revival of Gian Carlo Menotti's double bill of *The Medium* and *The Telephone* at the City Center. The

---

[6] An exponent of the comedy musical, Black may have thought the ballad-and-ballet format too elite, but he did produce *The Lisbon Story* (1943), a dire operetta about wartime espionage that concluded with the heroine's being shot to death (though the piece ran over a year). That finale is one of the two things this otherwise forgotten show is known for; the other is its Big Hit, "Pedro the Fisherman," recorded by Richard Tauber and Julie Andrews, among many others. It even found its way into the 1972 West End revival of *The Maid Of the Mountains*.

fighter was coincidentally playing just a block away at the Ziegfeld, in Agnes de Mille's eerie staging of Britten's *The Rape of Lucretia* with "simulcasts," one to sing and one to dance. A young bass named George (later Giorgio) Tozzi, fresh from the conservatory, was singing the villain of the piece, Tarquinius— "panther agile and panther virile," as the opera describes him—and Cochran had his man.

As always keen on character songs, Ellis and Herbert centered the score on the boxer's power and the princess' vivacity, effusive with vocal decorations. Tozzi sounded great, and if D'Attili's voice was on the thin and squeaky side, she was very musical. "Blood and Iron" typified Tozzi's music and the gentle "England Is a Lovely Place" hers, but somehow Herbert failed to pinpoint their appeal. It's a good thing Cochran never blamed his people for his flops, but Ivor Novello wrote Ellis one of those showbiz "sympathy" notes, helpfully suggesting that the audience just didn't care for either of the leads.

Ellis' next project with Cochran was to have been *Half In Earnest*, another of the countless adaptations of Wilde's famous comedy. Cochran didn't get around to putting it on (though Britons finally saw it at Coventry in 1958). And then came Cochran's terrible accident: he was boiled alive in his bath, because his arthritis kept him from being able to turn the faucet off and— in one version of the event—the maid's vacuuming drowned out his cries for help.

Given his arthritic condition, there would have to have been a safety schedule in the Cochran household whenever he stepped into the bathtub. But that may have been thrown off because the boiler pipes had burst and the Cochrans had only just moved back in after the repairs. When Mrs. Cochran finally stormed the bathroom and got her husband out of the water, it was too late, and he died in the hospital after nine days of agony—the strangest and most unforgivable death in the history of British theatre. Cochran was seventy-eight years old.

Meanwhile, working with other managements, Ellis continued to tinker with the instruments of his native form in ways neither Coward nor Novello had done. For *And So To Bed* (1951), "a comedy with music" on Samuel Pepys (the title revives the famous diarist's sign-off line), Ellis pastiched the seventeenth century. One imagines him relishing the chance to uncloak the sarabande and rigaudon, to penetrate the barcarolle for a choral piece, "Gaze Not On Swans."

Pepys, a surprisingly unpleasant character in his personal habits, was the subject of a much too forgiving 1926 play by J. B. Fagan with Edmund

Gwenn. And Leslie Henson—a low comic, remember, of the funny-faces kind—yearned to bring back Fagan's play, now with music. Ridi, Pagliaccio— except Henson was sincere in his dream, and, even after a long career, still a box-office draw. But poor Ellis had to fit his music and lyrics into a script with a non-musical integrity of its own. It didn't need and perhaps simply couldn't use songs. Yet *And So To Bed* ran 323 performances, a solid success.

Ellis was in rare form, however, in another duet with A. P. Herbert, drawn from an old Herbert novel, *The Water Gipsies* (1955). These are the folk of the Thames, living on barges and eking out livings in carting along the water-courses running into it, their boats towed by horses ambling along a parallel path. This is one of Ellis' most interesting scores, steeped in the narrative. He even shows a bit of the American influence in some brassy, conversational songwriting, though Ellis fiercely corrected anyone who suggested that the American musical was superior to the local form.

The Water Gipsies tells of two sisters, worldly Lily and naive Jane. Lily drives the action, because her every entrance promises comically crazy-smart observations on life, and, after years of revue, Dora Bryan became a star in the part. Merrily fighting with her beau (Roy Godfrey), establishing her daffy acumen in "Why Did You Call Me Lily?" ("Gardening names are silly," she explains), or counseling Jane in "You Never Know With Men," Bryan anchored the show in sheer musical-comedy fun.

Still, the piece was billed as "a musical play," and the plot line for Jane (Pamela Charles, a soprano to balance Bryan's belt) was serious, catching her among three suitors. One was a Communist (Wallas Eaton), because Herbert thought artwork without politics lacked flavor. Another suitor was a sophisticated older man, a painter (Peter Graves, late of the Ivor Novello stock company, still wearing his urbane little mustache). And the third suitor was a barge-runner (Laurie Payne), and we know we're supposed to root for him because he was strong and happy, in the big-hearted waltz "Castles and Hearts and Roses" (on the icons traditionally painted on the boats) and "Clip-Clop," echoing the pace of Beauty, the tow-horse Payne leads along the canals. Everything he sang was about living free in the outdoors; he was like nature in trousers.

After the stately pageant of *And So To Bed*, *The Water Gipsies* offered a liberated Ellis, for example reveling in the new character challenge of Lily, a Thames water-folk version of *Guys and Dolls'* Miss Adelaide. But Ellis was also as lyrical as ever; "This Is Our Secret," the love song for Jane and her painter, could have been written twenty years earlier, and Ellis closed the show with a quodlibet of "Clip-Clop" and "This Is Our Secret," running the two tunes simultaneously. If you've ever seen a photograph of *The Water Gipsies*, you've seen that moment, as Laurie Payne, standing on the barge at stage left, sweeps Pamela Charles into his arms while the chorus, at stage right, hails the happy ending. The moment really demanded the smashing "Castles and Hearts and Roses" to bring the curtain down, but apparently Ellis wanted to put the love theme together with the nature theme, because that's what is happening: Jane, so unsure of where she belonged, is finally marrying into a new community—her own.

Blending Ellis' characteristic love of romance with the new flashy style in musicals, *The Water Gipsies* was a big hit, but in the middle of what was going to be a long run it closed, as Dora Bryan had become pregnant. A valid understudy was ready in Vivienne Martin, but *The Water Gipsies* had become the Dora Bryan Show, and management gave up.

However, Ellis had already produced his career smash in *Bless the Bride* (1947). Another collaboration with Herbert for Cochran, it was Total Operetta in the tale of Lucy, an English girl who elopes with Pierre, a Frenchman just before the outbreak of the Franco-Prussian War of 1870–1871. Her family follows her to France and takes her back to England while her love stays to join the fighting. But he reappears in England, and now Lucy's former fiancé magnanimously pulls his engagement ring from Lucy's finger and gives it to Pierre. Reprise. Lavender spot on the two sweethearts. Curtain. No, wait: the curtain shoots up again on the entire company dancing a polka. *Fin.*

Note that, as so often before, a second act takes the audience across the Channel. If France had not existed, the British musical would have had to invent it, as those trips to France (which had been elemental for some fifty years) refreshed a skimpy plot with, if nothing else, a change of decor.

At that, *Bless the Bride* was an extremely lavish show. Everyone who worked for Cochran says the same thing: he was a spendthrift. So not only did he encourage designer Tanya Moiseiwitsch to run up a whopping bill but he commissioned Madame Sophia, the go-to milliner among ladies of rank, to create the heroine's chapeaux. *Formidable!*

The Bride's score is not only melodious but ingenious, as Ellis devised two completely different soundscapes for it—stately and diatonic for the Britons, lush and chromatic for the French. So Ellis establishes Lucy in "Any Man But Thomas T" (referring to her dull fiancé, one Thomas Trout), building it in a squared-off tune all in quarter- and half-notes. It's strait, dignified, limited, though Ellis tops this off with a long wordless phrase of silken longing (thus revealing the real Lucy, hungry for life) before the tick-tock tune returns.

The effect is almost pointillistic, a soul oppressed by custom, forced to live in bits of herself. But Pierre takes a mad fancy to Lucy, and suddenly it's Come with me to France:

PIERRE: [Where] all the stars together will not be so bright as my Miss Lucy's eyes.

Boy, she sure was never going to hear such ardor from Thomas T. Then, as in a fairy tale, Pierre takes Lucy in his arms and kisses her—and her world shatters as she is whisked into "I Was Never Kissed Before," a headlong waltz with plenty of altered chords. In other words: liberated.

Ellis is so sure that his English miss has gone over to the other side that he sets a bit of the number to that clomping "Thomas T" theme, to conquer it definitively with the "Kissed Before" music, Pierre carrying the tune while Lucy sings a descant over him. This is "light opera" at its best: the story doesn't tell the story. The *music* tells the story.

The entire score runs this way, but Ellis is not doctrinaire, so sometimes he's just having fun. Thus, he allows an ensemble piece, "Come, Dance, My Dear," to begin with a pianissimo trembling in the strings and then the girls' chorus vocalizing up and down glissandos on wordless chords of exotic construction. It's lovely but a meaningless sensuality. A decoration.

Nevertheless, Ellis makes narrative points all along the way, as when Lucy solos in "The Silent Heart," eerily intimate as the harmonic "middle voice" slides downward in half-steps, changing the chord structure as it slithers along. What does this represent? Guilt? Longing? Although Lucy is singing a song as party entertainment (which is why Ellis allows accompaniment on piano only), it is nonetheless about *her* heart. And it will no longer be silent.

Is this what the entire show is about? A young woman rebels against the order of things while her parents never understand what is happening. In Act Two, during the French episode, Lucy's father complains that "Every [news] paper in the [French] town seems to be printed in a foreign language." It's a comic bit, yet it does tell us that this is a man—even, this is a social class—that never has a clue. At least Herbert and Ellis get some music out of it, in "The Englishman," in faux Gilbert and Sullivan style. I say "faux" because there's no Sullivanesque vocal harmony till the last two measures, though there are plenty of G & S "fa la la"s.

Of course, a craftsmanlike score is not necessarily a hit score, but Ellis bestowed upon *Bless the Bride* some of his most "commercial" tunes. "Table For Two" and "This Is My Lovely Day" are almost a set: first, Pierre orders a dinner with his love to a seductive Tempo di Tango (with an anxious trio section); then Lucy and Pierre, at table, celebrate their love in music spotlighting an intriguing tonic major seventh chord. The music is like a dream, but even as Lucy cues in the number with "My only fear is that suddenly I shall wake up," we can see that the gang from home is in the restaurant, too, waiting to swoop down on her.

"Ma Belle Marguerite" was the Big Hit, another party piece, with an irresistible "ting-a-ling" refrain. Like all of Pierre's music, the song lies high. Lucy's role lies even higher, and one of the glories of the original production was the casting of Georges Guétary and Lizbeth Webb in the parts. Guétary's specialty was introducing the latest snazzy pop tune, not antiqued romances, and when Ellis first played "Marguerite" for him, Guétary cried, "C'est magnifique—mais ce n'est pas Guétary!" (It's wonderful—but not my style of music!)

"It soon will be," Ellis told him.

Bless the Bride was the great smash in the careers of everyone involved, running 886 performances. It should have placed Vivian Ellis firmly in the company of Coward and Novello, but Ellis lacked the public persona—the oomph, really—that substantiated their art with a household image to go with the household name.

They went to parties; he stayed home. Moreover, the *Bride's* Victorian atmosphere is too prim to revive easily except under limited-season conditions. Yet its subject is timeless, speaking to us all. Who doesn't wish to be free of the prison of etiquette like Lucy? Who doesn't nourish a secret heart?

7

Imagine the Duchess' Feelings

Noël Coward

Every writer says so: Noël Coward's masterpiece was Noël Coward, a personality towering above his works in a way unique in theatre history. Few other authors of musicals command a personality at all in the sense of being "known" beyond the theatregoing community, and even Ivor Novello, who was so known, could not rival Coward for opulence of profile.

Coward's ID, however, changes over the years—from an enfant terrible in the 1920s, to a written-out dinosaur derogating new young voices in the *Sunday Times* in the 1960s, and at last, rehabilitated, a national treasure. He is tensely patriotic yet a notorious tax exile in the Caribbean and Switzerland, pilloried in the press. And, though an alumnus of spotty schooling, he was so self-educated he was always the most sophisticated person in the room—for instance, so fluent in French that he played his own *Present Laughter* in Paris in *their* language. On top of all this, he was apparently apolitical yet, in private, so *parti pris* that when Novello wept with relief at Neville Chamberlain's appeasement of Hitler at Munich, Coward socked him.

The one thing that never varied in Coward was his sexuality: he was gay, everyone knew it, and nobody mentioned it. His sexuality may be the reason he was for so long passed over for a knighthood, but it enabled the outsider's powers of observation that gave his best work resonance. Still, his spoken plays in particular were dismissed by the intelligentsia—Aldous Huxley waved Coward away as "an omelette without eggs," and such dismissals came at him in a veritable chorus.

For all that, he never stopped coming back in return. He was implausibly productive in work and recreation both, for besides countless plays and musicals and a great deal of other writing, he performed, directed, painted (as an amateur, especially of charming studies to present to his collaborators), participated in charity work, traveled incessantly, and found time to contract and recover from rheumatic fever, lumbago, pneumonia, phlebitis, a urinary infection, conjunctivitis, and so on, till his journal reads like a medical textbook.

The best of Coward's writing is fast and smart, essential gay qualities, and while we can't penetrate the mystery of chromosomes, the gay ID in art is like jazz: indefinable yet unmistakable. It could be something as small as his penchant for precious character names (e.g., Elyot Chase, Garry Essendine, Eloise De Kestournel, Maimie [sic] Candijack, Eustace Dabbitt); or as arresting as his remark, in his diary, that straight writers never quite get gays because of "that dreadful, unconscious superiority"; or as broad as the suggestion, in *Private Lives*, that marriage works only when divorce is outlawed because people are too complicated to cohabit in peace.

Of course, we're here to consider the musicals, so let's put up the list, separating the revues from the story shows:

I. THE REVUES
London Calling! (1923)
An André Charlot production, only partly by Noël Coward (hereafter NC). The songs are never heard today, save "Parisian Pierrot," introduced by Gertrude Lawrence with her trademark plangent wistfulness, in an extravagant clown outfit.

On With the Dance (1925)
Initiating a fruitful nine-year partnership with Charles Cochran. Again, only one number makes the canon—"Poor Little Rich Girl"—and NC still shares the show's writing honors. But his work is more characteristic now, befitting the author and star of the shocking play *The Vortex*, with its subtext of homosexuality and incest. The revue's most wicked episode is set at a village church fête, with lyrics exposing the gleeful mischief of two clergymen, of "six dirty little choirboys," of the dourly "unenjoyed" church women. But did NC really get away with "Several old deans behind Japanese screens give naughty Cupid a chance"? Yes.

This Year Of Grace! (1928)
NC now the sole author, he henceforth would be in virtually all his musicals. Visually a triumph of style, with a very strong score: the teasingly driving "Dance, Little Lady," "Lorelei," the haunting "Mary Make-Believe," "Teach Me To Dance Like Grandma [used to dance]," ragging on the new music while exploiting it, and the Big Hit, "A Room With a View."

Words and Music (1932)

Another stylish production—Joyce Barbour (in white) leading the chorus women (in black) bearing cigarette holders for "Children Of the Ritz"; four different sets for the four strophes of "Mad About the Boy," as a schoolgirl, a Cockney, a prostitute, and a Society woman dote on movie star "Gavin Fortescue." Romney Brent sings NC's later trademark number, "Mad Dogs and Englishmen"— introduced, however, by Beatrice Lillie in New York in *The Third Little Show* the year before.

Sigh No More (1945)

A forgotten work that produced an NC ballad standard, "Matelot," a flowing paean to a sailor boy, written for NC's life partner, Graham Payn.

II. THE STORY SHOWS

Bitter Sweet (1929)

The ultimate operetta—sentimental, passionate, and quixotic, partly in period settings. Old-fashioned even when new but kept alive by a superb score, from the ruminative "If Love Were All" to the lush waltz "I'll See You Again."

Conversation Piece (1932)

Most unusual: a talky play with operetta songs. Keeping up the curious bond between the British musical and France, NC includes passages conducted entirely in French while telling of a Gallic fortune-hunting team (NC, Yvonne Printemps) out to snare an English lord. But will the pair fall in love with each other instead?

To-Night At 8:30 (1936)

Three evenings of three one-acts each, on a highly theatrical conceit: the same two stars (NC and his essential stylist Gertrude Lawrence) appear in all the plays, in very varied parts. Four of the titles have one or more vocal spots, including NC's most beguiling love song, "You Were There."

Operette (1938)

NC saw Fritzi Massary onstage in Berlin, marveled at her over-the-top bravura, and vowed to write a show for her. This was the show, a disaster because of extensive play-within-a-play scenes that confused the public.

Pacific 1860
Reopening Drury Lane after the war, with Mary Martin and Graham Payn romancing on NC's pet imaginary South Sea island, Samolo. (The accent is on the second syllable.) Martin, in reality a small-town Texan who combined naiveté and an iron will, was miscast as a worldly sophisticate and Payn suffered from a hunt-and-peck stage presence in dialogue scenes.

Ace Of Clubs (1950)
Breaking away from operetta with a piece about a Soho nightclub, unfortunately with Graham Payn again and the eight millionth imbibing of the old "stolen jewels" plot tonic. A failure.

After the Ball (1954)
Back to operetta, adapting Oscar Wilde's *Lady Windermere's Fan*, which NC himself called "dull" after seeing the 1945 revival. What's wrong with this picture? A failure.

Sail Away (New York, 1961)
Back yet again to musical comedy, loosely structured to allow a host of quirky shipboard travelers to come and go doing quirky musical-comedy things. An underrated work with NC's only truly "pop" story-show score.

The Girl Who Came To Supper (New York, 1963)
NC wrote only the score to this adaptation of Terence Rattigan's *The Sleeping Prince*. Reminiscent of *My Fair Lady*, with an offbeat romance between an older, somewhat non-singing grandee (José Ferrer in a charmless beard; NC had wanted Christopher Plummer) and a spirited maiden (Florence Henderson) in London in 1911 and, instead of a ball, a coronation (of George V). Famous now because the Welsh Tessie O'Shea tore the roof off with music-hall pastiche in an excrescent role that killed the story proper beyond resuscitation.

Perusing the list, we note that *Bitter Sweet* is the only classic—and more for its superb score than its no more than functional book, full of snobby folk fussing over etiquette. When we speak of Coward's musicals, we really mean just the songs themselves, especially the witty lyrics, because no one in West End theatre besides W. S. Gilbert rivals them.

Consider, from Coward's last revue, *Sigh No More*, the ironic rhumba "Nina," about an Argentinian lass who rejects the idea that South America is exotic. When Coward adopted the number for his club act, he delivered it—of course—in his usual clipped whimsy. But Cyril Ritchard, introducing "Nina" in the original show, was a florid performer, driving Coward crazy with moues and emoting. Still, let us note a brilliant triple-jump in the lyrics: "She declined to begin the beguine," Coward explains, "though they be*sought her to*." Here's the counter: "She cursed the man who *taught her to*." Now the topper: "She cursed Cole *Porter, too*.

Wit is elemental in Coward's prestige, not only in his art but his everyday as well. When the local curate paid a call and Coward's dog Matelot started humping the guest's leg, Coward dryly pulled him off with "Matelot, *not* the vicar." Or take Coward's most famous bon mot of all (though he always claimed someone else said it), when he and others, in London during Elizabeth II's coronation, took in a parade of foreign notables that included a very large black woman and a small man sitting next to her.

Well, of course that's Queen Salote of Tonga. But who was the gentleman with her?

"Her lunch," says Coward.[1]

Ironically, we find relatively little wit in the scripts of Coward's musicals, only in the lyrics and some of the revue sketches. Further, Coward's revue songs emphasize his musical-comedy side, while his story shows tilt toward operetta in whole or part. Further, there is his questionable love of writing "point numbers" for not only revues, where they belong, but for the book shows, where they don't.[2]

Another problem is Coward's musical illiteracy: he composed but couldn't write anything down. For most of his career he used Elsie April and then Robb Stewart as secretaries, hired to help organize the music on its way to the orchestrator. But how much "organizing" was there? Were Coward's harmonies improved? Was even the vocal line developed? April famously described

---

[1] Coward biographer Philip Hoare says David Niven was the actual quipster.

[2] The point number is autonymously self-contained, neither character nor situation song typical of a book musical but rather a one-off specialty bit riffing on some quirky idea. A typical point number is "Three Juvenile Delinquents," from Coward's *Ace Of Clubs*, in which the titular teddy boys simply appeared for an out-of-story serenade on their love of crime and rude retorts to critics, punctuated by a merrily nasty noise on the trombone. The trio had nothing to do with *Ace of Clubs*' narrative—the night club itself, though in Soho, is actually rather dressy—but the audience loved the number all the same.

her assistance as "soling and heeling," but that's awfully vague—and Stewart, also vague because Coward was alive at the time, seemed to imply that his assistance was more than perfunctory.

Let's consider one of Coward's best numbers, "Poor Little Rich Girl," from *On With the Dance*. The revue sited the song in a sketch in which debutante Hermione Baddeley suffered a lecture from governess Alice Delysia on Baddeley's dissipated life. Then came the song, a Zeitgeist item because it reflected a national scandal, the reckless anything-goes lifestyle of Mayfair's Bright Young Things.

Now, "Poor Little Rich Girl" is lush and elaborate, the refrain's phrases separated by twiddly rising triplets and, at the climax, a Gershwinesque cacophony. Yet the first four measures of the tune are smooth and wondering, perched on not the usual tonic chord but the dominant seventh with the melody touching the fourth and sixth of the scale, a shivering, haunting effect, a kind of witch's lullaby. The number as a whole is extremely craftsmanlike, not at all what you'd expect from someone who needed help "organizing" his music.

Then, too, how could the rich and diverse *Bitter Sweet* score have been "organized" by anyone but Coward? It is filled with arresting effects, such as the little arabesque in "If You Could Only Come With Me" that sounds like a singing teacher at the keyboard, nervously fingering a pretty phrase at random—which is exactly what is happening at that moment. And does an interloper "organize" a ballad as total as "I'll See You Again," *Bitter Sweet*'s theme song and one of Coward's most enduring melodies? It has been claimed that Elsie April devised its first few notes and Coward thought up the rest, but none of these criticisms comes with a proof.

In *Composers of Operetta*, Gervase Hughes, whose contempt for Coward is personal, dismisses Coward's singing as "a *parlante* croak" and claims that "the elementary fabrications which he fits to his own verses have to be written down, harmonized, jazzed-up and orchestrated" by others. Yet Hughes presents no support for the allegation—and why blame Coward for not doing his shows' orchestrations? Most composers of musicals lack the knowledge or are too busy with the production to find the time for instrumentation.

On top of all this is the great sense of cohesion in the *Bitter Sweet* score, driving the action in Act One, when the plot is at its most excitable; relaxing in Act Two, to fool the audience (because something terrible is coming up); and more or less expiring in Act Three, as the bitter overtakes the sweet. And remember, Coward wrote all of this show and directed it, and he knew exactly what he wanted it to accomplish.

Coward's second argument with the new generation of playwrights during the Coward eclipse was their (he felt) squalor and disillusionment. But his first argument was their lack of structure, of the timing of events, the entrance that focuses attention, the hint planted in the first scene that pays off in the last.

Bitter Sweet itself is structured around a suite of opposites, as the title anticipates. The story is simple: a well-born miss runs off with her Austrian vocal teacher and they live on love and art till a bully comes between them. But it's not the narrative that holds *Bitter Sweet* together. It's the show's collection of antagonisms: the elite vs. the bohemians; social protocol vs. impulsive rebellion; England vs. the Continent; the woman terribly in love vs. the woman with no more than "a talent to amuse."

And of course it is the wonderful score that made the original production the darling of London theatregoing, lasting a year and a half. Ballads rather than charm or comic songs are what everyone remembers—besides "I'll See You Again," there are "Zigeuner," "The Call Of Life," "Kiss Me," "[Dear] Little Café" and of course the Noël Coward ID piece, so to say, "If Love Were All." Like "Poor Little Rich Girl," it's very expansive, with an unusually interesting verse, and then there's the refrain's famed line about what separates those whom life loves from those who no more than get by on their wits, that oh so Cowardesque "talent to amuse."

They put the phrase on his death plaque in Westminster Abbey (though he was buried in his beloved Jamaica), and the number itself is presented by Manon La Crevette, a cabaret performer who turns up in *Bitter Sweet*'s second act, flamboyant and impetuous. Under Coward's direction, the original Manon, Ivy St. Helier—and it was Coward, not producer Cochran, who discovered her, years before, in a duo-piano act in Manchester—did not deliver the number tragically. Rather, it's a sort of regretful celebration, the *triumph* of the artist.

So "If Love Were All" plays as a character song, though it's actually a performance spot sung at a rehearsal. But the other Coward ID piece, "Green Carnation," is a point number, in which a male quartet pauses the storytelling to discuss the concept of what used to be called the "aesthetic" lifestyle, Coward's own. Unbelievably swishtastic for the era, the song by its very presence suggests that the Lord Chamberlain's censorship office was so straight-clueless that the people there couldn't tell a hawk from a handsaw. Because the piece is the ultimate forbidden fruit: guiltlessly gay.

"Green Carnation" bubbles up in a party scene in the third act, set in the 1890s, and as the ensemble heads off to the dinner table, Coward directs that "four over-exquisitely dressed young men enter—a poet, a painter, a 'dilletante,' and a playwright." As if we didn't know something was up by the exotic bloom in each one's buttonhole, the playwright of the group says, "It's entirely [the poet] Vernon's fault that we are so entrancingly late." Three lines later, they launch their number, a minty gavotte, with "Blasé boys are we" and move on to such parish key words as "porphyry bowls," "jaded," "[Aubrey] Beardsley," "Grecian," and, topping it all, "As we are the reason for the 'Nineties' being gay . . ."—the first instance I know of when the adjective was used on the British stage in its modern connotation.

It's all the more notable in that Coward intended *Bitter Sweet* as derrière garde, a purely reactionary flight into old-time operetta. It seems that Coward heard Strauss' *Die Fledermaus* on the gramophone and suddenly wondered where full-blooded operetta had gone to. His own work, till this point exclusively in revue, was chic and trendy—where, instead, was the passion of *Fledermaus*' czardas, the community warmth of its "Brüderlein" chorus?

Ironically, *Die Fledermaus* doesn't have a single genuine love song while *Bitter Sweet* is full of them, and while Strauss' show draws on standard operetta talents, *Bitter Sweet* was going to be hard to cast. Coward intended the heroine (Sarah, though she becomes Sari in Vienna) for Gertrude Lawrence, who we already know was his dear, dear Gertie when they weren't hacking away at each other like savages. But the music ran away with him, and he ended with a woman lead well beyond Lawrence's vocal range.

In fact, it appeared that there were only two ideal choices for Sarah/Sari, Edith Day and Evelyn Laye. But Day was tied up in American shows at Drury Lane, from *Rose-Marie* to *The Desert Song* to *Show Boat* to *Rose-Marie again*, while Laye was still mad at *Bitter Sweet*'s producer, Charles Cochran, for enabling the runaway romance of Jessie Matthews and Mr. Laye, Sonnie Hale.

Never mind: on one of his many trips to New York, Coward ran into Peggy Wood, an old acquaintance and one of Broadway's most gifted operetta sopranos. She could act, too, just then having temporarily left musicals for the spoken stage, taking in even a Portia with George Arliss as Shylock. Oddly, Coward had never heard Wood sing. But once she auditioned, he sent word to Cochran that they had a Sarah/Sari.

So there's the Girl; what about the Boy? He must be a tenor with a foreign quality, as part of *Bitter Sweet*'s plot turns on his being an alien amid the English. Yes, he's as well a lowly pedagogue, but Coward wants to underline how unlikely a suitor he is, how love sweeps all before it. That's why we first see him at the piano, accompanying Sarah as she sings: he's a servant, but also an outsider, a musician and European. So Cochran and Coward went off tenor hunting on the continent—and here we meet up with a *Bitter Sweet* legend that needs debunking, because they supposedly found the perfect Carl in one Hans Unterfucker. He was handsome and a wonderful singer, so we're told. But that name! As someone says in *The Good Companions*, two generations later, "It'll look rotten on the bills."

Yet, if this actor was that good, why does his name never turn up on con- temporary recordings or cast lists? We never hear of him except in this *Bitter Sweet* anecdote. "Unterfucker" means what it sounds like in German, too— change one letter, to "Unterficker," and you have, literally, the German for "under fucker." So this must have been a tall tale Coward invented to dine out on when he and Cochran got back to England. Somehow or other, it passed from a joke into gossip and thence into all the books. But it never actually happened, and, in any case, when *Bitter Sweet* opened in London, on July 12, 1929, Carl was played by the Romanian-Greek Georges Metaxa.

The critics were not quite as enthusiastic as the public, who kept the show on for 697 performances. One reason was the score; everyone had to revisit the show to hear it, as *Bitter Sweet* got four cast singles but no cast album— unusual for a West End hit even then. Further, there was Coward's love of surprising the house.

Thus, while billing *Bitter Sweet* as "an operette," Coward raised his curtain on a paradox. The first words we hear sung are "Play something romantic," yet the music is anything but: it's a snazzy fox trot with a charleston beat in the A strains, and the visual is young people dancing to a small band at a private party, fizzy, sophisticated, *today*. This is an operette? "We quiver to the saxophone" runs a line in the poem "The Women Of 1926," by James Laver (author of the novel *Nymph Errant*, one chapter ago). "The world is one huge dancing floor."

Yet soon enough the party's titled hostess (Sarah/Sari in old age) is lec- turing her guests on the timeless needs of true love, "tho' it may bring you sadness and despair," in *Bitter Sweet's* most passionate number, "The Call Of Life." The young people, seated on the floor around her, are cynical, responding, also in song, to one another. And now Coward sprang his sur- prise. As the music built in intensity, the lights started to fade, and when they reached full blackout, the music surged on in the orchestra alone while, in the darkness, a new set flew down in front of the old one, stagehands stole in to set up new furnishings, the chorus kids left the playing area, and dressers changed the heroine's appearance—the white-haired wig, the grande-dame gown. Then, without a transition, the orchestra cut out, leaving only a piano to sound as the lights came back up on the *young* Sarah finishing "The Call Of Life" as if part of her singing lesson with her teacher—Carl, of course—at the keyboard. The flashback had started and the real story had begun.

It was a stunning effect, because the optics had completely changed inside of twenty seconds. And not only the optics: the very tone of the show has been altered, as Coward opened with "jazz" only to subsume it in romance. And he had a second dramatic turnabout to offer, for the second act's cabaret introduced a figure twenties operetta couldn't do without, the uniformed baritone. This one, alas, is the evil version, getting aggressive with Sari (as she is now called) and forcing Carl to confront him. Within moments, they were dueling, though Carl is no match for a soldier. The villain struck him, and he died in Sari's arms, a shock of a curtain even for Coward, the enfant terrible of the 1920s.

The third act tells how Sari returned to England and became the Marchioness of Shayne, always ready to hearten young lovers to seize their own chance to answer that call of life. Still, Coward leaves us with his heroine alone and loveless but for the memory of what she had with Carl. She reprises "I'll See You Again" to bring down the final curtain, but what stays with us is: Carl died, and it's sadness and despair.

Bitter Sweet was a hit of such electric appeal that Florenz Ziegfeld and Arch Selwyn raised up a precise replica of the London staging on Broadway only four months after the London premiere. True, many thought G. E. (Gladys) Calthrop's and Ernst Stern's set and costume designs could hardly be bettered. Still, Ziegfeld was known above all for the unique look of his shows, not for hand-me-downs. Perhaps Coward, directing in New York as he had done in London, insisted; he all but banned the interfering Ziegfeld from rehearsals, at that in the Ziegfeld Theatre, the producer's own playhouse. Evelyn Laye (opposite Georges Metaxa's London understudy, Gerald Nodin) now claimed her rightful part (and even joined the London cast at the end of its run), and Coward thought her a distinct improvement on Peggy Wood. Yet *Bitter Sweet* lasted only 157 performances in New York.[3]

---

[3] One odd detail was New York's inclusion of "Evermore And a Day," a second-act duet for Sari and Carl. Dropped during *Bitter Sweet*'s Manchester tryout, it apparently was sent on to New York with the rest of the performing materials, and was in the show when it opened on Broadway. Cochran had probably cut it because it was sung before the Sari-Carl "café" duet, and the second act was overlong as it was. In New York, however, Coward was in charge, and he restored the piece. It was slipped unbound into the Chappell vocal score as a "new number," but to my knowledge it has never been recorded.

Coward tried his only formal experiment in the full-length musical (that is, excepting the *To-Night At 8:30* titles) with his next one, *Conversation Piece*. This could easily have been written as a straight play—thus the title—because the score is quite short, much of it is unnecessary, and the few numbers that do matter all belong to the heroine, Melanie.

A French ragamuffin, she has been coached and tutored by the suave (and much older) Paul, the two posing as a French duke and his ward to charm their way into a lucrative marriage in Brighton in 1811. Paul sings but little and the young English nobleman he has picked out for Melanie doesn't sing at all, so Coward filled out the music with those before-the-curtain point numbers he so loved—the quartet "Regency Rakes"; a few tarts making mock in "There's Always Something Fishy About the French"; a Fisherman's Quartet on how Brighton was transformed from a seaside village into the playground of the fashionable world, where "even the turbot know Mrs. Fitzherbert."

Ironically, *Conversation Piece* has a lot of script but not much plot: the parents of the young nobleman forbid his marrying Melanie, and a worldly socialite who knows Paul from before can expose him at any moment but decides to help him. "It should be amusing at least," she says. But, really, hasn't everyone in the audience assumed early on that Melanie is in love with her mentor in the first place?

Coward wrote Melanie specifically for Yvonne Printemps, a talent of the kind we no longer have: a beguiling personality that enchants rather than acts. Printemps had no English, which is no doubt why her most dramatic scenes are delivered in French; she learned the rest of her role by rote, coached by her grand ami Pierre Fresnay. One might assume that she eventually picked up some English from her colleagues, but, au contraire, Coward says that by the end of the London and New York runs, "most of the company spoke French fluently."

As for Paul, this is the Coward role clearly, for, as the stage directions tell us, "He appears to exude an aroma of perfection." As it happens, Romney Brent was cast in the part, but gave it up as "bloody awful," leaving it to not only Coward but Pierre Fresnay, who played much of the London and all of the New York runs. Still, why single out Paul when almost everyone in the show is a stick figure, from the young lord (Louis Hayward) besotted with Melanie to Melanie's more or less Cockney maid (actually, she's Welsh)?

The sole interesting character is Melanie, because she hates the phony disguise Paul has laid on her. This drives the show's best number, a musical scene of varying moods centered on "I'll Follow My Secret Heart." It's a duet, though Paul only speaks in time to the orchestra's melody (at that in just a line or two) while Melanie both speaks and sings. The show really comes alive here, with a lightly pounding accompaniment for the start of the scene and that lovely waltz tune for the climax. Yet all the rest of the entertainment is . . . well, a conversation piece. It does have a few musical highlights, especially in a busy street-scene pantomime very early on; and we should mention that very odd role of a Mrs. Dragon, one of the tarts (presumably their madam) who keeps turning up but never makes a sound, even when she's "in" a number. The work's quixotic nature makes it Coward's most fascinating title, but it has never caught on—the New York run, in a poor booking that dwarfed this chamber piece in a theatre built for spectacle, lasted less than two months.

The disappointing runs of *Operette* and *Set To Music* (even as Coward's spoken fantasy *Blithe Spirit* ran over four years) meant Coward needed to redeem his reputation, and the postwar reopening of Drury Lane seemed ideal. His history epic *Cavalcade* at the Lane, in 1932, was a tremendous hit, turning on his lovable and most genuine patriotism; at his curtain speech on opening night, he said, "In spite of the troublous times we are living in, it is still pretty exciting to be British." Now he wrote the Lane an operetta set on his idyllic Samolo, focusing on the romance of a cosmopolitan opera diva with a local fellow: *Pacific 1860*.

And everything went wrong. The theatre's restoration after its closing and then alternate use had been fitful, and when the show itself opened, it played in an unheated auditorium during a terrible winter. The heroine was the intensely uncosmopolitan Mary Martin, who commanded a broad range but not broad enough to play the diva. Worse, she came complete with a husband-manager, Richard Halliday, who was a drunken idiot full of grotesque suggestions, raging whenever he was thwarted.

Coward and Martin were natural partners, because there was nothing he admired more than a woman star with sensational stage presence, and Martin had it: everyone who played with her learned the secret of invisibility. Yet the two did not get on well on this outing, not least because Coward tried to stick her with a point number, "Alice Is At It Again." The song's premise is amusingly roguish—Alice is a country maid drawn to erotic adventure—but Martin refused to sing it because it was wrong for her character. Indeed, it's not really a woman's number at all, and Martin was adamant. Worse, she was right, and being in the wrong could bring out the tyrant in Coward, which made a difficult rehearsal process all the more fraught.

Worse yet, Coward had cast as Martin's opposite his lover, Graham Payn, an amiable chap of modest talents. He looked well, but he was the opposite of Martin; when anyone else was on stage, Payn disappeared. Too, there was something dodgy in Coward's showcasing his boy friend in lead roles. Ivor Novello's aforementioned partner, Bobbie Andrews, by comparison never played more than also-theres.

And Payn was again the male lead in *Ace Of Clubs*, another disappointment. Every manager had turned it down till Tom Arnold agreed to put it on provided Coward rewrite the book "drastically," as he noted in his journal. Imagine how he felt then: Noël Coward is told he doesn't know how to write a musical.

"This series of blows in the face is beginning to get me down," he admitted—and he was not yet aware that from then on every one of his theatre pieces would get blasted by the critics. Roddy McDowall told Philip Hoare that McDowall once asked Coward how he survived the relentless shellacking. "It's very simple," Coward replied. "They're wrong." Still, it was a terrible comedown to see *Ace Of Clubs* staged (in Coward's words) "as simply as humanly possible" and to have to put up two-thirds of the capitalization and receive no royalties till the show paid off.

It didn't. Was Coward losing his touch? *Bitter Sweet* had been a phenomenon—what others could boast of having written book, music, and lyrics to what was many theatregoers' favorite musical? Yet none of Coward's succeeding book shows was even remotely as successful. Again, many of the *songs* were; he was as good as ever in creating afresh while working in old forms, as in *Pacific 1860*'s grandiose waltz "This Is a Changing World" or *Ace Of Clubs*' wistful excuse for travel, "Sail Away" (which we'll hear from again presently).

It was the shows themselves that had lost the originality that made Coward the Dean Of the Twenties Musical. And what possessed him to adapt *Lady Windermere's Fan* (as *After the Ball*)? Coward loathed Wilde, though the Coward wit at times precisely echoed Wilde's, as when *Conversation Piece*'s Paul recalls his English governess:

PAUL: She had a very pink nose, but her syntax was above reproach.

Even worse, *After the Ball* was bound to be yet another predictable Coward operetta, with the "here we are in the time and place" opening, "Oh, What a Century It's Been" (with another Wildean usage, of trivializing the important, in the line "We thought the Indian Mutiny was extremely impolite"). And the point number trio, "Why Is It the Woman Who Pays?." And the eulogizing of the ordinary, from an older woman glad to turn in early with a nosh in bed, in "Something On a Tray."

And yet. With two lead sopranos to work with, the Novello specialists Mary Ellis and Vanessa Lee, Coward tried to exalt *After the Ball* in their music, writing almost on the operatic level. But Ellis was no longer able to encompass more than modest demands. Out of England by law because of his tax-exile status, Coward missed *After the Ball*'s rehearsals to catch up with the production in Manchester and find it dying alive.

The director, ballet choreographer Robert Helpmann, suffered from what Coward thought of as the dance world's fear of letting anyone just stand there and play. Thus, Helpmann had constructed a machine of endlessly moving parts, exhausting to watch. The conductor, new to the job, lacked spark. Even the orchestrations needed replacing.

Help! Yet for all Coward's cutting and coaching, *After the Ball* was still just another new antique—and who in 1954 cared about the social dislocations caused by a fan? *Plays and Players* magazine spoke for the younger half of the theatre world that year in giving Coward its Please Don't Do It Again award.

After a diplomatic retreat to pursue other goals, Coward returned to his first love, the musical, vowing to write something with contemporary *zing!*. *Sail Away* started as a movie idea for his character of Mrs. Wentworth-Brewster (introduced in one of his cabaret solos, "A Bar On the Piccola Marina"), a woman of a certain age who will find love on a sea voyage . . . with a younger man. It was daring, though many a matinee matron would surely find it resonant.

Then the idea reshaped itself as a stage musical, this time without the coquetries of operetta and those irrelevant point numbers. No, this will be a real musical comedy, snazzy and jazzy and WAIT!—what if I unveil it on *Broadway*? They still love me there, sort of. I'll have a smash with it and then bring it to London already pedigreed.

It was a fine idea, but Coward couldn't resist adding soprano numbers from *Pacific 1860* for the Wentworth-Brewster character (along with *Ace Of Clubs'* "Sail Away" for her younger swain). Coward would have bristled if any one dared challenge this; after all, they had never been heard in New York. Still, it shows how operetta remained basic to Coward's book-show style, even now that he was trying to rejuvenate it.

At least Coward thought to balance Wentworth-Brewster's soprano with a Cicely Courtneidge part, that of the ship's spunky social director, Mimi Paragon. Yes, those Coward names again. In the operetta corner was Jean Fenn, a glamorous Metropolitan singer, and of course Cicely Courtneidge was too old for Mimi, so Coward chose Elaine Stritch, queen of the mean-girl sophisticates, perfect for the sarcastic handling of demanding tourists and even a pack of bratty kids. James Hurst was Fenn's young man, Margalo Gillmore his domineering mother, Grover Dale and Patricia Harty filled in as the Second Couple to emphasize youth, Alice Pearce played the nuttiest of the passengers, and Joe Layton would stage the numbers, a superb choice as he was imaginative and could help Coward pace the show crisply. Operetta can take its time and hold a spotlight with passion, but musical comedy must *move*.

Sail Away's Boston tryout was a sell-out, partly because of the talkabout generated by celebrity drop-ins, from Judy Garland to the Lunts. And the show played well—except during the scenes between Fenn and Hurst. They were primarily singers, unable to accommodate Coward's brittle *marivaudage*. "The show sags," he wrote in his journal, "whenever they come on."

It was Joe Layton who devised a solution, during the similarly sold-out Philadelphia stand: drop Jean Fenn's character entirely and let Stritch play the romance with Hurst as well as her own part. With three weeks to go before the New York opening, it was not hard to implement—and with Fenn's Big Sing numbers gone, the score was finally pure musical comedy.

But what about the billing? In Boston, Stritch and Fenn (in that order) shared first credits but below the title. There was no star player because Coward was the star: he wrote it all, directed it, and even drew the key art, a colorful view of the passengers on deck with Stritch holding a string of balloons and a little dog, as on stage.

Still, with Stritch now the driver of the action from star entrance to eleven o'clock number ("Why Do the Wrong People Travel?"), surely her credit would be altered. And how would this affect the other players' billing? Rumor had it—and rumor rules all tryouts—that someone was going to be singled out. In my favorite Coward anecdote, Stritch confronted him, asking if it was true that a certain party who was not Elaine Stritch was going to have her name last, in a box, with the word "and" in front of it.

And Coward snapped back with "She shall have her name last, in a box, with the word 'but' in front of it!"

Still, "The next days are going to be exciting," he noted, on the eve of putting the new changes into the show—and, truly, it began to play quite well, though the New York critics, Coward admitted, would "make all the difference between a moderate 'season' success and a smash."

Joe Layton was the show's secret weapon; his musical staging seconded Coward's writing in making *Sail Away* a world apart from all other Coward musicals. How he must have ached finally to get to London to show the public The New Coward.

Take the opening number, no "Here we are again" chorus but a pantomime cued to music, as the travelers boarded the British cruise liner S. S. *Coronia*, each in characteristic fashion. Among them was the Second Couple Boy, Barnaby Slade, energetic with his books and cameras; the worst of the children, Alvin Lush, bombing past the stewards to bang luggage out of their hands; grande-dame novelist Elinor Spencer-Bollard (the Alice Pearce role) signing her autograph as her niece, the Second Couple Girl, smiled at Barnaby, who snapped her picture.

Then came the moment. "Mimi's late," a steward worried, and the diva staggered in:

ELAINE STRITCH: (covering the stage wait as the public applauded) Sweet God, I've made it. . . .
What sort of an assignment have we got this trip? Any drunks, junkies, or ladies of light reputation?

Yes, the dialogue is a bit weak, but the staging was tight, and, a few lines later, the stewards sprang into the intro to the first vocal spot, Stritch's disquisition on a social director's expertise, "Come To Me." She then chimed in to the music of *La Boheme*'s "Mi chiamano Mimi," and finally tore into the brisk, no-nonsense refrain of *exactly* the kind of music Noël Coward *had to write* if he was to *reclaim* his *reputation* as a *pathfinder*.

The script, too, was free of the neo-Wildean jests Coward was known for, as when Stritch admits to having been a theatrical:

STRITCH: I retired from the stage . . . owing to popular demand.
MRS. VAN MIER: Oh, I had no idea you were an actress.
STRITCH: Neither had anyone else.

In both words and music, Coward was stretching himself, even writing quasi-"pop" numbers for Barnaby, "Beatnik Love Affair" and "When You Want Me." But all of this put Coward under immense pressure, which led to a terrible scene when Alice Pearce improvised an exit poking fun at Jean Fenn's opera stuff. After the performance, Coward ripped into Pearce till she was in tears.

When *Sail Away* reached Broadway at last, it got mixed reviews. (One critic thought it "the musical of the year" of 1936.) The run ended before reaching five months, and though more successful, the West End production (with Stritch and Dale) failed to break Coward out of his eclipse. Maybe that streamlined script just wasn't sharp enough. And maybe Stritch, matchless in her own style, lacked the warmth needed for a Boy Gets Girl love plot.

In the end, it was not music that brought Coward back but one of his plays, *Hay Fever*, in the 1964 revival at the National Theatre that gave Coward, as director, a cast of experts to stimulate the text. Indeed, all of Coward's theatre is singularly dependent on the performing talent.

Because he himself was the performing talent: everything in his life took off from its presentation. Thus Coward became the grand old man again. He was arch and precious, yet he could sell out in Las Vegas—in the early 1950s, no less. And he earned fame's truest credential: every educated person knows what his name signifies.

In sum, he left a humble background through hard work to rule in entertainment. It's a very American paradigm, though Coward could be thought of as Briton No.1 because he made so much of the language, the culture, the attitude, that if Coward hadn't existed there wouldn't be an England. And he was gay, and if he never mentioned it, that was because his art mentioned it—relentlessly—for him. After all, straights don't write "Parisian Pierrot" or "If Love Were All" with that talent to amuse. And he even got his knighthood. He was generous and vindictive, amiable and grouchy, expansive and narcissistic, Noël Coward rolled into one.

8

It's Sort Of Romantic

The 1950s

"Big Hearted Arthur" was the user name of comedian Arthur Askey on the radio show *Band Waggon*, where he specialized in "silly" little songs about animals. With his horn-rimmed eyeglasses and skinny frame, Askey played the merry nerd, putting a spin on the pantomime dames he played and his stint in Jackie Gleason's Broadway role in the London staging of the down-and-dirty wartime musical *Follow the Girls*.

Then it came time to build a show around him. *Bet Your Life* (1952) cast Askey as a jockey in a piece so loosely structured that, when sales slowed, its producer, the bandleader-turned-impresario Jack Hylton, reimposed it in a much shorter version for a two-shows-nightly run. Though totally British in style, *Bet Your Life* made a point of including in its cast Julie Wilson, who had scored a major success as the Second Couple Girl in London's *Kiss Me, Kate* (1951). As the frisky Lois Lane, so Cole Porterish in her "Always True To You In My Fashion" credo, Wilson was a bawdy American sprite, and *Bet Your Life* played her in counterpoint to the show's other woman lead, Sally Ann Howes, Wilson the aggressive belter to set forth "I Want a Great Big Hunk Of Male" and Howes the soprano on the tender "I Love Him As He Is," whose release opens up with surprising grandeur for a musical comedy, *con espressione*. And when the two women duetted on the torcher "[All] On Account Of a Guy," Wilson still sang low to Howes' high, as if balancing the traditional sweet British heroine sound with the brassier noise popular across the Atlantic.

Thus, as in the 1920s, "American" was in again. The high-energy delivery of musical comedy and the keen character interaction of the Rodgers and Hammerstein musical play quickly became a thing amid the importation of Broadway hits, usually in replica stagings with some American leads. Certain works seemed for various reasons ill-suited to travel (such as *Li'l Abner* and *Jamaica*) and some hits, lacking popular scores (such as *Top Banana* and *Redhead*) also stayed home. And one commercial failure, *Candide*, sang too eloquently not to dare a London mounting, in a book revision, with Denis Quilley, Mary Costa, and Edith Coates. (In a curious footnote, Ron Moody, Lionel Bart's future Fagin and at best a George Grossmith sort of singer, played the demanding high tenor part of the Governor of Buenos Aires.)

The American influence on British shows obtained osmotically, as when producer Emile Littler commissioned the score to *Love From Judy* (1952) from Hugh Martin and Jack (later Timothy) Gray. The show was otherwise largely indigenous, even if adapted from American Jean Webster's novel and play *Daddy Long Legs*, about a wealthy gent mentoring a young girl from afar; romance ensues.

The novel, made almost entirely of the heroine's captivating letters to her unknown benefactor, appears to be set in Webster's own New York state, but the musical started in New Orleans to take advantage of the colorful locale. Better, the opening chorus, "Mardi Gras," gave a warning about the elusive nature of identity so pertinent to this story: "You can't tell who's a devil or angel at the Mardi Gras," the refrain began. Further, as Webster's stage adaptation opened up her story considerably, the musical's script writer, Eric Maschwitz, had little more to do than navigate between the musical numbers.[1]

Jean[nie] Carson played Judy, to Bill O'Connor's benefactor, winning rave reviews and making the show a smash. Besides the score and the hepcat vocal arrangements Hugh Martin was famous for, *Love From Judy* had two specifically American touches—Adelaide Hall as a maid, Butterfly, and a very creative psychological Dream Ballet (choreographed by Pauline Grant) encompassing all of the heroine's fears about her unknown background and the sense of unworthiness that her hideous institutional upbringing had instilled in her. Oddly, *Love From Judy* is in a general way an anticipation of *Matilda*: a heroine caught between a vicious schoolmistress and a sympathetic older "guardian."

Melodious as it is, the show had yet more to offer in especially beautiful scenery (by Berkeley Sutcliffe) to offset the monotony of the orphans' blue-and-white-checked uniform dresses. And note that the mean-spirited grownups oppressing the kids were cast with extremely tall men and women, to emphasize the orphans' vulnerability.

There was as well a wonderful first-act curtain, when Carson and O'Connor—her protector, remember—are at a dance, on the floor amid

---

[1] Amusingly, the musical did not cite its source material on the hoardings, crediting the book simply to Maschwitz "and Jean Webster"—who had died in 1916.

waltzing couples, and the lights faded on everyone but the two leads. *He* knew who *she* was—his ward, his responsibility, and now his love. But *she* didn't know who *he* was, just that he seemed different from other males, handsome and young. And she liked him. As the spotlight hovered on the two of them, lost to the world in a waltz, the curtain fell.

There were many "American" touches in the fifties musical, but one went completely American: *Grab Me a Gondola* (1956). Composer James Gilbert and wordsmith Julian More wrote it, collaborating on the lyrics and jumping off a central visual: the year before, movie star Diana Dors ("the English Marilyn Monroe") appeared in PR photos disporting herself in a Venetian gondola in the Grand Canal wearing a mink bikini.

The shots achieved the fifties equivalent of going viral, and Gilbert and More thought they could get a musical out of a Dors-like movie actress visiting Venice for the annual film festival. Of course they would include a number with that mink bikini, and there would be starlets, reporters and their "show page" (a newspaper's show-biz coverage), and an Italian count to complicate the relationship of the sweethearts (Denis Quilley, Jane Wenham). *He* gets too close to "Diana Dors," so *she* gets to know the count; thus the show had a plot as well as background. There was even a number based on and set in the famous Harry's Bar (here Jimmy's Bar), to name-check celebrities from Elvis Presley to Malcolm Sargent to Tessie O'Shea.

The whole thing was brash and vulgar, comparable to the much-reviled American show *Ankles Aweigh*. But that one was a floppo blunder while *Grab Me a Gondola* was a smash hit, in part because of its novelty as a British show in wholly American style. It even boasted a more or less terrible score that nevertheless was fun, with some tuneful ballads and chorus pieces so coarse they were thrilling. That mink-bikini number, "Rig O' the Day," offered not just "Diana" but all the chorus women in the indicated costume, a lapse of taste that was if nothing else bemusing, because, really, whose idea *was* this? There seemed to be no anchor for the craft; it sailed in many directions. "Diana" was established as uneducated and even scatterbrained, yet in "Cravin' For the Avon," she rattled off details worthy of an Oxonian. "Give me the works," she cried at the end, "of Shakespeare!"

Yet the show had a secret weapon in Joan Heal's Virginia Jones (the "Diana" part), strutting onstage for her first number, "That's My Biography," in a folded black sheath narrowing at the ankles, voluminous white fur over her bodice, and her dark glasses mounted on a lorgnette. Blonde and voluptuous like Dors herself, Heal suggested the celeb who never stops uttering pull quotes or posing for the press even when alone. She *lived* fame, and the two authors were eager to show us how intelligence has nothing to do with it. We're attending a film festival, right? So:

VIRGINIA: Oh, I do love it here in Cannes.
HER MANAGER: Venice.
VIRGINIA: Oh? Oh yes, Venice.

or, when asked if she's going for a swim:
VIRGINIA: What—and wash off all my tan?

One thing un-American about *Gondola* was its modest staging. The sets looked cheap, the orchestra counted but thirteen players, and the twenty-three-person cast didn't allow for enough chorus people in the production numbers. Nevertheless, the overall effect was that of a guilty pleasure, and the show's 673 performances convinced many a producer to find a way to slip American elements into British forms, even pantomime. Harold Fielding took advantage of an arresting coincidence: American television had aired original musicals by outstanding American songwriters—first Rodgers and Hammerstein and then Cole Porter—that happened to be based on two of the most popular panto subjects, *Cinderella* and *Aladdin*. Fielding staged them a year apart at the Coliseum at the decade's end, using the television scores (with added material from the respective writers' catalogues) in book revisions that transformed American art into British, complete with *Cinderella*'s Buttons[2] (Tommy Steele) and *Aladdin*'s Widow Twankey (Ronald Shiner), though *Cinderella* traded the principal-boy Prince Charming for a male (Bruce Trent). *Cinderella*'s step-sisters were the usual drag roles, here for one menacing hulk (Ted Durant) and one cutting queen (Kenneth Williams). Of course, Williams had all the lines, decrying Cinderella's entrance into the ball with "My dear, her eyes are so far apart I think I shall have to take a taxi." When his role was edited down, Williams began to sulk, but then Noël Coward caught the show, "the most beautiful-to-look-at pantomime" he'd ever seen. Visiting backstage, he heard Williams' complaint and suggested he slip his deleted lines back in. "Gradually," The Master advised.

[2] This venerably traditional role, a page boy named for the buttons on his tunic, became to an extent a synonym for the jeune premier. Vivian Ellis always referred to the hero of *Mister Cinders* as the show's Buttons. By slight extension, the protagonist of *Half a Sixpence*—another Tommy Steele part—could be called a Buttons role.

As for musicals free of foreign influence, many chose period settings, charm, a decorous attitude. A few writers even positioned them as The Resistance. *Dear Miss Phoebe* (1950), from Barrie's *Quality Street*, revived the world of bonnets as big as moons, of men in regimentals with sash and brushes, of the children's dance class with Miss Phoebe (Carol Raye) at the clavecin. It might have been successful with a tuneful score, but its one distinguishing feature was "Whisper While You Waltz"'s marked resemblance to "The Words Are In My Heart," from Warner Bros.' *Gold Diggers Of 1935*.

Peter Tranchell and James Ferman's *Zuleika* (1957), from Max Beerbohm's satiric Edwardian novel *Zuleika Dobson*,[3] was actually a college show, done at Cambridge in 1954. Tranchell's music, though harmonically advanced, lacked arresting melody, but there is something wonderfully provocative about Beerbohm's wicked tale of a woman magician who enchants Oxford undergraduates into killing themselves in her honor. For the West End, Diane Cilento was to have played the heroine opposite David Morton, but she left the production during the tryout, and Mildred Mayne was brought over from Ireland in Cilento's place. This almost never works out well, however good the replacement is, in the hurry-scurry of a last-minute Hail Mary play, and *Zuleika* lasted only 124 performances. Even so, it collected so many partisans it might be the first of the British cult musicals. Moreover, the authors found a way out of Beerbohm's impossible ending, wherein, having killed off the Oxford student body, Zuleika makes plans to move on to Cambridge. Tranchell and Ferman didn't end there: they added in a Cambridge sequence in which Zuleika is tamed by love.

Many of these period musicals tried to run on charm at a time when American sex and guts informed the new Zeitgeist style. True, *My Fair Lady*—the American musical of the age, at Drury Lane from 1958—was a costume show with a book virtually written by an Irishman and with numerous Britons in the Broadway cast. But *My Fair Lady* had more than charm. A West End musical such as *Marigold* (1959) didn't: it was a thin Scots piece based on a play over thirty years old, with a winsome lass of a heroine (Sally Smith) courted by an army officer (Jeremy Brett) amid constant invocation

---

[3] For a BBC radio adaptation of the book, Beerbohm facetiously warned the producer that the pronunciation of the heroine's name "is a matter of vital, of tremendous importance." To that end, he telegrammed, ZULEIKA SPEAKER NOT HIKER.

of Queen Victoria, who is just about to make an entrance when the final curtain comes down. Charles Zwar and Alan Melville's songs were pleasant and worth re-hearing, but not enough to excite ticketbuyers. *Marigold* was a "soft" musical, soothing to those who found *Guys and Dolls* or *The Pajama Game* . . . what? Rash? Blunt? Yet we note that Smith and Brett's lovely ballad "Wonderful View" slipped a Latin beat into its second refrain, as if admitting that the sweet old ways seemed feeble next to "Luck Be a Lady" and "There Once Was a Man."

It became a controversy, with many a journalist's paragraph on whether or not the American musical was "better" than the British musical, some writers scolding theatregoers for their preference. Vivian Ellis, as I've said, was adamant on the matter, because no, the American musical wasn't better. In a *Plays and Players* article in 1956, Ellis discerned "presentation" as the aliens' secret weapon. Americans were expert at getting attention for their products, and British opinion-makers were enabling it: "Each new American Musical [that comes to London] is acclaimed as a masterpiece—*before it opens.*" In other words, a new British show would premiere with no more backstory than what happened during the tryout, while American shows appeared having already been Broadway hits. Worse, dance bands and vocalists took up only the latest American show tunes, frankly ignoring the British ones.

So the infrastructure favored the Yanks, and even good British musicals could suffer—for example, *Chrysanthemum* (1958). This very funny, melodious, and even unique attraction was destroyed by one bad break after another; its authors, composer Robb Stewart and wordmen Neville Phillips and Robin Chancellor, suffered the Test Of Job. A period piece with much charm but also adventure and even horror, *Chrysanthemum* actually anticipated the plot of *Thoroughly Modern Millie*, a hit film and, later, stage show . . . for the Americans.

The subject was sex trafficking in Chinatown, though *Chrysanthemum* was also a wild spoof of antique melodrama. The husband-and-wife team of Pat Kirkwood and Hubert Gregg were the stars, he "singing" his numbers in the Rex Harrison manner and she getting plenty of main chances, especially in the raucous, music-hallesque "Saturday Night" and an ethnic comic bit, "Shanghai Lil." ("I was christened it," she assures us.) Set in 1911, when ragtime was just starting to enchant London, *Chrysanthemum* was filled with references to the old days: the novelist Ouida, *The Arcadians*, even the late-Victorian habit of naming girls after flowers—the heroine's sisters were Lavender, Lily, Rose, and Daisy. (And think of Maggie Smith's character in *Downton Abbey*: Violet.)

More important, *Chrysanthemum*'s worldview poked fun at the ancient belief that women are vulnerable so chivalrous men can protect them, as Kirkwood drove the action very independently while Gregg did a lot of bumbling. His big moment was "Sorry You've Been Troubled," a "telephone number" in which the operator keeps connecting him with irrelevant circuits while he's trying to report his sister's kidnaping to Scotland Yard. (And let's note that it's *Chrysanthemum* who saves the sister.) Of course, it's all the telephone's fault. "Why," Gregg laments, "did everything have to be invented during my lifetime?" The crazy operator has set him up with the Crystal Palace, a Euston boarding house, a Ladies Turkish Bath in Pimlico, "and then she got me Fortnum and—*Hello*?"

Chrysanthemum's problems ran from a first producer who wouldn't go with the Greggs and sat on his option for several years to the stars' several medical problems that necessitated understudies taking over headliners' parts. Worst of all was a short television showcase that failed to deliver because of technical difficulties, and *Chrysanthemum* folded just as word of mouth was saying that London was enjoying its latest homegrown smash. *The Stage* asked a question on behalf of the entire theatre world: "WHAT HAPPENED TO CHRYSANTHEMUM?"

One period show that became a classic was *Lock Up Your Daughters* (1959), the opening bill of Bernard Miles' "off-West End" non-proscenium Mermaid Theatre, in Blackfriars, nearer to St. Paul's than to the cluster of playhouses around Covent Garden. Miles himself wrote *Lock Up Your Daughters*' book, on Henry Fielding's *Rape Upon Rape*, and Laurie Johnson composed the music to Lionel Bart's lyrics, fashioning a score that observed period even while sabotaging it—the ensemble number "There's a Plot Afoot" was set as a cha-cha.

Yet the script rooted the piece in Restoration style, as in the corrupt magistrate Squeezum's remark on the two-tiered system of justice:

SQUEEZUM: The laws are turnpikes—only made to stop those who travel on foot and not to interrupt those who drive through them in their coaches.

Directed by Peter Coe in a unit set by Sean Kenny, *Lock Up Your Daughters* heralded a new style, moving past naturalistic scenery, even naturalistic plastique. Just before the show opened Coe gave an interview to *Plays and Players*, invoking, the unnamed interviewer said, the "Eastern [i.e., Asian] influence . . . felt through the plays of Brecht and his followers." Coe clarified: "When a Kabuki actor stops acting . . . he starts to sing. When he stops singing he begins to dance. . . . The blending of acting, singing and dancing is a thing of the future."

It was elemental in *Lock Up Your Daughters*, with the very game cast of sweethearts Stephanie Voss and Terence Cooper, roving seducer Frederick Jaeger, evil Squeezum Richard Wordsworth and his contemptuous wife Hy Hazell, and nineteen other name roles. (There was no chorus.) Some of the dancing seemed absurd—three buddies singing the title number just kicking about like this, like that, for instance—but then this was an above all playful piece. Sean Kenny laid out the acting area in a series of boxes representing various places and lit up only when in use, so the actors could sneak onstage in darkness and each new scene jump into the continuity right after the last one. Thus, the scenery danced as well.

If the music was fun, however, the singing itself was merely functional. Many of the characters were old clunkabunks, and no one expected them to field gala voices. Except for Voss, Cooper, and Hazell, the cast was not rich in tone. But Laurie Johnson cleverly tagged his music for actors, not singers. True, the sweethearts' "Lovely Lover," with Voss in one of the set's "places" and Cooper in another (a jail cell, in fact), was the outstanding ballad, a "fa la la" piece of sensuous grace. Still, much of the score was more wordy than lyrical, as with Hazell's racy "When Does the Ravishing Begin?" or two gallants' "Red Wine and a Wench."

West End audiences love elegant bawdry, and *Lock Up Your Daughters* quickly became the show everyone had to see, from the intellectual disdainful of "musicals" (but wasn't this one really a Restoration comedy by other means?) to the common-or-garden theatregoer. The show closed after its season, returned, then moved to Her Majesty's, totting up some 1,000 performances, and it will never date because of its bonding of the antique and the newfangled.

The title, incidentally, came from Antony Hopkins, the composer of the musical *Johnny the Priest*. Bernard Miles wanted to go with Fielding's original title, but a musical with "rape" in its name was "a little too warm for the City," he thought. Showing Hopkins around the new theatre, Miles offered him a glass of wine and a cigarette; Hopkins declined. He didn't drink and he didn't smoke: "But," he said, "lock up your daughters."

If the avant-garde could co-exist with the old-fashioned, why not bring back the comedy musical, with a nonentity of a score but a favorite star jester? Tremendously popular through films and recordings, George Formby was now to make his book-musical debut in *Zip Goes a Million* (1951), from George Barr McCutcheon's *Brewster's Millions*, the tale of a lad who must spend, to the last penny, a million dollars, throwing the money away yet oathed never to tell why. Eric Maschwitz wrote the book and lyrics to the music of his usual partner, George Posford, using no more than McCutcheon's basic premise and one episode on a boat from the first adaptation, a hit play in 1906.[4]

In the George Formby iteration, Brewster—renamed Percy Pigott, of Lancashire, complete with a northern twang, ba goom—was in America backing a Broadway musical. After all, what better way to lose a fortune? Of course he was driving his Lancashire fiancée crazy, because one of the conditions Maschwitz added to the deal was "No matrimonial entanglements whatsoever." Percy refuses, till he sees the actual currency:

PERCY: I'll get over it *some* road!

Formby offers a curious case of stardom, as he wasn't talented except in his banjo playing (chordal rather than melodic, and not virtuoso but sturdy). He always impersonated the likable dope, singing numbers that he co-wrote—"Why Don't Women Like Me?," "The Lancashire Toreador." An all but vacant personality with a disarming innocence when touching on the risqué, Formby tells in "Chinese Laundry Blues" of how the proprietor has "a naughty eye that flickers," followed by "You ought to see it waffle when he's ironing ladies' blouses."[5]

Despite the dull score, *Zip Goes a Million* really was George Formby, and Formby was a West End smash. Even after a heart attack drove him off the stage, the show sailed on, now with Reg Dixon, who then toured the piece for two years. That seems odd, as Formby had virtually trademarked his "dumbest person in the room" persona. Even his star entrance was dumb, cleverly so. After a get-the-curtain-up dance to establish that we're in a small Texas town and a bit of exposition to introduce the Second Couple (show-biz types, to hustle Percy into capitalizing their musical) and prepare us for Percy's arrival, someone cries, "The taxi's just comin' up the highway!" The

---

[4] There have been many versions of the story, and even the new title had been used before, for a little known Jerome Kern show based on McCutcheon that closed in tryout.

[5] This is a typical Formby bait-and-switch: "flickers" anticipates "knickers" (underwear) but gets the safety word "blouses."

crowd surges as two chorus men carry someone in on their shoulders. Cheers from one and all till the new arrival shouts:

NEWCOMER: Put me down! You daft gormless lot!

Oops. He's from Lancashire, but he's actually Percy's fiancée's dad. *Now* the star comes in—but the chorus blocks our view. We only hear him, arguing with a cab driver:

FORMBY: Four dollars, just from station? Your clock must be fast. I've been in
    taxis before. *Twice*!

The Star called *Zip Goes a Million* "a real British Musical show," but let us note that there was a great deal of America in it, in the setting and the many numbers slated for the Broadway musical that Percy will pay for. At that, the Second Couple, Warde Donovan and Barbara Perry, were actual Americans. (Donovan later married Phyllis Diller, and if that isn't American, I don't know what is.)

And of course the story's origin itself was American. Where else on earth, in the very early 1900s, could a character toy with a million dollars? Maschwitz updated the narrative to his present, and he also, as with *Love From Judy*, fudged his source billing, crediting "an idea by Winchell Smith and Byron Ongley" (authors of the *Brewster's Millions* play) without naming the play or mentioning George Barr McCutcheon at all.

One sub-group all but untouched by the American influence would have to be the colonial British shows, few of which traveled to London. Yet Africa took stage in the West End with *Golden City* (1950), entirely by one writer, the South Rhodesian John Toré. *Golden City* was not an import, but rather a brand-new show for London, set in South Africa during its gold-rush days.

With the usual lusty miners and saloon hostess, Mabel, the piece had the air of an American western, but Toré's very melodic score was traditional British theatre music, even when singing a bit in Afrikaans. The First Couple (Norman Lawrence, Julia Shelley) got "One White Glove" and "Moonlight On the River"; the Second Couple (Roy Buckingham, Judith Whitaker) got the more colorful numbers; earth-mother contralto Muriel Brunskill delivered the sermons, such as "All Will Come Right"; and Mabel (Eleanor Summerfield) got the earthy solos. *Golden City* must have seemed like a valid novelty, but despite wonderful choral writing and flashy Zulu dances, it lasted only 140 performances.

Australia's *Lola Montez* (1958) covered much the same territory with its own period tale of gold rushing and young sweethearts backing the relatively true-life saga of Montez, the infamously manipulative adventuress. It's a tricky part to cast, as the performer not only sings and dances but has to justify a legend as a woman of fascination and power. As it was, the show's main production had to import Mary Preston, the second Anita in the London *West Side Story*—and Anita is kind of Lola Montez in her own way. Preston was game, but the role is poorly written, with an establishing number, "Let Me Sing! Let Me Dance!," that is too raucous for a fatale.

That said, *Lola Montez*'s appeal lies largely in its marvelous score, by Peter Stannard and Peter Benjamin (alongside Alan Burke's book), unusually story-oriented for the period, with lovely ballads but also solid dramatic numbers. "There's Gold In Them There Hills" and the wistful "Southerly Buster" (on the miners' anticipating a cooling wind) give the men's ensemble real presence, and the women of Ballarat, the mining camp Lola visits, get their innings in snippy and even shrill numbers on the timeless envy of the town girl for the games of the siren who can enchant kings.

The ballads, too, are very winning, as in one miner's "'Til Summer's Been and Gone," as he tells us how the vast natural panorama of Australia's outback invigorates him. "A man forgets his cares," he explains—but, all the same, so touchingly, he misses his "pretty wife and his five little steps and stairs." *Lola Montez* was never given a major staging in London, but it remains the Australian National Musical, often revived and broadcast.

Moving to South Africa, we find comparatively little except productions of English or American shows. But let us consider Ralph Trewhela's *Eldorado* (1960), whose score sounds like music hall. It's even scored that way, complete with the trombone's insolent "have a banana" riff. The song titles warn us that this yet another gold-rush tale will not be crowded with dramatically pointed numbers: "Modern Young Ladies," "Free As My Fancy," "[Do you believe in] Loving At Sight," and the noisy, repetitive "Take Out an Option On Me." Least persuasive is a dowdy samba called "Tant Sarie Has Been Baking," wherein the singers look forward to a feast of desserts only to be punished like the three little kittens, though at length Tant Sarie relents.

On the other hand, one original South African musical was seen in London: *King Kong* (1961), first staged in 1959 all over the homeland and based on the true tale of a champion boxer who destroyed his career, murdered his girl friend out of jealousy, and killed himself in prison. The musical, composed by Todd Matshikiza to Pat Williams' lyrics, was at first a somewhat cooperative project, not surprisingly in a country without a tradition in the making of original musicals. In her memoirs, Williams claims that *King Kong* was taken out of the authors' hands by the credited bookwriter, Harry Bloom, who passed off others' work as his own.

South Africa's first black show, *King Kong* seems almost absurdly fresh and imaginative—"naive" in Friedrich Schiller's formulation of art conceived without program, a creation that just happens. The Sunday funnies. Apples. The blues. What makes *King Kong* so special is Matshikiza's jazz-flavored music; from the start, it was the sound of the show that enthused everyone involved in it. The sound, really, of the place that gave it birth.

The cast was perforce inexperienced yet well chosen; Pat Williams speaks warmly of the company's feeling that they were making history. The protagonist himself, Nathan Mdledle, had the build of a boxer but a beguiling light baritone that floated his numbers above the violent story. "That's me," he sings early on, "I'm him, King Kong," as a sort of burly Nat King Cole—and, lo, Miriam Makeba was his opposite. Yet when Jack Hylton agreed (reluctantly, it appears) to host a London visit for the full cast, Makeba had suddenly become celebrated in a documentary and was off to the US, replaced in *King Kong* by Peggy Phango.

Williams says that Hylton's choice of theatre, the Shaftesbury, hurt *King Kong*'s London season, as it was a hard-luck house seating three thousand. In fact, it seated less than half that, though it *was* regarded as an unhappy venue despite many a hit's having played there. *King Kong* prospered there for about seven months, and one wonders how it might have fared on Broadway. There were talks of this, even of casting Muhammad Ali as the boxer. But there are always "talks" when something clicks and the carpetbaggers converge. Then, in 1979, a ghastly revival in South Africa, debauched by vast book and score revisions by interlopers, destroyed the piece forever.

Unusual as *King Kong* was, the most offbeat musical of the 1950s was *The World Of Paul Slickey* (1959), by professional Angry Young Man John Osborne to Christopher Whelan's music and the most famous catastrophe in British theatre history between Noël Coward's *Sirocco* and Lionel Bart's *Twang!!*. After *Slickey*'s premiere, Osborne declared, "It's an honour to be booed by certain people," and he has confirmed the legend that he was "pursued down the London streets by an angry mob." He says also that "Anyone reading the play may well wonder what the fuss was all about."

Actually, it was about Osborne's casually scathing assault on everything and everyone British, which the public was not used to after only three West End attractions bearing his byline. He called theatre critics "predators," but Osborne had attack words for every segment of the population while recounting his tale of a reckless gossip columnist whose name referenced the real-life journalists William Hickey and Paul Tanfield.

Why did this have to be a musical? And *Paul Slickey* really is one, with a strange score, including for instance "Bring Back the Axe," about capital punishment. Composer Whelan was uncelebrated, but the choreographer was Kenneth MacMillan, and let us note that the script and some of the songs were published. Furthermore, *Slickey* lasted five weeks at the Palace, so why does this show seem to be such a mystery? Is Osborne right to ask what the fuss was about?

Oddly, it was partly about transsexualism, as one of the characters crossed over, and 1959 was too early to expect support. Naturally, that naughty Osborne placed a song about it, "A Woman At the Weekend [and a man all the week]," whose next line is "Two days as Madame Pompadour and five as an Ancient Greek." Clearly, Osborne didn't want support; the entire evening was meant as spit in the public's face. That's why they called them Angry Young Men. You have to shock the audience with 2,000 volts to get just fifty through.

And that's because nobody is listening, not really. Yet what outraged the theatre people in the house was how poorly put together the piece was. (Osborne directed it himself.) "Bad lyrics," Noël Coward wrote in his journal, "dull music, idiotic, would-be daring dialogue." At least Coward liked the lead, a handsome pop singer with a smooth baritone named Dennis Lotis (whom Osborne had preferred to another candidate, Sean Connery). Let's leave the last word to Osborne biographer John Heilpern: "Had [*Paul Slickey*] really hit its targets, the Lord Chamberlain would have banned it from the stage."

Interestingly, Osborne's show arrived in the middle of a fascinating cycle of dark or at least naturalistic musicals that bore some relation to the Angry movement: *Expresso Bongo* (1958), on shady trade in the pop-music world; *Fings Ain't Wot They Used T'Be* (1959) and *The Crooked Mile* (1959), treating Soho gangs; *Make Me an Offer* (1959), on slightly dodgy dealers in second-hand merchandise; and *Johnny the Priest* (1960), about a vicar's attempt to save a lawless youth.

Expresso Bongo derived from the explosive popularity of then rock and roller Tommy Steele and the growth of coffee bars, where urban youth congregated to support "their" music. From the first seconds of *Expresso Bongo*'s overture, the public heard something new to the West End: blaring brass mixing swing with the Elvis sound, and the score pursued also Latin rhythm in a kind of mission statement to feature not only pop music but the attitudes impelling it.

The title role was that of Bongo Herbert, the latest pop idol, played by James Kenney with an idiomatic portrayal complete with the rocker's typical elision of consonants—"We onna" for "We're gonna [have a party]." Kenny looked great and sang well—but he was not the show's protagonist. Rather, Paul Scofield was, as the agent who discovers Herbert. Scofield was what I call a Novelty Star: an actor from the spoken stage or cinema brought in because the writing needs more psychological presence than we expect from performers who interpret Vivian Ellis or Sandy Wilson. In truth, even Phyllis Dare, who started her career in *Bluebell in Fairyland* (1901) and ended it in Ivor Novello, complained at how limited musicals were, made as they were of "songs and little scenes" instead of "a study of character." She felt like a charm machine: "I have always got to be smiling."

Scofield did a lot more than smile in *Expresso Bongo.* He was greedy and desperate, a mean-streets hustler. And Hy Hazell, an older woman "adopting" Bongo for her own purposes, was an elegant hustler. And Meier Tzelniker, as a recording impresario, was a music hustler. In a number late in the continuity, "Nothing Is For Nothing," these three laid out quasi-Brechtian rules for survival in the "business" of celebrityism: "Man must live on man." Millicent Martin played opposite Scofield as his more or less naive sweetheart; everybody else in the narrative was a user.

"He's got the slinky figure," Hazell sang of her Bongo, "he's got the face." She's like Vera in *Pal Joey*, and many have compared *Expresso Bongo* to the Rodgers and Hart show of 1940, not seen in London till 1954 (with the Joey of the Broadway revival, Harold Lang, succeeded by another American, Richard France). However, the character distribution of the two shows does not comport. Just for example, Joey's agent is relatively minor, and while both works explore a seedy subculture, *Joey* is a sexy musical comedy while *Expresso,* billed as "musical play," is very dark and almost sui generis. Thus, *Joey* ends with a joke—he's off after a chick again—while *Expresso* ends with its leading man shattered.

The British Musical: A Scrapbook

The Beggar's Opera

Above, William Hogarth's famous depiction of The First Musical (actually a "ballad opera," 1728) shows a performance in progress, with audience VIPs sitting on either side of the playing area. At far right, the demanding Lord Bolton gazes territorially at the show's heroine, Lavinia Fenton (as Polly Peachum, kneeling in white), who became Bolton's mistress and then wife. Note the show's other heroine, Lucy Lockit, with her jailer father, at left; Polly's father, the head of a crime family, is at right; and lovable rogue Macheath is in the red overcoat. John Gay, author of the piece, can be dimly seen immediately to the right of Peachum.

The Beggar's Opera is a merry piece, for all its talk of hangings and transportation (to the penal colony in Australia). But Peter Brook's 1953 movie adaptation shows us the danger of the outlaw life most blatantly, as here *above*. Laurence Olivier's Macheath (right) sported the by then traditional red coat; what does he think of the man at left, a symbol of Macheath's possible future? The sign reads, "Ned Harris, highwayman, hanged Sept. 24th, 1721."

TOWER, LONDON.

Gilbert and Sullivan

G & S "reformed" ballad opera's borrowed tunes with wholly original music, though Gilbert maintained John Gay's salient quality of satiric wit. Yet one G & S title is more serious than frolicsome, *The Yeomen Of the Guard* (1888), set in the Tower of London (*top right*), not as a tourist stop but a place of terror, as the show's original poster art (*top left*) warns us. After G & S, Edward German used their format in *Merrie England* (1902), here depicted in the cover art of its ancient 78 album, sung by His Master's Voice's G & S specialists. The inset shows Elizabeth I, a character in the show.

The Gaiety Era
Top, the Gaiety Theatre itself (second of the name), looking westward in the Strand. *Center*, a poster for the Gaiety smash *A Gaiety Girl* (1909), and, *bottom*, a scene from *Our Miss Gibbs*, as milliner Madame Jeanne and assistants pitch their ware in "Hats." They're all about glamor, she sings: "Men will wait outside on the mat if you have . . . that *hat!*"

Top, the girl (here Gertie Millar) and the clown (Edmund "Teddy" Payne) centered the fun. Millar wears the blue Punchinello outfit for *Our Miss Gibbs'* "Moonstruck." *Bottom left*, the very influential performer, writer, and producer George Grossmith Jr. In *The Orchid*, he sang to his love, "I'll be your Hayden Coffin if you'll be my Evie Greene." And here they are (*right*), in another Edward German title, *Tom Jones*, after Fielding.

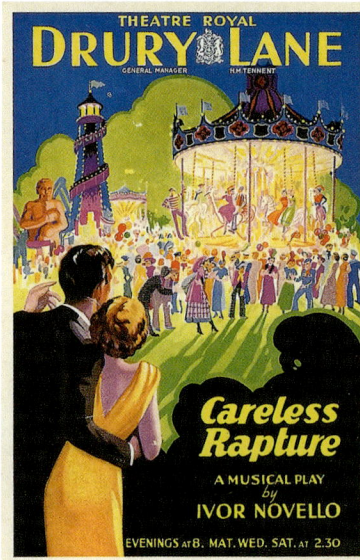

Between the Wars

Top, a PR postcard for *Mr. Cinders* (1929), given out at the theatre for patrons to send to friends. *Left*, the second of Ivor Novello's Drury Lane spectacles, *Careless Rapture* (1936), with a carnival scene and an earthquake. *Right*, the West End's biggest song hit before Andrew Lloyd Webber.

The sheet music helpfully lays out the steps, so let's all try it! Form Lambeth Walk clubs! Hold Lambeth Walk contests! As the lyrics urge, "Why don't you make your way there?—Go there—Stay there?"

(HOW TO DANCE THE LAMBETH WALK)

Description by:
ARTHUR MURRAY, AMERICA'S FOREMOST DANCING INSTRUCTOR

1 Partners march side by side, gentlemen on the left. Strut forward 8 steps (4 bars); swing the arms, walking jauntily in cockney fashion.

2 Link right arms, walk around in circle to right 4 steps. Quickly reverse, linking left arms, and walking 4 steps in circle to left.

3 Strut side by side again 8 steps (same as figure 1.) Partners separate, face each other, taking 4 very short steps backward. Close heels on 4th count.

4 Slap knees in time to music.

5 Ending with pointing thumb over shoulder, in hitch-hike fashion; and yell loudly, "Hoy!" Repeat from beginning. It is necessary that the steps fit the music. Dancers should start on the very first beat of the chorus.

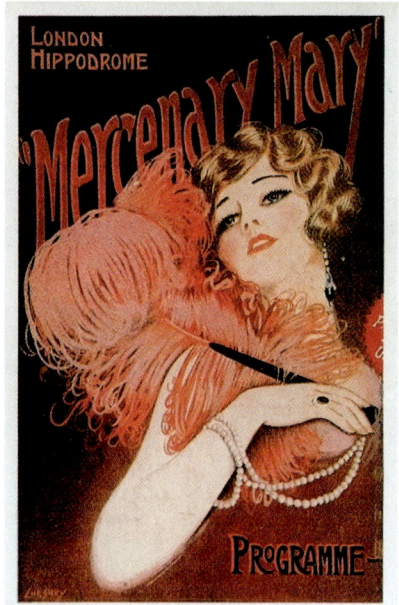

Foreigners

From about 1860 until World War II, London hosted countless musicals from Paris, Berlin, Vienna, and New York, both established hits and new titles written for the West End. *Top left,* Lily Elsie and Joseph Coyne, who opened London's version of Franz Lehár's *The Merry Widow; right,* Broadway's racy *Mercenary Mary* fed the British interest in sexy American attitudes; and, *bottom left,* Fred Astaire and Claire Luce repeated their New York roles in Cole Porter's *Gay Divorce.* The sci-fi spectacle *Metropolis* (*right*), had a German source, a French director, and an American robot, Judy Kuhn.

A BLOCKBUSTING SPECTACLE

TIMES

FROM ITS BEAUTIFULLY CHOREOGRAPHED OPENING OF A CHESS MATCH
BETWEEN PURE IVORY HUMAN CHESS PIECES, TO ITS LAVISH ANTHEM FINALE
'CHESS' IS A BEAUTIFULLY WRITTEN AND SUPERBLY STRUCTURED
ENTERTAINMENT THAT IS WARM, EMOTIONAL, INTELLIGENT AND CONSISTENTLY
ENTHRALLING

BBC RADIO

Metropolis failed, but Sweden's ABBA collaborated with Tim Rice on the very popular *Chess* in the mid-1980s. *Chess*' PR brochure (pronounced "*bro*-shur," by the way) recalls the original's high-fashion staging, played on a vast chessboard. In the bottom photo, note the dancers costumed as playing pieces in the prologue, "The Story of Chess."

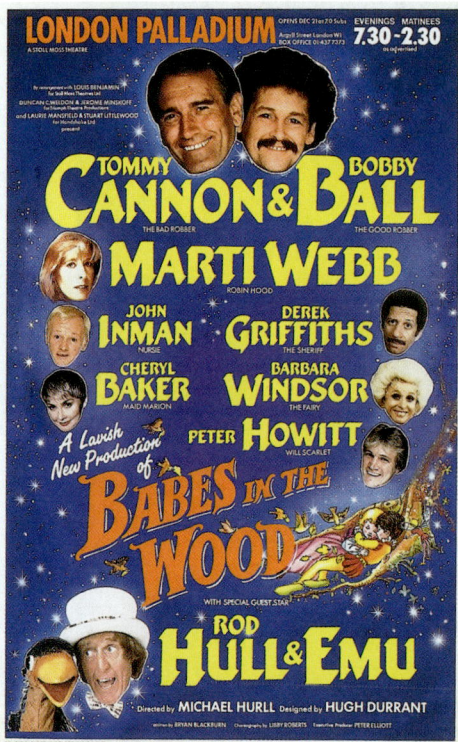
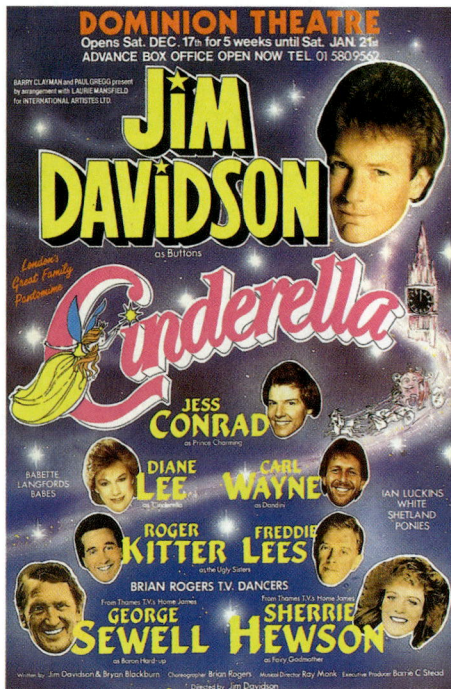

The Pantomime

More brochures, these heralding annual Yuletide bookings, adhering to the time-honored panto storylines though casting television personalities rather than theatre specialists. Marti Webb (*left*), at least, was a veteran stage ingenue. Note that she graced *Babes In the Wood* in the Principal Boy track, playing Robin Hood in trousers, a venerable tradition. Note as well *Cinderella*'s top billing for the Buttons (*right*), the servant named for his livery fastenings, another panto hallmark. Tommy Steele made his musical-comedy debut as a *Cinderella* Buttons in 1959 in a production on the grand scale, while today the decor usually resembles Rumplestiltskin's garage sale.

Me and My Girl

The cast of the 1984 revival changed often during the show's eight-year London run, but the brochure didn't, rephotographing the same shots with the new people.

The Movie Versions

MGM's *Bitter Sweet* adhered to the show's narrative, though Noël Coward hated it as a coarsening of his characters. Typically, "Ladies Of the Town" (*above*) no longer represented the glad cry of prostitutes, even slipping heroine Jeanette MacDonald (at center) into the number. *Opposite top*, director Ken Russell thought *The Boy Friend* too corny to film straight; instead, he framed it as a third-rate touring company *presenting The Boy Friend*. This created a backstager complete with sweethearts Christopher Gable and Twiggy. Comparably, Norman Jewison filmed *Jesus Christ Superstar* (*below*) as a passion play mounted by performers outdoors in Israel. Here, in the number "The Temple," lepers mob Jesus demanding cures. "Don't crowd Me!" he cries. "Heal yourselves!"

2057-15

Half a Sixpence's 1967's film version, on the other hand, was quite faithful to the stage original, though it troubled to move much of the action not only out of doors but wherever possible into roomy vistas. *Above*, legacy heir Tommy Steele enjoys his fortune in a brand-new, ritzy motorcar. *Opposite top*, Steele anticipates a wonderful outing (with the wrong girl!) amid a bunch of adorable kids in "If the Rain's Got To Fall." *Below*, a mere line in the stage show about "the regatta on the old Military Canal" engendered a full-scale boat race with Steele taking part. The *Oliver!* movie was so popular it won the Best Picture Oscar, but *Half a Sixpence* did poorly despite preserving a major performer in his major role.

Noël Coward

His musicals are seldom revived except by amateur groups, and his debonair-to-a-fault persona is as dated as a fan dance. Yet Coward (*above*) remains the most renowned among the notable makers of the British musical. He lacks the historical prestige of G & S and he never enjoyed the tremendous commercial success of Andrew Lloyd Webber. Yet his songs are still very much with us, and something in his out-in-all-but-name sexuality holds our attention. He was gay and he didn't care who knew it, an all but modern attitude for someone who came of age in the 1920s. Long may he reign.

Just to complicate matters for us, *Expresso Bongo* has four authors, and they shared the composition unconventionally. Wolf Mankowitz thought it up and wrote the book with Julian More. Meanwhile, More collaborated with Monty Norman and David Heneker on the lyrics and Norman and Heneker co-composed the music.[6] The show gave 316 performances—a surprising run for so bleak a piece, even given how smart the score is. In a cute touch, Meier Tzelniker told us what he thinks of pop music in "Nausea," rhyming "Meistersingers" with "shyster singers," and both words and music to Martin's "Seriously" and "I Am" broach the subject of romance without quite believing in it, as if she senses that Scofield is focused on ambition, not affection. Moreover, the scoring's use of brass, electric guitar, and Latin rhythm instead of strings and fox trots gave the show its own tinta—and some bright soul thought of ending the big ensemble "He's Got Something For the Public" with a quotation of the fanfare that launches *Carmen*'s prelude to Act Four. It's the sound of the torero entering the bullring and thus ironically—sarcastically—frames Bongo as a warrior of style and technique when he's really just a butcher's boy in luck.

Hard upon *Expresso Bongo* came *Fings Ain't Wot They Used T'Be*, and here we meet Joan Littlewood, the showrunner at the Theatre Royal, Stratford East, off the West End in the land of the Cockney. Littlewood didn't just happen to be there: a left-winger, she saw theatre as a means of communication rather than entertainment. The latter was for the burzhui play boutiques of Shaftesbury Avenue and their (in Terence Rattigan's not derogatory term) "Aunt Ednas." Communication, on the other hand, was for the people who thought theatre had nothing to say to them. Yet it did, and Littlewood would say it, using a rehearsal process in which the actors improvised in collaboration with the playwright. It was Experience Theatre, Democracy Theatre. Of course, it was chaos as well, but at least it was left-wing chaos. And Frank Norman, who, with no knowledge of the theatre, wrote *Fings* (as a straight play), declared himself content with the show's communal authorship. So Littlewood's co-operative plan had a certain artistic "truthiness."

A Littlewood show had spark. She wasn't an ideologue as much as a magician: she pulled real life out of a hat, but a life stimulated by theatricality. *Fings*' pimps and touts and sex workers spoke the language they were born

---

[6] This is why these three very gifted songwriters have next to no reputation outside the theatre community: it's too hard to keep straight exactly what job they hold, because they keep trading positions, as we'll continue to see.

into, not as actors did—said Littlewood—"when every actress had roses 'round her vowels and a butler's suit was an essential part of an actor's equipment." But Littlewood's naturalism wasn't merely natural; somehow, despite her distaste for "entertainment," she still managed to put a hat and cane on everything.

Indeed, the language of Soho was an entertainment in itself. "Give 'im a butcher's, Lil," says Fred Cochran, the closest thing *Fings* had to a protagonist (in—I say again—the ancient Greek meaning of the character whose story is being told). Cochran is the proprietor of a "spieler": a hub for outlaws and their marks, and a "butcher's [hook]" was Cockney rhyming slang for a "look." The score, by Lionel Bart, was similarly set within the patois, yet there was a strange moment in the lively "Contempery" [*sic*], in which a gay character (described in the text as "queer" in "tight-fitting white trousers") plans the spieler's redecoration. Quoting the music Harold Fraser-Simson wrote for A. A. Milne's poetry, a performer billed as "Mystery" (at the first performances, this was Shelagh Delany, a Littlewood playwright for *A Taste Of Honey*, here doing a walk-on in her trademark trenchcoat), sang, "They're changing the style at Buckingham Palace," to which the gay decorator replied, "Oliver Messel is full of malice." (The Milne line is "Christopher Robin went down with Alice.")

What Littlewood's East End public made of this in-crowd persiflage we do not know, but then all of *Fings* was offbeat. It had no plot to speak of, and Bart's score gives no hint of what he would do in his coming shows. Here he sounds like a former writer of rock and roll (which Bart in fact had been) trying to go straight with show tunes. In *Plays and Players*, Caryl Brahms called *Fings* "a rudderless gas-inflated airship," but after a revision and another brief run at Stratford East, the show moved to the Garrick and played for two years.

Littlewood directed also *Make Me an Offer* (1959), another Stratford East title that moved to the West End. This one told of the objets dealers of the Portobello Road outdoor market. *Fings'* people were outlaws; these people were guilty at most of sharp practice. So their show does not precisely belong to this cycle, save for the participation of *Expresso Bongo*'s Mankowitz (for the book, from his novel) and Norman and Heneker (for the score) and also for its interest in characters heretofore unknown to the musical.

They're colorful folk, as in the dialogue between two ever-bickering partners, played by Meier Tzelniker (another *Expresso* alumnus, remember) and

Wally Patch. While Americans are browsing the market, Patch starts quoting Karl Marx, so:

TZELNIKER: Oi! Manners! Diplomacy! You mention Karl Marx in the presence of America? *Schlemiel!*

This was no doubt when actors threw away their butler suit—and this revolutionary attitude permeates the songs as well. "I will give you the entire history of commerce," Tzelniker announced, "whilst standing on one leg," whereupon he went into "All Big Fleas [have little fleas]." The show's big up-tune was a "Portobello Road" chorus, and there was a climactic set piece, "The Auction," over a room with Wedgwood decoration. The songs seemed born straight out of the way these people talked, as in Tzelniker's use of Hebraic recitative, and the orchestra was small and piano-dominated, as befits action based on secondhand sales. At the same time, though, Norman and Heneker filled their music with counterpoint—whistling, aah-ing, solo singing against the ensemble, and so on.

The plot itself concerned a married couple beset by money troubles. He (Daniel Massey), a Wedgwood dealer, longs for a shop rather than a mere road-cart, and his "I Want a Lock-Up" was thus a key number, easygoing and amiable rather than intense, to a soft-shoe rhythm as the other dealers filled in with their own vocal accompaniment: a beguiling sense of community amid the naturalism. And with Diana Coupland as Massey's wife and Dilys Laye as a dealer who owns a Wedgwood vase that Massey desperately wants—the show's maguffin—Mankowitz had his first-act suspense curtain: she demands that Massey spend the night to bargain for the vase . . . and when the curtain went up on Act Two and the pair duets on the jaunty "Whatever You Believe," we don't know whether or not negotiations turned fleshly.

Now we return to the criminals of Soho for *The Crooked Mile* (1959), by wordsmith Peter Wildeblood and composer Peter Greenwell, from Wildeblood's novel *West End People*. *Fings* is a chamber piece; *The Crooked Mile* is opera stacked on musical play atop a musical comedy. Its core is simple: the ne'er-do-well outlaw Jug Ears (Jack MacGowran) partners Sweet Ginger (Elisabeth Welch), who is temporarily attracted to an American businessman (John Larsen). So already the tone is rich, as Welch was a pop vocalist, MacGowran an actor who sang (but tonelessly), and Larsen a powerful tenor. These three are thus at odds with one another every time they start singing—and in this show, the singing is all-important. And that's because the music drives the action far more than the action itself does, in powerful chorales as good as anything in Benjamin Britten or Arthur Bliss and a collection of songs that might have been gathered from three or four different scores. And somewhere in all this is Millicent Martin giving another of her Miss Adelaides and duetting with Welch in the jaunty "Meet the Family" (marked Tempo di Schottische") or trying a comic solo, "Horticulture," in the mixed rhythm of $\frac{5}{4}$ vying with $\frac{4}{4}$. It's a daffy sound, fit for the character.

When Greenwell first played his music for the actors, Welch expressed mild alarm at the composer's "Chinese harmonies"—that is, his broad palette of shapes and colors, restless and demanding. And it's amazing that this expansive work was produced by the Players Club, where *The Boy Friend* had its start, with its paper-thin action and piano accompaniment. *The Crooked Mile* got a huge orchestra, and its first audiences were so responsive to the music that the cast recorded the album before the London premiere.

The show earned wonderful notices, and it ran 164 performances, a good stay for so quixotic a work, for Wildeblood's script tried to fit too much of his novel into too little space. It is worth noting that the show's director, most unusually, was a French thespian, Jean Meyer—what feeling did he have for the Soho milieu? At first an actor (everything from Feydeau farce to Javert in a *Les Misérables* adaptation) and then a director, both at the Comédie-Française, Meyer later ran Lyon's Théâtre des Celestins, arguably the second stage company in France, taking in now Racine and now Yves Montand. So Meyer was a kind of "polyartist": merging the grandeur of the classical with the gaiety of pop. And that does sound like *The Crooked Mile*, after all.

Speaking of France, we should note *Irma La Douce* (1958), a bit like the Parisian equivalent of *Fings Ain't Wot They Used T'Be*, but with marvelous tunes by Marguerite Monnot (a constant composer of Édith Piaf's best numbers) and an untranslatably droll book and lyrics by Alexandre Breffort. It had been playing in a very small house in the Opéra neighborhood when that ubiquitous trio Julian More, David Heneker, and Monty Norman found a way to Anglicize it without turning all the *mecs* (pimps) and their *poules* (prostitutes) into Cockneys.

So Pigalle remained Pigalle, with the authentication of argot, as in this new title for one of the Monnot-Breffort songs: "Le Grisbi [money] Is le Root Of le Evil In Man." Further, where the original French Irma, Colette Renard, was an actress with a light voice, the West End Irma, Elizabeth Seal, was a dancer who could really belt. This gave the creatives the chance to beef up

Irma's musicality, from a play with songs to a full-fledged musical comedy, complete with a Big Ballet in Act Two, albeit on the small scale, as the cast consisted entirely of Irma and her handful of admirers. The most joyful of the "lowlife" cycle, *Irma* ran 1,512 performances, sent its three leads (Seal, Keith Michell, and Clive Revill) to Broadway, with heavily revised lyrics, new dance arrangements by John Kander, and choreography by Onna White. Then it tracked the world, and is still with us here and there.

"What dear, old-fashioned things American musicals now seem to be," *Plays and Players* observed, after the first night of *The Lily White Boys* (1960). Here was the grimmest entry in the cycle, in a tone that reminded many of *The World Of Paul Slickey*. Billed as "a play with music," the show gave just 45 performances at John Osborne's old haunt the Royal Court, and its music, by jazzmen Tony Kinsey and Bill Le Sage, to Christopher Logue's lyrics, is as unknown as *Slickey*'s. Still, the show's premise is arresting: three nihilistic teddy boys named Ted, Razzo, and Musclebound decide to ditch petty crime for big-time larceny as would-be leaders in law enforcement, politics, and business.

Albert Finney was Ted and Georgia Brown, five months before *Oliver!*, was in it as well, but *The Lily White Boys*' place in the annals was usurped almost immediately by Antony Hopkins and Peter Powell's *Johnny the Priest* (1960), the climax of the movement to bring the Hard Life into the musical. Thus the show is historically important, though its run was a mere two weeks. Produced like *The Crooked Mile* by the Players Club, *Johnny the Priest* brought near-classical lyricism into contact with jazz, reminding everyone of *West Side Story*, as a wistfully expansive number such as "Be Not Afraid" shared *Johnny*'s stage with the jagged "Doin' the Burp" just as *West Side Story*'s "One Hand, One Heart" abutted "Cool." Then, too, *Johnny* told of the relationship between criminal youth and grownups. But *Johnny the Priest* was altogether different from *West Side Story*.

For one thing, *Johnny*'s source, R. C. Sherriff's play *The Telescope*, had been produced (regionally) in 1957, before Britain knew of the Bernstein musical, and rather than clan war and star-crossed lovers *The Telescope* treats a vicar trying to save a promising teen while resisting pressure from the conservative faction in his parish.

Raised in the narrow culture of the East End Docklands, the boy—Johnny—becomes enraptured gazing at the stars through the titular telescope and steals it. Clearly, Sherriff meant this metaphorically: a slum kid tries to escape his destiny by reaching up to the lights of heaven while the vicar sees this as the awakening of a love of God: the rebirth of a soul.

This is a heavy assignment for a musical, especially in the cavernous Princes Theatre (again, now the Shaftesbury), even as Hopkins' avant-garde music was bound to ire critics who hated musicals, especially ambitious ones. *The Evening Standard*'s tone-deaf Milton Shulman complained of "atonal" sounds, apparently thinking "atonal" means "music I don't like." No—the word is a non-judgmental technical term relating to Western harmonic structures. It has nothing to do with what a bitter clown like Milton Shulman doesn't like.

Further, Hopkins was lumbered with a Johnny, Bunny May, who could get through a fast-moving song but had no legato or sustained notes for a ballad. This left a hole in the score: how are we to know how Johnny feels if we don't hear him sing? The crucial scene in which he comprehends his searching, needful love of the stars demanded a big solo, but Hopkins perforce had to settle for giving May a few lines, and the actor couldn't manage even that much.

So the bulk of the vocals was left to Jeremy Brett (of *Marigold* and later famous as a television Sherlock Holmes) and Stephanie Voss as the vicar and his wife. In a way, Johnny's mother (Hope Jackman) had to do the singing for her son, as a figure allied with not the vicar but his enemies, Johnny's gang.

When she and the resentful kids went into "Johnny Earn Peanuts" and "The Little Box," *Johnny the Priest* was mapping out grim terrain—"and you know what you can do," Jackman spat out, "with the [collection] plate!"

Where *The Crooked Mile* sprawls in gala crowd scenes—a panorama— *Johnny the Priest* is penned in, even walled up. A trio among the vicar, his wife, and his severest critic in the parish, Miss Fortescue, "Vicarage Tea," though tuneful (Hopkins set it to a Latin beat) underlined how the vicar was trapped between his vocation as a pastor and a flock that wanted him to stay out of the reforming business. "He'll let you down," the kids gleefully warned Johnny. And he did: when Johnny begs the vicar to protect him by lying about the telescope's theft, the vicar refuses, and the kids have the show's last words: "*He let you down!*"

Oddly, one musical that dealt with the criminal underworld—in part grimly—is not thought of as belonging to this cycle, and ended up as one of the biggest hits in theatre history: Lionel Bart's *Oliver!* (1960). We already know Bart as the composer-lyricist of *Fings Ain't Wot They Used T'Be*, another underworld piece. But *Fings*' slapdash crooks are nothing like the cunning housebreakers and pickpockets of Dickens' tale. And consider David Lean's famously creepy *Oliver Twist* movie, with Alec Guinness' louche Fagin and young Anthony Newley's sinister Artful Dodger, not to mention the gigantic torch-bearing crowd chasing after Robert Newton's vicious Bill Sikes. An astonishing shot: they watch from below as Sikes forces the helpless Oliver to climb up on the roof, some five stories in the air. How could a musical of 1960 accommodate any of this, especially Newley's truly black-hearted Dodger? Was the very form of the musical too thin for Dickens?

However, in writing both book and score, Bart had a plan: to temper many of the story's unsavory elements. *Oliver!*'s director, Peter Coe, who edited Bart's drafts, kept trying to drag the villainy back to Dickens, but Bart kept pulling the action away from the brink of depravity. Yes, Bill Sikes (respelled "Sykes" in the musical) is an utter terror. But Bart's Fagin is pleasantly avuncular and the Dodger lovable. And Nancy, caught between her love for Sikes and affection for Oliver, is sympathetic even in Lean.[7]

The more original the idea, the more the gatekeepers resist it. Every management turned *Oliver!* down till Bart sang the score (to a taped accompaniment) to producer Donald Albery, who took it on the condition that it would cost no more than £15,000 at a time when a good-sized musical could run upwards of £50,000.

So *Oliver!* came cheap. But let us call it rather a neighborly or unpretentious show, because Peter Coe heard in Bart's score a music-hall atmosphere, authentic, populist, and intensely English. These were songs Marie Lloyd might have sung—"Oom-pah-pah" (which is in fact performed in a music-hall atmosphere, complete with the "chairman"), "Consider Yourself" (in the $\frac{6}{8}$ meter so popular in Lloyd's day), "It's a Fine Life."

True, some of the numbers are contextual (such as two villains flirting in "I Shall Scream," the title words taken right out of Dickens) or beyond music-hall's emotional reach (such as "As Long As He Needs Me"). Even so, *Oliver!* begged to be staged as a bill on your local variety house, just around the corner or so. Thus, while a number of choreographers, especially Eleanor Fazan and Malcolm Clare, rehearsed "Consider Yourself" and "Who Will Buy?" as typical "production numbers," Coe finally threw their work out to get his people moving as characters in a story rather than as dancers in a musical.

---

[7] There is as well the mysterious involvement of Joan Maitland, who sustained a close relationship with Bart at once personal, secretarial, and artistic. A shadowy *Oliver!* associate, she is possibly an unbilled co-librettist and possibly not.

And what, now, of the narrative's relentless shifts in locale, with concomitant blackouts while the sets were changed? In the introduction to the published text of a later Dickens musical, *Pickwick*, Coe observed that blackouts "make things more difficult for actors and stage staff." The audience knows what's going on in the darkness, so why not show them? Coe humorously adduced to all this the remark by comic Frankie Howerd that the backstage help "should be heard but not seen."

Sean Kenny, who, we remember, kept Coe's *Lock Up Your Daughters* staging mapping about the stage from "place" to "place," hit upon a way to keep *Oliver!* moving seamlessly from the workhouse to street scenes to Fagin's lair to the Three Cripples tavern, and so on. All of *Lock Up Your Daughters'* action fit neatly into a unit set, yes—but *Oliver!* was too big, with its crowds and London panorama. So Kenny designed arguably the most influential set structure in theatre history.

We're still working with it today. Instead of the backdrops, side pieces on wagons, and other habilitated elements of the classic musical's itinerary, Kenny fitted his stage with five distinct components:

1. A painting on the theatre's back wall of nondescript London buildings, behind a fence running the entire length of the stage.
2. A central playing area bounded on either side by rickety wooden staircases capable of revolving slightly or completely to alter the view.
3. More wood: structures on either side of the staircases, also mobile and useful to offer small sub-scenes, such as a bedroom at upper stage right or Mrs. Corney's parlor at lower stage left.
4. Separate pieces flown in from above to establish locale—a "GOD IS LOVE" sign for the workhouse dining hall; a bookseller's façade; even a flat walk-on connecting the two structures of component 3 to create London Bridge.
5. The black-metal lights casings above the playing area, completely unmasked in quasi-Brechtian mode, to underline the presentational aspect of the production, setting the action within theatrical scare-quotes. Yet the story was so compelling that the audience would fall helplessly into the narrative's emotional power.

All this enabled *Oliver!'s* continuity to *flow*—every writer uses that verb—naturally from scene to scene. For example, after Mr. Bumble and Mrs. Corney's duet episode in her parlor, two of the workhouse attendants brought

Oliver in, and at the Widow's "Get a good price for him, Mr. Bumble," he led Oliver off through Kenny's London as the great wooden constructions began to move. Just when Mr. Bumble reached the last phrase of "Boy For Sale," a suite of coffins came down from the flies to identify the undertaker's shop, the proprietor came forward at Mr. Bumble's "Liberal terms, Mr. Sowerberry, liberal terms," and a new "chapter" was already unfolding.

Kenny's contribution formed the biggest part of *Oliver!*'s budget. Marc Napolitano, in *Oliver!: A Dickensian Musical*, breaks down the show's capitalization item by item, and "Scenery" along with "Wardrobe, Properties, and Equipment" ran Albery £6,260, not much less than half the £14,717 the production cost in toto through its Wimbledon tryout and first week in London.

A great look and a concise, fleet book are invaluable, but *Oliver!*'s glory remains its score, a unique creation that doesn't sound like Bart's other titles, much less anyone else's. Think of the deviously playful "Pick a Pocket Or Two," couched in the minor with a sneaky vamp between the verses that suggests a thief sidling up to a mark; or the quasi-operatic "Boy For Sale"; or the quixotically humpty-dumpty "Oliver" after his iconic request for a second helping; or Bill Sykes' "My Name," his establishing solo after a long-delayed entrance right behind the slatternly "Oom-Pah-Pah." The latter is in D Major, but suddenly the orchestra jolts us into d minor, dangerous music whose first chorus is capped by Sykes' knocking out someone Nancy has been flirting with and then shouting his name like a gorilla pounding his chest after a kill: "Biiiiiiill . . . *Sykes!*"

There are flaws. In this show, Bart dealt heavily in cliché lyrics, as in "Where Is Love?"'s "Who can say where she may hide," answered by "Must I travel far and wide?" Then, too, "Consider Yourself" is completely wrong in story content. Yes, it gives the audience a rousing number just when the continuity needs one. But Oliver is supposedly being surreptitiously lured into Fagin's gang—not more or less adopted by the population of London.

All the same, the show's sense of its own esprit de corps—its mission to reply to the American musical with a great *British* musical—disarms these cavils. And if Bart was such a primitive at composition, how did he work two quodlibets into the piece, on either side of the intermission, in "Be Back Soon" and "Oom-Pah-Pah"? The quodlibet isn't merely any two (or more) themes mashed together: one *complements* the other, to avoid cacophony, so the different strains have to bond harmonically. These two examples do just that—and "Oom-Pah-Pah"'s so to say togetherness mates its verse with its chorus. This just doesn't sound like the work of someone singing ditties into tape recorders, but rather a talent that transcended its own limitations with the genius of instinct.

And yet the rough music-hall ethos rules the music. Eric Rogers' orchestrations, for thirteen players, deliberately imitated a modest pit band (albeit with vibraphone and glockenspiel) rather than the richer noise of West End professionalism, and there were no choral arrangements in soprano-alto-tenor-bass block harmony or big high notes. The chorus ensemble singing sang as plain people sing: in unison. And if you can't sing good, sing loud.[8]

Thus, the show's subject was classic, a story everyone already knew. But the show itself was innovative. Is that why the week's tryout in Wimbledon went over to no discernible enthusiasm? The town's eponymous theatre, built in 1910, looks handsome from the street, fronted by a four-story turret surmounted by a dome and a statue of a pagan goddess; inside, it's a barn of a place that, before the days of theatre miking, left half the audience unable to hear the actors. Yet its location, within suburban tube reach of central London, meant that devoted theatregoers from other districts could easily drop in to get an advance view.

Some did, and they liked what they saw. Who wouldn't like *Oliver!*, even in its messy pre-premiere state? There must have been excitement, too, in being the first to watch the all but unknown Ron Moody and Georgia Brown break through to certain stardom as Fagin and Nancy. Further, Coe had cast so efficiently that the action got off to a sure start with the Mr. Bumble and Widow Corney of Paul Whitsun-Jones and Hope Jackman, who set the show's tone in the three numbers after the opening "Food, Glorious Food." Jackman, who had just come off playing the mother in *Johnny the Priest*, generally sang in chest voice, but slipped into head voice for the top note in "I Shall Scream," a dandy effect. Even the Bill Sykes, Danny Sewell, was excellent casting in what could have been a routine villain, as the towering Sewell had been a boxer in his youth, even a contender for world heavyweight champion. His Sykes was so persuasive that Sewell virtually built his career on the part, as there's always an *Oliver!* going up somewhere.

So the Wimbledon break-in should have told Albery that he had been right all along. But there were technical problems, as Kenny's big pieces required time-precise movement between scenes. There was the acoustic problem.

---

[8] Fagin's boys, exceptionally, break into thirds at the end of "Be Back Soon."

And even enthusiasts would have found it awkward trying to cheer for the show while the rest of a sparsely sold house sat on their hands.

There was one advantage, in the development of Oliver's experience at the undertaker's. Though rich in Dickensian flavor, it seemed superfluous, a detour between Oliver's leaving the workhouse and being impressed into Fagin's gang. In fact, it's the young hero's one chance to claim some of the drama for himself, as he is largely a passive figure elsewhere in the show. The undertaker episode gives him his only ID number—"Where Is Love?"—and then the fight with Noah Claypoole for vilifying Oliver's mother.

So the undertaker sequence is essential, and Bart was so taken with the Sowerberry of Barry Humphries (later the naughty drag performer Dame Edna) that Bart wrote a number for him, "That's Your Funeral." An eerily dainty little mourning call, it's yet another of the unique *Oliver!* numbers that separate the work from the *Dear Miss Phoebes* and *Wild Grows the Heathers*—adaptations without innovation.

Oliver!'s London opening caught everyone by surprise, and the show has traveled the globe as a citizen of world theatre. Still, it *is* wholly British. It's worth noting that, for the first American production, in 1963, David Merrick brought over the original Nancy, Bill, Widow Corney, and Sowerberry (and replaced Ron Moody's Fagin with another Briton, Clive Revill), to substantiate ethnicity. The Big Hit on Broadway that season was "What Kind Of Fool Am I?"—but the melody that everyone was humming was that devilish "Pick a Pocket Or Two."

9

Behind the Times

Sandy Wilson and Julian Slade

Wilson and Slade are often paired for discussion because: both first appeared in the early 1950s, both wrote shows originating outside the West End, both seemed unaffected by the American influence, both had one outstanding hit (respectively, *The Boy Friend* and *Salad Days*), and "Julian" and "Sandy" were two gay characters on the BBC radio program *Round the Horne* in the late 1960s, throwing off wildly campy double-meaning jokes.

However, the two are unalike in important ways. Wilson was the sole author of his shows, while Slade had collaborators, especially actress Dorothy Reynolds, who co-wrote with Slade the book and lyrics to most of his best-known titles. Then, too, Wilson enjoyed basing songs on earlier models, while Slade used pastiche rarely. Most important, Slade's musicals are innocent and sweet-hearted while Wilson's are worldly, satiric, and cynical. Thus, Slade's *Salad Days* is the perfection of lovable twaddle while Wilson's *The Boy Friend* is an *analysis* of lovable twaddle, a resuscitation of the twenties musical to ask what it was made of.

Let's begin with Wilson's chart, a selective one, limited to work playing major venues in London:

1. **The Boy Friend** (Players' Club, 1953; West End, 1954) An original story with songs largely styled on older ones.
2. **The Buccaneer** (New Watermill, 1953; Lyric, Hammersmith, 1955) The title refers to a boy's adventure magazine, in danger of being taken over by Mr. Maximus, an American publisher of horror periodicals. *The Buccaneer* is a very personal show, expressing Wilson's distaste for the possibility of a Maximized England. The American's strident credo is "It's Commercial," while a Briton's sad confession is "Behind the Times."
3. **Valmouth** (1958) The gayest musical till *Everybody's Talking About Jamie*, closely based on Ronald Firbank's novel, the gayest book till *Little Me*. *Valmouth* is the very opposite of *The Boy Friend*: complex,

mischievous, and campy. It is also Wilson's most expansive score and, some feel, among the best ever written.

4. **Divorce Me, Darling!** (1964) *The Boy Friend*'s sequel, as the old gang returns in a big, plot-heavy piece overthrowing the original show's simplicity. A failure that closed major stages to Wilson's further work.

The Boy Friend started as an hour-long diversion at the Players' Club, a thespian cabaret devoted to preserving The Traditions, as in the "Late Joys" concerts of old music-hall numbers by high-tech talent in an informal atmosphere. (The audience would frequently call out the name of the next artist along with the Chairman, and after the accompanist inserted a dramatic riff into the introduction to "Waiting At the Church," Hattie Jacques told him, "I hope we're not going to have too much of that, dear.")[1]

The Players' entertainment included ancient melodramas, but there were original works, too, and Wilson's first stab at *The Boy Friend* went over so well that he expanded it, filling out the script with a lot of "Do you think so?" lines, breaking Act Two into Acts Two and Three, and adding songs. A five-year run at Wyndham's Theatre inaugurated global popularity, even in cultures baffled by the show's primary elements—English girls at a "finishing" school in France; a young aristo posing as a shop assistant; a crew of people who have nothing to do but gambol about; and of course the rigid class system. Perhaps these were seen as charming fantasies, for *The Boy Friend* became a classic, ever ready for revival.

Of course, it's a twenties musical. Not *Betty In Mayfair* or *Mister Cinders* twenties but a new show supposedly cut to their pattern. Writers assume that Wilson had not *Betty* or *Cinders* in mind but rather *No, No, Nanette*, an American piece but very popular in England. However, *No, No, Nanette* is very plotty, with three storylines; *The Boy Friend* is frightfully thin, a Players' Club bauble with some extra glitter. Still, how did Wilson know what these old shows were like? In the intro to *The Boy Friend*'s published text, he surmised that "people who have not met me imagine I am three old men." His research was old sheet music and touring revivals, but also instinct. *The*

---

[1] "Late Joys" is a pun. The Players first set up shop in King Street, where—so legend tells—music hall was invented by an actor named Evans, who opened a room where the public could take in variety turns while enjoying food and drink. The building had been a hotel run by a man named Joy, so the new management raised its sign as "Evans'—Late [i.e., formerly] Joy's."

Boy Friend's director, Vida Hope, staged the First Couple's duet "A Room In Bloomsbury" with the pair miming the action on a repeat of the chorus, only to learn from Binnie Hale that *that* was how they did such numbers in the 1920s. How did Hope know? "It just happened," she said.

First Couple Polly and Tony fall in love instantly. The Second Couple is Maisie and American Bobby. Three other schoolgirls love three Frenchmen. Polly's father once dallied with Polly's headmistress, Mme. Dubonnet. Hortense, the school's maid, passes colorful remarks and is oo-la-la French. Tony is cut off from his parents for reasons that are never explained. The climax is a costume ball at which everyone who isn't already married gets engaged except Hortense, and that's all that happens. An ensemble show to the nth, *The Boy Friend* has no star roles, though Polly's Anne Rogers (in London) and Julie Andrews (in New York) went places, and the two main seniors can be given the celebrity treatment—Anna Quayle and Derek Waring got top billing in these parts in the 1984 Cameron Mackintosh revival.

This show is easy to stage and easy to enjoy, because the text is amusing and the next number is never more than minutes away. The suspense finale finds Polly hurt by Tony as the police (and his parents) chase after him. So he is a common hustler?—and note the repetitiveness, due to Wilson's rather lazy expansion of the original script:

DULCIE: Polly? Did he steal something from you, too?
POLLY: Yes, Dulcie, he did.
DULCIE: Not your gold bangle?
POLLY? Not my gold bangle. Something much more precious.

Her heart! As I tell it, it sounds spoofy, but if the actors play with sincerity, it comes off as fond satire.

Another example: *The Boy Friend* opens with Hortense on the phone, Wilson's sneaky way—in the twenties manner—of telling us where we are and what will happen tonight. (The ball.) Then the four schoolgirls who aren't Polly breeze in carrying hat and dress boxes, wild with excitement over their outfits for the big do:

HORTENSE: Mam'selles! Silence, s'il vous plait! 'Ave you forgotten who
    you are?
GIRLS: Forgotten who we are? Of course not!

And they burst into "Perfect Young Ladies," which, for the oldsters in the house in 1954, recalled the way *No, No, Nanette* began (with Binnie Hale as the "Polly," so to say), back at the Palace in 1925). *Nanette* not only took off on a scene between a comic maid and young girls entering to sing about themselves (in "Flappers Are We"), but gave Sandy Wilson the inspiration for his music, which echoes the *Nanette* intro of a descending scale and even suggests without actually copying the outline of "Flappers Are We"'s melody.

This is part of *The Boy Friend*'s archival trick: many of the songs are hommages to twenties originals—not replicating them note for note but following the general feel of their A strains. Thus, the title song uses the harmony and, somewhat, the vocal line of a Rodgers and Hart number, "The Girl Friend." However, other *Boy Friend* tunes are new compositions respecting old genres, so "A Room In Bloomsbury" simply "remembers" songs like another Rodgers and Hart piece, "A Tiny Flat Near Soho Square" (from the aforementioned Hulbert-Courtneidge show *Lido Lady*), and "Fancy Forgetting" does the same with the old "fancy" songs, such as "Fancy Me Just Meeting You" (written for the London staging of Vincent Youmans' *Hit the Deck*).

The most stealthy of Wilson's hommages has eluded writers because it's *really* obscure: *The Boy Friend*'s "The 'You-Don't-Want-To-Play-With-Me' Blues" is a direct reworking of "Atlantic Blues," another *Lido Lady* title. Wilson really knew his London shows, and this particular song is a doozy, with a refrain that starts on a supertonic ninth chord, a rarity indeed. Wilson's refrain starts on the supertonic $\frac{7}{4}$, rarer yet.

Of course, most listeners are unaware of all this, and *The Boy Friend*'s songs stand on their own as ideal melodies: for all their archeology, they sound just like the characters who sing them, from Bobby and Maisie's "Won't You Charleston With Me?" to the Flirtation Duet of Tony's father and one of the schoolgirls, "It's Never Too Late To Fall In Love," with its mincing little rhythm and "Wackadoo" replies. The score is so basic yet beguiling that it has crossed cultural barriers with ease, as when, in Germany, Mme. Dubonnet upbraids Polly's sulky father (in the aforementioned "blues" number) with "Percy, nun regier' doch nicht so 'englisch' auf mich!" (roughly, "Percy, why must you always be so English with me?").

The first British musical to try Broadway since Noël Coward's *Conversation Piece* a generation earlier, *The Boy Friend* suffered a famous historical snafu when the American producers banned the complaining Wilson and Vida Hope from rehearsals while demanding the mostly English cast camp the show up (which is why Wilson and Hope were complaining). It was a hit even so, spinning off an off-Broadway revival two years after it closed that ran even longer, albeit in a theatre one-quarter the size of the Broadway house. This smaller *Boy Friend* returned it to its original spirit, so, for instance, the "Fancy Forgetting" waltz of Mme. Dubonnet and Percy, buffooned on Broadway, became stiff and a bit sad, he holding her not close but rather with his right arm around her waist, their bodies almost a foot apart.

In a shocking stylistic turnaround, Wilson's *Valmouth* was everything *The Boy Friend* was not, especially lewd and cynical, even blasphemous. Yet it's Wilson's most adorable score, richer in both melody and harmony than *The Boy Friend* and, interestingly, built on characters from a different planet than Tony and Polly: sizzling young people and debauched elders, a woman sex worker from India, an oily Catholic cardinal, and, in particular, a visiting noblewoman hot for a young shepherd who's immune to love. "He's awfully choice, my lady," the sex worker agrees, and milady cries, in a line right from the source, Ronald Firbank's wicked novel, "I want to spank the white walls of his cottage!"

"HAS THE CENSOR QUIT?" ran the headline of one startled review. What kind of musical *was* this? There weren't even any dance numbers, like *The Boy Friend*'s "Won't You Charleston With Me?" or "The Riviera." But Valmouth and its visitors don't dance: they lust. The milady above enjoys a big solo devoted to it, "Only a Passing Phase," a catalogue of her conquests, as when she recalls, "One of our footmen, as they oft do, looked so handsome with his livery on, and off too." Note the sly delicacy of the wording. Wilson is celebrated for his stylish music but too seldom for his wit. *The Boy Friend* was his valentine, *Valmouth* his pasquinade.

A succès d'estime among the cognoscenti, *Valmouth* was revived in 1982 at Chichester with some of the original principals, including Bertice Reading as the sex worker and Fenella Fielding as milady with the too-too Firbankian name of Parvula de Panzoust, with ballerino Robert Helpmann as the Cardinal. It almost *had* to be revived, like a mummy in a horror movie, too famous to rest in peace. Still, *Valmouth* remains the British musical's UFO, Sandy Wilson's own passing phase. "It's over now," milady lets out at the end of that big solo, to the notes traditionally used for "Good evening, friends," concluding inconclusively.

Then Wilson returned to *The Boy Friend* for a sequel, *Divorce Me, Darling!* (1965), Polly and Tony now restless in the 1930s. Wilson brought all the old characters back (along with two new ones), yet this show is more sophisticated than the old one—and there is no attempt to parody the thirties musical. Who knew in 1965, what Britain's thirties musicals even were? *Mr. Whittington*? *Me and My Girl*? *Operette*?

It must have seemed a valid project, because the first show had been so easy to love, and, as one of the new numbers testified, here they all were, "Back Where We Started." However, the problem with sequels (which will come up again when Andrew Lloyd Webber tries to revisit *The Phantom Of the Opera*) is that music defines character so explicitly that, by the final curtain, we have collected all the information we need about the story and its people. Another visit would be redundant.

On the other hand, some argue that Wilson's generic *Boy Friend* songs never actually define the characters. Do the title tune, "A Room In Bloomsbury," and Polly's soprano descant in "Poor Little Pierette" really match? Rather, Wilson was defining early musical comedy as a form, just as when, in *Divorce Me, Darling!*, Polly's four old school chums cap "Here We Are in Nice Again" by suddenly breaking into a dance using the taps we didn't know they were wearing. Or when Hortense recognizes the disguised Mme. Dubonnet and the latter retails her recent past. It seems that Percy went bankrupt in the Crash:

> MME. DUBONNET (now known as Madame K): Then he was accused of selling shares in a non-existent platinum mine . . . . He was forced to flee to South America, and I—I became a Cabaret Star. But I did not wish little Polly to be ashamed of me, so I also became a blonde and changed my name.

This is virtually what happens to Marlene Dietrich in *Blonde Venus*, and within moments Madame K is ripping into "Lights! Music!," a pastiche Dietrich number (in her Universal phase) —and this, too, is meant not as characterization but as hommage to genre.

Still, *Divorce Me, Darling!* is not filled with pastiche the way *The Boy Friend* was. Wilson gives us a Cole Porter list song in "You're Absolutely Me"; an Eleanor Powell MGM rave-up in "Swing Time Is Here To Stay"; and a tintype of *Footlight Parade*'s "Honeymoon Hotel" in "Paradise Hotel." Madame K even gets a *second* Dietrich number (in her Paramount phase) in the purring "Blondes For Danger." But most of the score is simply Sandy Wilson writing songs in his usually ingratiating style and at his best in "Together Again," for the four main leads.

Alas. *Divorce Me, Darling!* had too busy a script with too many people con-stantly running around in it, and the show died in 87 performances. Wilson pursued his career in minor venues till Trevor Nunn offered to give *The Boy Friend* a gala revival at the National Theatre. Yes, huzzah. But when Nunn proposed to itemize the changes he wanted to make in the show, Wilson told him it was fine the way it was and Nunn dropped *The Boy Friend* and put on *Anything Goes* instead.

On the Brighter Side was a typical "small" revue of 1961, with a cast of versa-tile comics led by Stanley Baxter and Betty Marsden and written by a host of contributors including Vivian Ellis and *Chrysanthemum*'s Robb Stewart and Neville Phillips. The topics, treating everything from a nightmare of a hon-eymoon to the resurgence of Nazism in Germany, peaked in the hysterical (if cruel) "A Resounding Tinkle," in which Jolyon and Dotty are the guests on a television show recalling the events of their lives.

The authors of the hit musical *Follow That Salad*, the two are fiercely mocked, Jolyon as a writer of infantile jingles and Dotty as an elfin frump. At one point, she recounts a wartime dream of entertaining the troops with a fey babble of coloratura while the boys shout, "Show us your legs!," "No, don't!," and, after a high note, "All clear!" Jolyon and Dotty's latest production is *Let's Make a Daisy Chain*," and Dotty explains, "It's about a magic cow, and I play the leading role."

Jolyon and Dotty were Julian Slade and Dorothy Reynolds, writing part-ners (though only Slade composed) specializing in a soft-toned world that knew nothing of Sandy Wilson's gay divorces or titled wantons. *Salad Days*, Slade and Reynolds' biggest hit, is so unworldly that it's about uncles. Or is it about Timothy and Jane, coming down from university to marry on a whim and take charge of a magic piano that makes people dance?

The young are enchanted and the old overbearing, so Timothy's and Jane's parents have plans for them. The kids secretly resist, though Jane keeps a bit of company with Nigel, the lord her mother chose for her, mainly to teach him music—because it's always just the right time for Slade-Reynolds playroom karaoke—in "It's Easy To Sing [a simple song]." And Tim sort of connects with his uncles, who are to give him a position. There are five of these uncles, asserts "crazy" Aunt Prue:

TIMOTHY'S PARENTS: Four! And the one we don't mention.

The piano is the property of an old tramp, strangely low-key in style considering his piano—Minnie by name—is disrupting what the authorities call "order" by provoking dance parties in the parks. When the piano goes missing, Jane asks if the Tramp is angry, and his reply is essential Slade-Reynolds:

TRAMP: It's too hot to be angry.

The piano's disappearance is almost the only thing that happens in the entire evening, though *Salad Days* is crowded with events. Timothy's uncles help keep the action moving, as at the Foreign Office, where Uncle Clamsby and his aide sing the stealthily minor-key "Hush-Hush" and the aide gets a dance break in the major, doing that low-to-the-ground Russian can-can. Another uncle takes the kids up in his flying saucer. Other episodes move to a beauty salon, a fashion show, and an Egyptian-themed nightclub, while the cast (all drawn from the Bristol Old Vic, where Slade was the music director and house composer) doubled and tripled in the script's many roles. Reynolds herself played eight different parts.

All along, those simple songs that are easy to sing kept *Salad Days* joyous but occasionally pensive, for all the folderol covers the parable of two young people defying the authority of parents, the constabulary, and especially the Minister of Pleasure and Pastime, another of Timothy's uncles. The footloose gaiety of "Oh, Look At Me (I'm dancing!)," when Timothy and Jane first encounter Minnie is balanced by the sentimental "We Said We Wouldn't Look Back," as the pair contemplate the start of their adult lives. For all its silliness, *Salad Days* has an emotional core that explains why it was, for a few years, the longest-running musical in history: looking at the world through Jane's eyes,[2] the show sees it as beautiful, as long as you make it yours, not theirs.

Jane has the key number in this matter, "The Time Of My Life," a lovely waltz, and she caps it with the key visual when, after the vocal, she dances with the Tramp, thereby symbolically embracing his way of life, that of the individual. And this being a Slade-Reynolds show, the Tramp of course turns out to be the fifth uncle, the one we don't mention. The uncles all have offbeat names; his is Barabbas. And with all the plot lines tied up, we realize that the show isn't about

---

[2] During the Brighton tryout, somebody realized that Timothy lacked a defining solo. One was written for him but quickly cut, leaving him as a kind of ballet partner in the grand pas de deux, spending the adagio lifting the ballerina.

uncles or even about Timothy and Jane. It's about youth finding its way after expulsion from the playroom. The two sweethearts have amused themselves with one last toy—Minnie—and now pass it on to Nigel and his new friend Fiona, who sums up the whole show for us at one point with:

FIONA: I don't understand a single thing that's happening.

Salad Days ends very simply. The Tramp warns, "Don't look back." Timothy and Jane married for fun but are now truly in love, because they learned something important together: life is beautiful if one ignores the tyrants. Alone on stage, they reprise "We Said We Wouldn't Look Back," with just a little harmony on the very last phrase, and the curtain is already falling.

Noting Slade's fondness for "diatonic harmony with almost no chromatic coloring" and "standard metrical strophes," historian John Snelson likened *Salad Days* to an amateur show "in the parish church hall with limited resources, and shared bonhomie through the self-aware result." I saw the original production, and it did indeed have exactly that feeling. Even the scenery was far below West End standard, with one backdrop of a small-town skyline (though the action is set almost entirely in London), a black traveler curtain, and small pieces at center stage for some interiors. The breakfast nook of Tim's parents' house looked especially makeshift.

However, the next Slade-Reynolds title was much more professional, even slightly cynical and jazzy. But let's set out the Slade chart first, again listing only major works playing London:

Salad Days (1954)
Innocent fantasy or revolutionary subversion? The chorus people enter, hunting for a piano. "Not any old pia—?" and "No," comes the answer. "the one that makes you gay." Another aspect of the show's urge to conquer tyranny with nonconformism.

Free As Air (1957)
A sleepy Channel island invaded by mainland sophisticates. After *Salad Days'* modest presentation, here was a busy big ensemble, a full orchestra, and lots of scenery.

Follow That Girl (1960)

A reworking of *Christmas In King Street*, one of Slade and Reynolds' holiday shows at their home with the Bristol Old Vic. Again, a low-budget mounting as the entire cast was chasing after Susan Hampshire, great company even if she couldn't sing.

Wildest Dreams (1961)
An attempt to do without the quaint eccentrics of the three shows above, unfortunately with a tuneless score. Its failure ended the Slade-Reynolds partnership.

Vanity Fair (1962)
Alan Pryce-Jones and Robin Miller wrote the book and Miller the lyrics to this disastrous adaptation of Thackeray, produced on the grand scale with Frances Cuka as Becky Sharp and Dame Sybil Thorndike as Miss Crawley. The novel is a joyless compendium of mankind's faults, and Slade's was a joyful art. Thus, faced with a host of morally indecent characters plus one prig and the idiot he foolishly loves, Slade had nothing to say worth hearing.

Trelawny (1972)
Another adaptation, from Arthur Wing Pinero's play about an actress who marries into a family of rank and a playwright eager to bring real life onto the stage. With characters both lovable and talented to write for, Slade (with two new collaborators on the book) produced his finest score.

Free As Air, set on the imaginary Channel island of Terhou,[3] retained a bit of *Salad Days'* lightheaded ambiance, as in a trio for island dignitaries, "Let the Grass Grow [under your feet]," a soft-shoe (marked "Tempo di Schottische") salute to lotus-eating. "A man's life is longer if he lazes," the three sing: "Make time last by wandering through the daisies." And Dorothy Reynold's role, Miss Catamole, is so reticent that when a man proposes to her, they duet on the dainty "We're Holding Hands." There was as well a taste of collegiate cleverness in "Testudo," on Terhou's ancient Roman occupation, its name in each strophe inflected in the Latin third declension (e.g., Testudinis, Testudinem, and so on).

[3] The authors presumably used as their matrix the actual isle of Jethou, though it is quite tiny and privately inhabited by lease, while "Terhou" boasts a community of people.

But note that one of Terhou's visitors is a character clearly modeled on that ultimate urbane icon Jack Buchanan. He's called Jack and even sings like Buchanan, especially in a number that could easily have been written for one of Buchanan's twenties musicals, "Her Mummy Doesn't Like Me Any More." Later, Jack interrupts a big chorus number to imitate the patter of those insincere radio emcees:

JACK: Well, here we are on Terhou. . . . You come here a bachelor, you'll take home a wife. You come here with a wife, you'll take home two. . . . We've got a grand comedy swimming gala. Don't forget your water-wings.

There was nothing so racy in *Salad Days*—so aware, really, of the modern world. And Terhou's anthem, "Free To Sing"—another plea for individual liberty—was eventually sung by all the islanders in a choral arrangement far beyond anything heard in the earlier show.

Most important, Slade now threw off his "simple song" manner for a more eliciting sound. To capture Jack's extravagant narcissism in the aforementioned "Mummy" number, Slade roamed all over the black keys. As early as the first measure of the refrain (in E Flat Major), he reached the almost unnotatable chord of d flat minor over c minor, and five seconds later lit on a g minor diminished fourth over a B Flat seventh, becoming one thing no one would ever have taken Julian Slade for: wild.

Free As Air was a hit, but *Follow That Girl*, despite a fine score, failed. The sets were cheap-looking (though the Victorian costuming was persuasive) and the episodic continuity came off as a Slade-Reynolds grabbag. The cast included two of the era's best singers in Peter Gilmore and Patricia Routledge, and the songs boasted one of the strangest numbers of all time, "Shopping In Kensington," a gavotte about a kidnaped baby, brilliant in its oh so measured bitterness. And just as *Salad Days'* Tramp turned out to be Timothy's long-lost uncle, the baby, now a policeman, was Peter Gilmore.

When Dorothy Reynolds decided she was done with catamoling, Slade was on his own, and not till *Trelawny*, a decade later, did he redeem himself—because Pinero's characters were the kind Slade loved and knew how to write for. *Trelawny* is the world of theatre folk, along with a few outsiders who, through love of the actress heroine, become admirers of the stage.

As so often before, Slade launched his piece at the Bristol Old Vic, where Hayley Mills (to be replaced in London by Gemma Craven) played Rose Trelawny "of the Wells": charismatic yet no diva, but rather a simple,

clear-eyed young woman surrounded by the usual Slade eccentrics (even
if they all come straight from Pinero's play). *Trelawny*'s credits are confusing: the work is "by Aubrey Woods, George Rowell, and Julian Slade." But
Slade wrote the music and lyrics and Woods the book, so what was left for
George Rowell to do?

However it was worked out, the adaptation is masterly, as Pinero's original is sedentary while *Trelawny* the musical is mercurial and imaginative.
Take the opening, set on the stage of Sadler's Wells itself (which, by chance,
is where *Trelawny* first stopped when it arrived in London). The house has
cleared out after a performance, except for one young man, Arthur Gower
(John Watts), of the ruling class and engaged to Rose Trelawny. There's to
be a farewell party for her, and her beau is nervous about having to speak.
Music sneaks in for "Pull Yourself Together" as various members of the Wells
company come in and the number builds into a full-scale "opening chorus"
complete with a quodlibet section so Arthur, singing against the ensemble,
can establish himself with us.

It's a great way to introduce some of the principals—the madcaps Gadd
(David Morton) and Colpoys (Teddy Green), who play, respectively, the
Demon and Widow Twankey in the annual pantomime; the pompous company heads, the Telfers; and "walking gentleman" (i.e., extra) Tom Wrench
(Ian Richardson), a would-be dramatist fed up with the shrieks and poses of
the prevailing acting style. Pinero molded Wrench on the real-life Victorian
playwright T. W. Robertson, the revolutionary in naturalistic writing and
staging, an inspiration to W. S. Gilbert. Rose's theatre is one of quaint charm.
Tom Wrench wants a theatre of life.

Thus, when Rose retired from the stage to live with Arthur's family, Tom
told the audience exactly what it was going to be like. He counted off the
furnishings as if designing a set, and the pieces then appeared one by one in
spotlights, all of them practical—"real locks" on the doors, "handles to turn."
Tom was demonstrating what naturalism looks like. "And when evening
falls," he announced, "and the moon hanging [outside the windows] casts its
shadows across the stage"—here the lights faded to present exactly what Tom
was describing—"the curtains my actors draw against it will be real!"

Richardson threw himself into his part with such thespian self-belief that
he became the show's protagonist: helping the authors to tell Rose's story,
Tom Wrench was really telling his own. Through Slade's intensely personalized score—the aggression of Arthur's haughty grandfather (Max Adrian)
in "On Approval"; Rose's rebellion in "Rules," including a wicked imitation

of Arthur's naggy great-aunt; Gadd and Colpoys' anticipation of the panto in "We Can't Keep 'Em Waiting" (and even a bit of the show itself on stage, in "Hail To Aladdin")—Pinero's too limpid story became a battle as in *Salad Days* between youth and power. The driveline was Rose's defiance of that controlling grandfather, but also Tom's of lifeless art.

Trelawny marked a tremendous advance on the shows Slade was (and still is) known for. Yes, it's sentimental—but it's on fire as well. And of course Grandad and Rose make peace: the intolerant old conservative actually joins the Wells company in listening to Tom read his new play.

So we'd reached the final curtain. Yet there was one last theatrical trick to come. Gadd and Colpoys got into a lavish competition over where to sit, drawing the public's attention as Ian Richardson slipped offstage, his place taken by a double, facing the cast with his back to the auditorium. As the lights dimmed, Richardson shocked the house by re-entering from the wings as if, once again, taking over the action, now for his great solo, "Life." A yes-and-no singer but a valiant actor, Richardson seized the show and shook all the fluff out of it, out of Slade, out of the musical as a form. He had the last line, too, as Rose brought Grandad over to Arthur for *their* reconciliation, and the chorus began a last hearing of the show's anthem, "Trelawny Of the Wells":

TOM: Oh, my dears, let us get on with the rehearsal!

And to the last strain of the song, Tom began to direct his players in his new art of Theatre As Life. And there the curtain fell.

10

Sweep Me Off My Feet

The 1960s

Could we consider Lionel Bart as kind of holy fool, one without education who is nonetheless ennobled by rare gifts? He was friendly and filled with ideas, impetuous and inclined to double down on bad decisions, yet his successful music-and-lyrics credits—*Fings Ain't Wot They Used T'Be*, *Oliver!*, *Blitz!*, and *Maggie May*—form a cornerstone in this history.

And *Blitz!* (1962) seemed monumental after the artfully unpretentious *Oliver!*. Now Sean Kenny's structures were fully mobilized pieces, each driven by a stagehand hidden inside and decorated to resemble buildings. They could turn, advance, and retreat, constantly reshaping our view of the London streets. At one point early on, the very stage seemed to rise to create a tube station in which the locals took refuge during a bombardment.

The cast, too, was huge, and a big orchestra emphasized the drama in the lives of two families, whose chieftains, respectively Mrs. Blitzstein and Mr. Locke, are engaged in a verbal war of their own even as her Carol and his Georgie fall in love. Carol is blinded in an air raid—yes, Kenny simulated them on stage—and another Blitzstein, young Harry, deserts the army. A soap opera, you might say. But Bart's score, astonishingly craftsmanlike despite his lack of musical science—lifted *Blitz!* above the ins and outs of its plot. As with all of Bart's shows, there had never been anything like it.

It's a somewhat contrapuntal score, too; we always seem to be hearing rebuttals during the numbers. When Mrs. Blitzstein starts berating her offspring, in "Be What You Wanna Be," her neighbors quietly sing, "She's at it again" between her lines, at first staccato but then holding out the *n*, simulating a lingering worry in the air. And when children imitate grownups in "Mums and Dads," it becomes a quodlibet, as the "wives" nag while the "husbands" alibi their way out of trouble, singing first separately and then simultaneously.

Thus the show is much larger than its two central families. The Victorian *Oliver!* was something of a fantasy, but much of *Blitz!*'s audience had lived through its events, making it a kind of unbearable nostalgia; while the show was playing, whole blocks of London were still empty spaces filled with gravel, not yet rebuilt. It must have been extraordinary for the public to hear wartime sweetheart Vera Lynn's voice on the radio singing "The Day After Tomorrow" (newly written to sound like a forties ballad) as the entire cast started singing along.

Bart credited a book collaboration with Joan Maitland, but he directed the show himself, guiding a cast of unknowns. First billed was Mrs. Blitzstein, Amelia Bayntun, who seemed to come from nowhere (and return to it, after *Blitz!*'s 568 performances), and Bob Grant, Grazina Frame, Graham Jones, and Thomas Kempinski were similarly uncelebrated. Everyone got major opportunities in the music, however, as this is a long score, with all sorts of incidentals to fill out the neighborhood panorama—"Petticoat Lane (On a Saturday Ain't So Nice)"; children evacuating the war zone in "We're Going To the Country"; "Leave It To the Ladies"; and the show's hit, the Blitzstein girl's wistful "Far Away."

Most notable are the solos for Bayntun's matriarch, finding—as everyone did—that war breaks all the rules, including the protocols of one's native culture. She even becomes a bombing victim, and when her favorite enemy— no, not Hitler: Mr. Locke—pulls her from the wreckage, she gets out a furious "You took long enough to get here, didn't you?," to the ensemble's inevitable "She's at it again!"

With its huge cast and technical demands, *Blitz!* is seldom seen, though the National Youth Theatre revived it at the Playhouse in 1990, with a ton of scenery and a game if unseasoned cast. But Bart's *Maggie May* (1964) is even harder to bring back, though it was a hit, as it demands two extraordinary singing actors, originally Novelty Stars Rachel Roberts (as a prostitute) and Kenneth Haigh (as a dockworkers' leader, the man she loves). Alun Owen's book, set amid labor troubles in Liverpool, created two truly big characters, thought to be modeled on the Magdalene and Christ, and, amazingly, Roberts and Haigh unveiled excellent singing voices.

Haigh's was an amiable baritone, placed with an actory zest, though Haigh was personally a very angry fellow with a dangerous vibe that came out in everything he did. As for Roberts, despite a raspy quality she hit every note with a pungent blend of determination and vulnerability. The pair gave two of the most powerful performances in theatre memory (though Roberts, understudied by Julia McKenzie, missed many a show), and it's worth noting that between the goofy *Fings* and the zany *Twang!!*, Bart kept inventing acting challenges for special performers—Nancy and Bill, Mrs. Blitzstein, and, here, Casey and Maggie May.

The show was optioned for Broadway but never put into rehearsal, probably because (besides a very depressing plot denouement) the two leads would have been impossible to cast, and not just because of the required regional accents. Even in London, during the show's fourteen months, while Roberts was succeeded by *Oliver!* Nancy's Georgia Brown and Judith Bruce, Kenneth Haigh's replacement was an unknown.

As to the show's score, we think of Bart as an essentially melodic composer, but *Maggie May* is the work of a dramatic composer, intent on the story's driveline of a vibrant working-class world looking for a hero. As in *Blitz!*, many of the songs step around the romantic plot to spend time with the "folk": "Shine You Swine," the call of the milkman, in dada-like phrases; "Right Of Way"; the heavily infuriated waltz "Dey Don't Do Dat T'Day"; "We Don't All Wear D'Same Size Boots." With a terrific men's chorus and brilliant orchestrations by Ray Jones, *Maggie May* was highly musicalized, a refined piece about rough people. At one point, the dockworkers sing, "This lousy job isn't worth the pay" as they walk out in a boisterous march, "Leave Her, Johnnie, Leave Her." This is then juxtaposed against one of Maggie May's ID numbers, "The Land Of Promises" after Casey abandons Maggie May to join his buddies. Thus, "Leave her" takes on new meaning even as the hopeful but now embittered "Land of Promises" battles with it. And again we have a quodlibet—how does a non-musician effect this if he isn't some kind of genius?

But then came *Twang!!*, the super-flop that destroyed Bart's career and impoverished him. While planning *Quasimodo*, his projected musical drawn from Victor Hugo's *Notre-Dame De Paris*, Bart jumped at the idea of a Robin Hood spoof. But he chose as director—of a Big West End musical, now—that queen of bohemian experimentation Joan Littlewood. The cast was caught between Bart's professional protocols and Littlewood's improvisations, as if Starfleet Command was allied with the Katzenjammer Kids.

Littlewood abandoned the production after the first night of the tryout, and Burt Shevelove took over, but the book (by Bart and Harvey Orkin) was incoherent and the score, except for the plangently medieval "What Makes a Star," was astonishingly poor. Clearly, *Twang!!* was an idea for a show rather than a story Bart needed to tell. In a television documentary on him, Barbara Windsor, top-billed with the Robin Hood, James Booth, recalls Booth's refusing to risk a curtain call before a hostile house and telling him, "It's not *our* fault. It's *their* fault"—meaning the producer, the director, and writer, all of whom were Lionel Bart. He insisted that the cast sing reprises at the end while the audience "were almost snarling at us." On and on the players sang, while the public simply got up and left. There was no booing, but before the reprises were finished, the huge Shaftesbury auditorium was empty.

Yet Bart left his mark on the era, partly in a renewed interest in adapting classics (in the *Oliver!* manner) and partly in a yen for experimentation. In fact, the first British concept musical came along just a year after *Oliver!*: Monty Norman and Wolf Mankowitz's *Belle; or, The Ballad of Dr. Crippen* (1961).

Billed as "the music-hall musical," *Belle* recounted the notorious 1910 murder case in which a doctor killed his wife in order to be with his secretary. But the show did this—to the critics' fury—in the ironic detachment typical of music-hall performers. A troupe of them ran the narrative, commenting on the story while telling it, one of the elemental qualities of the concept show. A long score made of short numbers in the old style seemed to relish the violence of the tale, taking stage in galumphing up tunes such as "Meet Me At the Strand," while the three principal actors in the actual narrative (doctor George Benson, victim wife Rose Hill, secretary Virginia Vernon) sang a completely different set of numbers, apparently sincere—or were they? The wife, herself a music-hall performer, offered "Bird of Paradise," which, after an intro of pure Kurt Weill, went into a ridiculous soprano ballad that the music-hall people booed off the stage, while the secretary got the numbers supposed to move us—"You Are Mine," "Don't Ever Leave Me." Or were they spoofs, too?

Belle was one of the quirkiest shows of its time, but then the concept musical is quirky by nature, as witness the second British example, *Stop the World—I Want To Get off* (1961). But this one was a hit. Co-written by Anthony Newley and Leslie Bricusse, it set the life story of Newley's clown-like Littlechap in a simple circus-tent unit set, playing opposite Anna Quayle as his wife and three others—German, American, and Russian—with whom Littlechap dallied, each given an establishing number of the same music with different lyrics observing stereotype. (For example, the German: "And on Adolf Hitler's birthday, in our sentimental way . . .") There were no other leads; the rest of the cast were the couple's twin daughters and a small girls' chorus, everyone in fifty-cent costumes that were never changed. Newley wore suspended trousers cut off at the calf over a black top and Quayle was in grey one-piece pajamas with a white collar.

Unlike *Belle*, *Stop the World* was transparent in tone with a commercial score topped by a Big Hit, "What Kind Of Fool Am I?" Further, Newley was a wow—there were no wow roles in *Belle*. Three generations earlier, he would have been a music-hall star, capitalizing on that nasal voice and guiltless ego energy, but the Edwardian musical wouldn't have been able to place him, which tells us how expansively the British musical had developed, even how many eclectic influences it was eagerly toying with.

Thus, historian David Cottis discerns in *Stop the World* a number of inspirations for its non-realistic presentation, among them the "Theatre of the Absurd, the mime of Marcel Marceau, kitchen-sink films and novels." Indeed, *Stop the World*'s plot suggests John Braine's novel (and its film) *Room At the Top*. The Absurd and its habit of treating serious material as a loony lark permeates the musical's action, and Littlechap constantly mimes his way through scenes, as in a meeting about Quayle with his boss, unseen and impersonated by a grouchy bassoon:

NEWLEY: *That's* your daughter? . . . No, of course you wouldn't want her going out with a member of your staff.

(He mimes leaving the office and goes over to Quayle.)

QUAYLE: I'm going to have [your] baby.
NEWLEY: *Stop the world!*

Taking in the show's Manchester tryout, David Merrick, who routinely brought West End hits to Broadway, was enchanted with *Stop the World*'s staging, because Merrick was cheap and the show looked cheap. Just think— no scenery, just a . . . thing with bleachers. One set of costumes. Two leads and staff. There was a rumor that Newley and Bricusse wrote the show (or at least the first draft) inside of a month, that the production had cost only £2,000. While seizing the rights to bring *Stop the World* to Broadway, Merrick wondered if the authors could embark on a series of musicals played in a unit set with two stars and staff in fifty-cent costumes.

Oddly, the authors did, though their second entry, *The Roar of the Greasepaint—The Smell of the Crowd* closed on its British tryout tour with Norman Wisdom in the Newley role, despite another score rich in promotable numbers—"A Wonderful Day Like Today," as lilting as it sounds; "Who Can I Turn To (When Nobody Needs Me)"; and a bitter Newley specialty,

"The Joker," which Newley got to sing when Merrick, who had seen the tryout, took the show to Broadway. A third entry, *The Good Old Bad Old Days!* (1972), lasted 309 performances, but its raucous score and silly back and forth between the devil (Newley) and God (Paul Bacon), amusingly portrayed as a little old guy with a Jewish accent, terminated the cycle.

Most experimental of all was Joan Littlewood's *Oh What a Lovely War* (1963), another collaboration between her Stratford East troupe and a writer, here Charles Chilton. A revue using the songs and people of World War I, the show presented the cast in Pierrot costumes, varied as needed to assign the players specific characters, all on an empty stage backed by period slides and surmounted by a news-headline panel.

It was a clever idea superbly executed, very precise in its delineations of history. On one hand, the audience heard Field Marshal Douglas "Butcher" Haig talking evil nonsense against a photograph of soldiers crossing a field while an unseen voice sang "There's a Long, Long Trail A-Winding." And we hear "The men are forbidden under pain of court-martial to take cover in any shell hole or dugout" from Haig, and "The loss of, say, another 300,000 men may lead to really great results."

Of course it led to nothing, and Littlewood's valor in this project was to make this and other enormities all but elemental in the entertainment—for *Oh What a Lovely War* truly was entertaining, as if the ultimate truth of life was hidden in the cymbal playing of a toy monkey. This was that rare thing, a genuinely unpredictable musical, as when a sergeant-major (a Pierrot with cap and baton) screamed incomprehensibly at recruits for what seemed like hours till one of them charged into the audience and went after a young woman (a plant, be it said), who ran out of the auditorium while the officer called out, "I'm very sorry, madam, we were only doing bayonet drill."

Much less remembered (and less experimental than historical) was Ron Moody's failed labor of love, *Joey, Joey* (1966), on the famous pantomime star Joseph Grimaldi. Moody, the sole author, had been tinkering with the piece for years, yet he failed to create much of a show except when reconstructing the vanished art of the harlequinade. This he did complete with Grimaldi's invariable starting line, "Hello, here we are again!" and his theme song, "Hot Codlins" (candy apples), with its interactive menu when the "little old woman" selling the apples felt a chill in the air:

GRIMALDI: So to keep herself warm, she thought it no sin
  To fetch herself a quartern of—
THE AUDIENCE: *Gin!*

Also less than experimental but still advancing the sound style of the musical were *Passion Flower Hotel* (1965) and *Canterbury Tales* (1966), reaffirming the strong use of brass at the expense of the strings and giving all but the ballads a trendy air. *Passion*, with music by John Barry, occasionally tootled with the sounds Barry was known for from his film work. One number, the duet of two schoolboys discussing how to court girls, "What a Question," took off on a vamp that suggested the James Bond Theme was coming up. And the Chaucer, using some of the better known tales, balanced antique caroling with the patterns of rock.

The comedy musical was still vital; the Whitehall Theatre enlightened its series of sex farces with a musical farce, *Come Spy With Me* (1966), a spoof of James Bond thrillers with drag artist Danny La Rue donning wild disguises in a hunt for the usual criminal mastermind. Bryan Blackburn, who devised La Rue's club acts, was the show's sole author, and along with the joking in the script were some truly funny songs. Agent V.O.3—the James Bond character (Gary Miller)—used the title tune to recount his busy itinerary ("Wednesday in Rangoon, I blew up a dam—well, that's how I am") and, when everyone onstage ingested sodium pentothal, all began blurting out personal secrets in "The Whole Truth," from "I'm Anastasia, pretender to the throne" to "I hated My Fair Lady"[1]

Come Spy with Me occupied its own zany genre, but many felt that *The Four Musketeers!* (1967), a burlesque of Dumas, was totally ersatz in every way, including its score, though *Lock Up Your Daughters'* Laurie Johnson composed the music. "A comedy musical!" the heralds cried—and note that Peter Coe and Sean Kenny, the director and designer of the age, were in charge of this Drury Lane spectacular about what happens when D'Artagnan is not a Gary Miller but Harry Secombe, the pop Pavarotti of *The Goon Show*. Later in the show's long run, he lost his voice for a bit and had to sync to a tape. On the night I saw it, there was no announcement to that effect, and Secombe mimed his establishing number, "A Little Bit of Glory," persuasively. But when he and Constance (Stephanie Voss) reached their romantic duet, "What Love Can Do," Secombe pretended to have a drink of something while his taped voice was on, thus to toy with the problem and beg the public's indulgence. It was that kind of show.

---

[1] Sadly, Miller suffered a heart attack just before the opening (Dennis Lotis, the original Paul Slickey, deputized on the cast album), and though Miller did eventually rejoin the cast, he died a year later.

And what were the opinion-makers to say of *Charlie Girl* (1965), the only musical to win universal loathing and still run over five years? A modern *Cinderella* (instead of sitting by the fireplace ashes, she gets dirty souping up motorcars), *Charlie Girl* was an assembly of clichés—the aged woman star floating down a staircase to dance with dressy young admirers; the sudden intrusion of a music-hall rave-up about something banal (here a fish-and-chips shop); and so on. Worse, the show's star was Anna Neagle, one of a number of very popular show-biz names whose very purpose confounds intellectuals. At least Gracie Fields, a dour actress with the charm of a cleaning lady, had her interesting high notes. And George Formby had that banjo. But Neagle seemed to coast along on the eerie charm of being blithely talentless, sort of a posh version of America's Annette Funicello. Neagle's *Charlie Girl* rest periods were assigned to Evelyn Laye, so the producer, Harold Fielding, came up with a second musical using the same ingredients, this time for Laye: *Phil the Fluter* (1969). The show concerned (and used some of the numbers of) the supposedly beloved late-Victorian songwriter Percy French, but this one flopped.

Adaptations from the classics might have soothed the critics' impatience with musicals, but shows based on Dickens, Barrie, and so on only made them angrier. *Pickwick* (1963) was a smash, though, and a follow-up to *Oliver!* in Peter Coe and Sean Kenny's again using mobile constructions instead of conventional scenery. The actors appeared to move Kenny's big wooden pieces themselves, and as the action was told in flashback, at the start and end of it the chorus very obviously changed costumes in full view of the audience.

Book writer Wolf Mankowitz followed previous adaptations of *The Pickwick Papers* in centering on the most familiar episodes—Winkle's duel with Dr. Slammer, Miss Wardle's foiled elopement, Mrs. Bardell's suit against Pickwick for breach of promise and the ensuing trial. This necessitated very lengthy testimony—in fact, a ten-minute monologue—by Sgt. Buzfuz, as whom the gloomy comedian Peter Bull registered an arresting cameo. It was a daring sortie—one man, one voice, one endless speech—but Bull was hypnotically intense and always got a tremendous hand in the calls.

As *Pickwick*'s characters are mostly quite formal people, the show was a bit formal, too, including dance numbers and even a skating scene, when Pickwick learned of the case against him and promptly crashed through the ice for a shocking first-act curtain. However, the creators avoided letting the evening get too mannered, by giving a lot of stage time to the novel's

SWEEP ME OFF MY FEET   153

two unruly principals, Pickwick's Cockney manservant Sam Weller (Teddy Green) and the charming rogue Mr. Jingle (Anton Rodgers), with his habit of speaking in telegramese, as here when things are going badly for him and he leans on Pickwick:

JINGLE: Not too fast—legs shaky—head queer—round and round—earthquaky sort of feeling—very.

As for Pickwick, he was Harry Secombe, here not joking around but acting, and his piercing high notes, always the delight of the house, seemed to emphasize the precise way Pickwick has of going about the business of life. Though Secombe did, at one point, turn a cartwheel.

One reason *Pickwick* lasted 694 performances was the score, by Cyril Ornadel and Leslie Bricusse. It's extremely tuneful, from the waltzy "That's What I Want For Christmas" to the duet of Sam Weller and his father, "The Trouble With Women," into each strophe of which Ornadel slipped a sudden, lunging change of meter, reflecting a dramatis personae made almost entirely of Dickensian eccentrics. There was a Big Hit as well, "If I Ruled the World." For a season or two, the song was everywhere—but *Pickwick*'s best number was "The Pickwickians," our introduction to the four central figures of the protagonist and his comrades in a strutting gavotte that Coe insisted be not just sung but danced, in little hopping steps.

Other adaptations fared less well, despite having wonderful scores. James Bernard and Paul Dehn's *Virtue In Danger* (1963), from Vanbrugh's *The Relapse*, was the Mermaid's attempt to install a second *Lock Up Your Daughters*, and Dehn's lyrics are sharper than Bart's at that. Dehn draws closely from his source, even "Stand Back, Old Sodom!," a young man's rebuff of an elderly admirer. *Virtue In Danger* (the subtitle of *The Relapse*, by the way) was more seductive than *Lock Up Your Daughters*, even wittier, which is a real compliment. But ticketbuyers felt one such outing was sufficient.

David Heneker and Beverley Cross' *Jorrocks* (1966) also suffered a disappointing run, considering the fame of its source, R. S. Surtees' novels of the blustering Cockney tea grocer obsessed with fox hunting. There had been a popular television adaptation with Jimmy Edwards earlier that year, so theatregoers would have recognized the title, and besides Heneker's mostly quite wonderful songs was director Val May's decision to let his cast play with a sassy cartoonish emphasis—from Cheryl Kennedy's almost turbulent heroine to Thelma Ruby's spoofy high notes—to match star Joss Ackland's stuffed lobster of a Jorrocks: lots of bite and a ton of content.

Jorrocks was an above all lively show, then, deliberately gloomed down in Heneker's best number, "Toasts Of the Town," in which Mrs. Jorrocks, a doctor, and an army captain looked back on their youth in a woebegone waltz. These weren't characters we liked, yet Heneker caught the pathos of the situation so well that it became a noble moment. Even critics who panned the show singled out this number in grudging admiration.

Another failure with a memorable score was Ian Kellam and Michael Ashton's *The Young Visiters* [*sic*] (1968), from Daisy Ashford's novelette, written at the age of nine in a little composition book with an amusing innocence of spelling and punctuation protocols. *The Young Visiters* tells of clumsy Mr. Salteena's wish to become a gentleman, all in the language of a child who has been listening to adults and wants to use their every word. This is the story's charm, as when Mr. Salteena's friend invites him to visit with "Please bring one of your young ladies whichever is the prettiest in the face," or when, at table, Mr. Salteena gets "rarther flustered with his forks."

Kellam and Ashton's adaptation respected the book's tone, with delightful songs full of Daisy Ashford's naive wonder. Yet the show lasted only 63 performances. True, it did open just before panto season, so people may have assumed it was another children's Christmas special, like Harold Fraser-Simson and Julian Slade's *Winnie the Pooh* (1970), giving matinees at the Phoenix during the run of *Canterbury Tales*. Did *The Young Visiters'* whimsy give off too dear an air for the age of rock? Or was the cast's lack of star power the problem, good as Alfred Marks, Jan Waters, and Anna Sharkey were?

Mr. & Mrs. (1968) had stars—John Neville and Honor Blackman, along with a behind-the-scenes star in Noël Coward, as the show was John Taylor's musicalization of *To-Night At 8:30* one-acts. First was the one about the henpecked husband who turns, and after the intermission came the one that became the movie *Brief Encounter*.

This was an intriguing idea, for how many dual roles do we ever get in musicals? However, the first piece is dreary (though Coward loved playing it back in 1936). And the only halfway-decent number was third star Hylda Baker's "If The Right Man Should Ask Me," with its concluding repeated "yes"es on ever higher notes. Worst of all, Honor Blackman couldn't sing.

The show came off after just 44 performances at the palace—and *Two Cities* (1969) ran exactly as long in the same house. Musically the work of an immigrant American father and son, Jerry and Jeff Wayne, *Two Cities'*

Dickens was damned as being too literal—it opened with the novel's first line and ended with its last, both sung. And while the score is not as vapid as that of *Mr. & Mrs.*, it seemed to submit to rather than illuminate its subject.

But we were speaking of failed adaptations with good music, and *Ann Veronica* (1969), from H. G. Wells' feminist novel of 1909, is one. Wells gives us a young woman who rebels against her tyrannical father, gets caught up in the suffragette fight, and openly offers herself to a married biology professor with "I want you to be my lover." He sees "hardship and danger" in it, yet he succumbs to her determination and Wells, a closet humorist, assigns him the line "Biology was beginning to bore me a bit."

The novel was shocking in its day, because Wells had created a strong and vivid heroine. She "was assailed," he said, "as though she was an actual living person." In fact, her lover disentangles himself from his marriage and they wed. His are the novel's last telling lines, because Ann Veronica's problem is that men do not listen to women. "Blood of my heart," her biologist tells her, "I know. I understand."

The musical, with a libretto by Ronald Gow and Wells' son Frank and a score by Cyril Ornadel and David Croft (who also directed), hewed very closely to the book. The show even started exactly where Wells did, in a railway carriage as Ann Veronica, in her dark skirt-suit, embroidered white blouse, and banded straw boater, rides home prepared to confront her father over an outing he has forbidden her.

True, some of Wells was softened—the father, who in the novel gets nearly violent with his daughter at the front door as she tries to leave, was gentled down, and an elderly reprobate's assault was played for comedy. So was the important role of Miss Miniver, a feminist leader, though Wells himself had fun with her: "If once she lost her faith in Tolstoy's sincerity, nothing she felt would really matter much anymore."

One imagines the authors thinking, This character cries out for Hy Hazell, with her fussbudget presence and rampaging chest register. The rest of the support was less distinctive—Charles West as the father, Peter Reeves as the biologist, and Arthur Lowe as the old roué. But Ann Veronica herself had to be a star—pretty, vivacious, and possessed of a thrilling soprano.

There are not many such actresses around in any age. So the creatives were delighted to get Dorothy Tutin, a go-to for charismatic roles—Anouilh's Joan of Arc, Sally Bowles in the London *I Am a Camera*, Polly Peachum. But Tutin's workload created delays, and when at last she gave her Ann Veronica before an audience, in the Coventry tryout, she felt that the music was beyond her. It was too late to recast, so the showrunners tried to finagle the numbers to protect their star. But she soon gave up, and her understudy stepped in.

This usually means catastrophe. However, Mary Millar proved a real find, resourceful, believable, lovable—and she handled the singing with a vibrant soprano. Alas, on the first night in London, the complex scenery acted up, which was all the excuse the critics needed to wallop the show. After some five weeks it closed, though the cast album testifies to how tightly the numbers held the story.

Yes, there were the exuberant ensembles—"Opportunity," "Sweep Me Off My Feet"—whose purpose was simply to make merry. "Sweep Me" was especially deft in this, as a pulsing waltz punctuated by the percussion. There was as well a Heroine Anthem—as so often in sixties American shows the title song, sung by the heroine herself, then a cute neighborhood boy of no importance (Ian Lavender), and the chorus, as the scenery shifted to take Wells' budding world beater into her new life while the music kept pausing for deflating vignettes:

LANDLADY: Sorry, Ducky—we don't rent rooms to unaccompanied females.

and:

JOB BOSS: We don't employ women. It upsets the men. (Dismissing her) Go on.

Yet she went forward, undeterred in a conclusion of choral rhapsody and pounding tympani so exciting it threw the first act off a bit, sounding like a finale when only partway through Act One.

Of course, there were political numbers on The Vote ("Seek fair play," Miss Miniver sang, "for the mothers of your sons!"), hastening to a first-act finale in which the chorus women chained themselves to a barrier at 10 Downing Street while the cops and some reactionary louts chimed in with a condescending reply, the two melodies then combined in a quodlibet.

It was the character songs, I'm guessing, that most irritated scoffers, because nothing infuriates the music hater like a number with dramatic content; it's his idea of Little Tommy Tucker playing King Lear. *Ann Veronica* was loaded with these outpourings, most notably her "Why Can't I Go To Him" and "If I Should Lose You," cutting right to her blunt sense of independence—the reason the scoffers of Wells' day so hated the novel. Interestingly, Ornadel and Croft gave the biology professor—the man who inspires Ann Veronica's most provocative act, giving herself to an adulterous union—a number devoid of sensuality, "Chemical Attraction." Well, of course: he's a man of science, methodical, professional, detached.

Yet why was she drawn to a man of such prim little music? The *other* man, the one her father chose for her, got the big courtship number, "One Man's Love," and poor Simon Kent had to sing it groomed as a plop with a goon's haircut. But what a voice!—a booming, eloquent baritone. It's *Ann Veronica's* flaw that, in the middle of Act One, we anticipated Kent's make-over provisioning the happy ending when, on the contrary, she's destined to run off with Peter Reeves and his microscopes.

There was no such confusion at Ron Grainer and Ronald Millar's *Robert and Elizabeth* (1964), from Rudolph Besier's *The Barretts of Wimpole Street*, a thirties stage hit in London and New York and a touring favorite of Katharine Cornell. Almost from the first moments, it was clear that Robert Browning (Keith Michell) loved Elizabeth Barrett (June Bronhill), she loved him back, and the only impediment was another tyrannical father (John Clements). This was an operetta, spendthrift with music, so it opened with a lengthy song-and-mime scene-setter on Wimpole Street, taking in workers, passersby, and the Moulton-Barrett family, marching in strict order while Father Barrett tries (and fails) to stop an army officer from slipping a love note to one of the daughters. So we knew what Clements was like: a control freak, but one who can be defeated.

Then, indoors, the Barrett offspring explained matters in "The Family Moulton-Barrett," anxious and fidgety, even neurotic, with constant lashings from the orchestra of a chord made of a tritone and a diminished octave, the two most unstable intervals in the catalogue. Next we visited Elizabeth Barrett's room, for she is bedridden, crippled by an unknown malady (which we know is fatheritis). In "The World Outside," she gives us the show's first wave of the lyricism with which this score is flooded, and there remained only for us to meet Browning.

And it was then that a merely nicely imagined period piece turned dazzling, for the scene changed from the serene world of Wimpole Street to the bedlam of theatricals during a dress rehearsal, as the stage of the Haymarket in the 1840s thronged with actors in wigs and robes and poses, even the great William Macready, in a verse play about Savoy and Sardinia—a "deplorable piece," according to Macready. Still, he gives his all on a line calling for a momentous pause, and he gets so momentous about it that, suddenly, from the back of the auditorium in which *Robert and Elizabeth's* public was sitting, came a booming voice:

ROBERT BROWNING: Well, go on, man, go on! We haven't got all night!

and Keith Michell came striding up the aisle to take control of the play—his own, it turned out:

MACREADY: Mr. Browning, you are not *yet* William Shakespeare.
BROWNING: And . . . you never *will* be David Garrick or Edmund Kean.

Came then a note from Elizabeth inviting Robert to tea, leading to the exuberant "Moon In My Pocket," Michell soaring over the chorus in bliss, and from then on the suspenseful story of the knight, the damsel, and the dragon (and especially the Grainer-Millar score) took the audience into that territory only the musical occupies, mixed of fascinating personalities, stimulating ideas, and wonderful music: a poetic world, better than ours.

This rich show even found room for a subplot for that officer and Barrett daughter from the first scene. Of course, they're the comic pair, not least when she begged him to loathe her, out of fear of her father's fury.[2] Grainer and Miller got a song out of it, "Hate Me, Please." Still, the show's elemental power lay in the music for the First Couple, and as Michell and Bronhill were the best singers of the day, their scenes really took flight. More: it wasn't just a love story, because he was coaching her in learning to walk again and we wondered what her father would do about that.

We found out at the first-act curtain, in the Barrett garden, when, just after a passionate love duet, "I Know Now," she began to take a few steps on her own. But the dragon came upon them; his fire was her guilty memory of her dead brother: "*Wasn't* Edward's death enough?"

Bronhill froze, wobbled, and went down, unconscious. The beast had won. Carrying her inside, he whispered, "You're safe, my darling" as a lover might—an awfully dire moment for an operetta. Curtain.

During the intermission, some might have been wondering why Elizabeth seemed so attached to her father when he was so cruel, even to his own children, her siblings. But they are the products of lust, he explains. Of sin. He actually sang about it, in "What the World Calls Love," but she responded with the spectacular "Woman and Man," driving and tumultuous and carrying her ever higher to a non-optional top D.

---

[2] The real-life Edward Moulton-Barrett was so possessive (and rabid about even marital sex) that he disinherited each of his children when they married.

At last! We think. She has refuted her father's worldview—his place, really, in her life—and after torturing us and Browning (he, too gets a song out of this, the desperately staccato "Frustration") by Thinking It Over, she runs off to Italy with her lover, as she did in life. In the show's last moments, a train pulled into Florence in the brightest light the theatre can project, as Robert and Elizabeth disembarked to lead the chorus in a reprise of "I Know Now."

At 948 performances, the show should have been a smash, but there had been a booking crunch and for some reason producer Martin Landau settled for the Lyric Theatre, too small for the production's heavy running costs. A New York staging was planned, but a certain Fred G. Morritt had laid claim to the project in the first place with a terrible adaptation of his own. He had been edged out with a line credit, but was lying in wait in the US, threatening lawfare on any further production of *Robert and Elizabeth*. When New Jersey's Paper Mill Playhouse defied Morritt in 1982 with a lavish mounting led by Mark Jacoby and Leigh Beery, Morritt sued . . . and lost. Still, wasn't it now too late for a Broadway operetta? Chichester revived the piece in 1987, with Mark Wynter and Gaynor Miles, but the sun has set on this form of musical.

Let's close the decade on an up note, with a tale of *Belle Starr* (1969), the ghastly western starring Betty Grable. On the first day of rehearsals, everyone was expecting the manifestation of a Queen Of the Lot, but the artless Grable came through the stage door without an entourage or even a bodyguard, in street clothes with her hair in a babushka.

So a stage hand pointed at a nearby closet and told her, "The mop and bucket are right in there, luv."

11

The Little Things We Used To Do

The 1970s and 1980s

The small-scaled "clever" revue reached its apex in the late 1950s and early 1960s, leaving scarcely any memory, though John Cranko's *Cranks* (1956) was thought worthy of a visit to New York with its original cast (including Anthony Newley), mainly because Cranko thought up offbeat staging scenarios for the songs. Other revues simply sang the music; Cranko dissected it.

Replacing the revue was the review (of old music), as in the Mermaid's *Cowardy Custard* (1972) and *Cole* (1974), stylish recapitulations of Noël Coward and Cole Porter with flavorsome casts, though the singing was variable. Coward himself dropped in on *Custard*, and his blurb was ready: "I came out humming the tunes." *Cole* attempted a chronological tour through Porter's career, but *A Swell Party* (1992) offered just the tunes, letting Martin Smith sing "Love For Sale" as an escort in a hustler bar. While the music faded out, he said, "Good evening, sir."

There were comparable outings in *John, Paul, George, Ringo . . . and Bert* (1974); [John] *Betjemania* (1976); Lewis Fiander and Patricia Hodge doing *Noël and Gertie* (1986); and *Underneath the Arches* (1981), recreating [Bud] Flanagan and [Chesney] Allen and the Crazy Gang's bygone heyday at the Palladium. While singing the old songs, the show brought back the old routines, as when Christopher Timothy as Allen would correct Roy Hudd as Flanagan on a blooper and get cries of the working-class "Oi!":

FLANAGAN: I saw all the sights of London, [such as] Expensive End.

• • •

ALLEN: You saw Cheapside.
FLANAGAN: Oi!
THE ORCHESTRA: *Oi!*

The offbeat entry in the cycle was *Songbook* (1979), as it reviewed the catalogue of someone who never existed: Liverpool-born Michael Mooney, who emigrated to the US and, adopted by a Jewish couple, changed his ID to Moony [*sic*] Shapiro:

MOONY: I . . . decided to become Jewish. I went to see Rabbi Kotschinsky.
RABBI: You realize, my boy, you'll have to be circumcised.
MOONY: I decided not to become Jewish.

Five actors—Anton Rodgers, Gemma Craven, Diane Langton, Andrew C. Wadsworth, and David Healy—played countless roles in Monty Norman and Julian More's fictional biography of a songwriter who experiences the ins and outs of Broadway, Hollywood, war, McCarthyism, and so on. And all of "Shapiro" 's songs were pastiche.

There's something wrong with that, as it ended up a show about nothing, like those drag artists who imitate Judy Garland. Further, the book hit only obvious points, and the song copies lacked suasion, except for a Parisian episode, with Rodgers whispering à la Jean Sablon in "Je Vous Aime, Milady" and Langton urging, "Drink onion soup with your hand on my knee" in the waltzy "Les Halles," the show's little band gamely trying to imitate an accordion.

Two adaptations interest us. *The Good Companions* (1974), from J. B. Priestley's huge backstage novel, had been filmed twice (once with Jessie Matthews) when André Previn and Johnny Mercer collaborated with bookwriter Ronald Harwood (later the author of the play *The Dresser*). Priestley's tale focuses on three unconnected people fed up with their lives, hitting the road, and finding a new vocation with a touring Pierrot troupe. These are star parts, and this *Good Companions* had (top-billed) John Mills and Judi Dench, with Christopher Gable (and his opposite, Marti Webb) below the title. The score is wonderfully tuneful in the old-fashioned style that *Jesus Christ Superstar* was to send to the retirement home, but there's a problem built into Priestley's structure: much of it is backstory on how his three each found a way into show business. It works in the novel and, somewhat, in the films, but in a musical the songs put too much weight on all that prelude—Act One is almost over before the actual story gets going. Like so many shows, this one faltered in the theatre while leaving behind a lovable cast album.

Peg (1984), from the wildly successful American play *Peg O' My Heart* (1912)—written, be it said, by an Irishman, J. Hartley Manners, for his wife, Laurette Taylor—offers a comparable failure. Billed as "a romantic new musical," *Peg* closely followed Manners' tale of an American waif fostered by an English family.

Too closely. Though it ran 603 performances in New York (the straight-play record to that time) and 710 in London, *Peg O' My Heart* harks back to the era when the actor, not the script, was the draw. Alas, the musical *Peg*, which reached the West End without a bookwriter credit, simply added songs to an extremely dull and talky script. Why hire Siân Phillips in the so to say Wicked Stepmother role without giving her the patented Siân Phillips persiflage and snark? American Ann Morrison as Peg matched Phillips well in the first-act "quarrel" finale, "There's a Devil In Me" (from a line in Manners' play), as the two hurled cherry bombs at each other. No, literally. And if Phillips' big solo, "The Fishing Fleet," was sheer floppo, Morrison's exhibition piece, "Manhattan Hometown," sung in front of New York's twinkling lights and a big white moon, sounded like somebody's eleven o'clock number by Harold Arlen and Johnny Mercer.

In fact, *Peg*'s score was by David Heneker, at his best here even given the modest range of the characters. He gave Patricia Michael "When a Woman Has To Choose," soft and pensive yet jolted by a darksome chord on her last use of "choose," a tenderly dramatic touch. And to spark sympathy between Morrison and her opposite, Martin Smith, "Peg and Jerry" is sportive, as she slowly warms up to him and he sings his hope that they can meet "with reg." She: "Reg"?

HE: . . . ularity.

It's sweet, but it's outdated, leftovers to be remaindered at a discount. And pop opera's Big Sing histrionics were not the only reason why: nine years before *Peg*, Richard O'Brien unleashed *The Rocky Horror Show*, a spoof of fifties sci-fi B-movies spiced with camp and bisexuality. "Rocky Horror" can be read as "the scary power of three-chord rock and roll," and the piece could not have become the classic it now is if O'Brien had written a score of the easy-listen kind. This musical is friendly but dangerous.

Two innocents, Brad and Janet, attend a wedding—a symbol of the prelapsarian society that the counterculture will overturn. As the show's action proper begins, Brad and Janet are now caught on the road in a storm and happen upon the castle of Dr. Frank 'N' Furter (Tim Curry), a leather-and-fishnet drag queen Frankenstein whose monster is a muscleboy clad in nothing but passion shorts. The good doctor, his henchman Riff Raff (O'Brien himself), and the rest of his entourage hail from the planet Transsexual in the galaxy Transylvania, and the somewhat incoherent plot simply enables loony vignettes and those noisy songs. To add to the anarchy, the movie version, now *The Rocky Horror* Picture *Show*, encouraged audience interaction—but not in the family-approved manner of panto: spectators maintain a conversation with the action in set anticipations and replies varying from obscene to silly. A sample, after the wedding:

JANET: An hour ago [the bride] was plain old Betty Munroe, and now...
AUDIENCE: She's still plain!

Talk of film brings us to a feature of the late-twentieth-century, the staging of movie musicals, a bit like trying to eat the same sandwich twice. We've already dealt with Harold Fielding's two direct-from-television Coliseum panto-spectacles; later, Fielding went on to build a *Hans Andersen* (1974) around his favorite star, Tommy Steele. This was a Palladium spectacle, based on the Frank Loesser movie with Danny Kaye but with a different storyline and an adulterated score, partly of extra Loesser numbers and partly by one Marvin Laird.

This is not a genre to make major history, obviously—but one such title is now a secret classic, Alan Parker's staging of his movie *Bugsy Malone*, in 1983. A take-off on gangster films but cast entirely with kids (Jodie Foster was thirteen when the film was shot, and some others look nine or ten), *Bugsy Malone* substituted custard pies for bullets and pedal-driven kiddie cars for the real thing, even as Parker's script was of the hard-boiled Warner Bros. school. (Protagonist Scott Baio to Foster: "Careful, Tallulah, you're racing my motor.")

The staging retained all ten of the movie's numbers without emendation, and while the entire cast was dubbed onscreen, Parker had his stage cast doing their own vocals. A natural choice for the National Youth Theatre, the show has become a staple of the high-school dramatics club—so much so that many Britons know this musical better than *The Boy Friend* or *Half a Sixpence*: they were in it themselves.

Billy (1974), too, had been a movie (and novel, play, and television series, all as *Billy Liar*), but it was a musical for the first time, a surprisingly tart one.

Think of the elders' trio in *Salad Days*, "Find Yourself Something To Do," as they urge the family scion onward to a merrily flowing accompaniment. *Billy* had a comparable trio, "And," as Billy's parents and gran whacked away at him in disgust to a clunky wind band with a bass-drum chaser. How they hated him, despite the parents' duet, "Remembering," later on, recalling his happy youth.

But Billy wasn't happy anymore. Seeking escape from his humdrum life, he creates a fantasy world, and Patrick Garland's Drury Lane staging gave the public the big visuals the Lane was famous for in substantiating Billy's imaginary world, Ambrosia. From a colorless Yorkshire, the stage would explode in high-fashion crowd scenes. The first of these gave Billy an unprecedented star entrance, dropping in by parachute. And the moment Billy unhooked himself and took stage, a star really was born:

Michael Crawford. In a cliché of his bio, he had won renown in the television sitcom *Some Mothers Do 'Ave 'Em*. But that was Crawford playing an earnest, bewildered screw-up. In *Billy*'s script, by Dick Clement and Ian La Frenais, Crawford was reinvented as a cagey fabulist visualizing himself as a philosopher-king in gala production numbers.

This suggests a traditional star-turn musical comedy, but *Billy* was so tensely delineated that even the score was cut with uncomfortable honesty into this tale of a young man terrified of breaking loose while relentlessly scheming to do so. Meeting his insipid girl friend (Gay Soper), who sings a hymn to corny marriage, Crawford interjected bitter insults at her—and the number was called "The Witch."

He wasn't any more content with a second girl friend (Elaine Paige), a flashy horror, and he despised even his hometown in "Happy To Be Themselves," as Canadian-American choreographer Onna White filled the big stage with tintypes of a northern community—the butcher, the nurse, the charwoman—while they, at the same time, felt absolutely at home. Other numbers charted Billy's explosive fantasy world, here in Jack Buchanan tails and there in rock-star glam tights.

Which Billy would prevail—the drudge or the adventurer? A third girl friend (Diana Quick) encourages Billy to seek his fortune with her in the real Ambrosia, London, and he's set to go. Yet, as in the source material, he manages to miss the train. Back in his bedroom, Crawford looked at the audience with an inscrutable expression and said, without affect, "I'm home." A burst of jubilation from the ensemble, and the curtain came down.

Depressing! Is that why this smash hit—904 performances in London's biggest playhouse—never came to Broadway? *Billy*'s cast album was produced by American Columbia's Goddard Lieberson, *the* honcho of the form, so wasn't he expecting a Broadway staging? There's a story about this: someone asked Onna White why *Billy* wasn't coming over, and White replied, "That show wouldn't last two weeks in New York."

A bitter reality without the lift-off of dreams was to be found in Howard Goodall and Melvyn Bragg's *The Hired Man* (1984). This show looked at a young man named John (based on Bragg's grandfather) caught between the miner's life and (his preference) farming: between the dangerous blackpits and the green world under the sun. John has a wife who loves him but also loves another man as well—a case of the good guy vs. the charismatic one. But Bragg was more interested in showing how the well-off are free while the poor have few if any options. Consider the first dialogue scene, at a job fair, where would-be tenant farmers audition for the landowners. One applicant tries to seal the agreement, but:

FARMER: Don't rush, lad. . . . There's a lot of good muscle about today.

and a woman offers to work as hard as any man, and she has no "family to feed":

OTHER FARMER: I'll look about.

The Goodall-Bragg score has a folkish lilt, with powerful male choruses, Irish in tone but bearing a Welsh solidity in the harmony. It's an astonishing show, but a brutal and sad one and, as timeless tales of The System must, it ends where it began, because nothing changes for working folk:

FARMER: Are you for hire?
JOHN: Aye, I'm for hire.

Willy Russell's *Blood Brothers* (1983) was another tale of (partly) working-class life, and Russell, a newbie to the musical, broke every rule in the handbook, with strange song ideas, adult actors playing young children, and an ending foretold as soon as the curtain rose. But then, *Blood Brothers* recalled the old Greek theatre, with oracular prediction, a chorus (here a sole Narrator), and the concept of ineluctable destiny—rare in the musical, which favors characters who outwit fate (though this is much more elemental in the American form).

Barbara Dickson played the mother who gave away one of her twin boys for adoption, despite the warning that if they ever divine their true relationship, both will die. Despite Dickson's winning performance, the show didn't register strongly with the public till a few years later, when a regional tour with Kiki Dee and a very strong supporting cast came into the West End and played for a whopping twenty-four years.

What happened? This isn't a two-visit show that takes some getting used to, especially with its catchy though surprising score, filled with objets trouvés, for example the recurring "Marilyn Monroe," which sounds irrelevant to English life on the back streets but actually fills in plot material.

On a completely different note was Peter Nichols' campier-than-even-*Valmouth* "play with songs" *Privates On Parade* (1977). Note the title pun: this dark comedy on a British military entertainment troupe in southeast Asia was filled with gay humor, especially from the chief drag artist (Denis Quilley). A knock at the door, and:

QUILLEY: Come in if you're pretty.

Based on Nichols' own experiences in the years just after World War II, *Privates On Parade*, with music by Denis King, used the sounds of the late 1940s in an entirely pastiche score. Most writers don't classify this show as a musical per se, but it had ten vocal numbers, not just "entertainment" spots but character and situation songs. This is a fascinating but troubling show, as Nichols deals in sometimes unpleasant surprises. Further, there's a lot of military jargon, pidgen, and even a bit of Polari.[1] And an extremely dodgy sergeant major ends one scene by warning the audience not to give him away, in the style of a panto figure: "Anyone I hear saying, 'Look out, he's behind you,' will answer to me. Savvy?"

Speaking of panto, the Royal Shakespeare Company tried putting on a few of its own. *The Swan Down Gloves* (1981) was the traditional one (with a cute touch in that the protagonist, Will, "a simple scrivener," turned out to be William Shakespeare), but *Poppy* (1982), again by Peter Nichols, to Monty Norman's music, was the meta-panto, on the Chinese Opium Wars. The Fee

---

[1] This was the British gay dialect, designed to shield homosexuals from eavesdropping outsiders in the years when the communicants' very lives were illegal. "Bona [good] for you," Quilley said at one point, and "Vada the little tiaras," which he then translates as "Look at the crowns on your sleeve."

was Queen Victoria, the Demon King the Emperor of China, and Nichols included the Dame, the Principal Boy, and the animals. (There were three, two horses and an elephant.)

Unlike *The Swan Down Gloves*, *Poppy* filled its score with devious, ironic, and even risqué numbers. The Dame (Geoffrey Hutchings, of course a man in drag) had a song about the sexual urge to mate with a bit of rough, in "Nostalgie de la Boue," and the title tune, the first-act finale, found the British characters high on opium.

Nichols' script, too, kept edging into taboo. The Dame's son is Dick Whittington and the Dame is going to London, where the boy happens to be. So:

SOMEONE: In London you may come across Dick.

THE DAME: Well, I wouldn't have put it quite so bluntly. . . . Oh, you mean my son?

Meanwhile, one of the panto horses, Randy, keeps trying to mount the mare, Cherry—but later, during the war in China, Randy, who has been rather personified by his two human players under the "skin" suit, must be shot during a food shortage.

Good gracious. Is this really a panto? It didn't attract a panto audience, because panto is family fare and the Royal Shakespeare puts on intellectual theatre. So *Poppy*'s spectators weren't prepared for the traditional immersive byplay of the form. Amusingly, Nichols had to write two different outcomes into his script each time the spectators were to take part (as they almost never did), and when *Poppy* was filmed for television, after the final curtain there were retakes in which the house was carefully prepped in the "improvisational" spirit of pantomime's audience interaction with the players.

Perhaps the most English of all these breakaway shows was *Andy Capp* (1982), with novelty star Tom Courtenay as Reg Smythe's comic-strip wastrel with the flat cap over his eyes and the pigeons and the national record for being able-bodied yet unemployed. Trevor Peacock wrote the script and collaborated with composer Alan Price on the song lyrics—a real challenge, as Smythe's typical three or four panels were narrative-free. Now Peacock and Price had the characters—Andy; his wife, Flo; the publican; Percy the rent collector, who never collects any yet never stops trying; and other locals of the strip's Hartlepool, in the far northeast. Still, the authors had to invent a storyline: even to figure out who in the world Andy Capp really was.

Rejecting every first idea, they finally settled on the simplest plot possible: Andy's nephew Elvis is getting married, so there's a lot of preparation for the event and a handy Second Couple in Elvis and his Raquel. A subplot: Andy races those pigeons and will come into money if his prize bird wins the competition.

Interestingly, Alan Price was in the cast, singing his own music onstage as a kind of narrator as well as the pianist at the pub Andy frequents. This sounds a bit fantastical, but in Braham Murray's non-realistic staging, sets were minimal, bits and pieces against a blow-up of newspaper cuttings, so the visuals lay entirely in Johanna Bryant's bigger-than-life costumes. Too, the actors came and went in quasi-Littlewood fashion, presentationally rather than naturally.

At that, while Price wrote strictly theatre music for the characters, his own solos were pop-flavored, which emphasized the meta-theatrical staging concept. Thus, the show opened with Price singing the very personal "On My Street." But Andy had the customary establishing number, "I Ought To Be Ashamed Of Myself," Elvis' future mother-in-law berated her husband (who never utters a word till the very end of the show) with the expenses for the wedding in "Goin' To Barcelona," and poor Flo ruminated on her bad yet irreplaceable marriage in "When You've Lived In Love With Someone." It's an excellent score because it sounds like the individuals singing it; when Andy and a pal stagger home from the pub in "Good Old Legs," the music itself is drunk.

Andy Capp honored its source, then. Yet the show lasted only 99 performances, because the authors and Murray had indeed figured out who Andy is: a terminally selfish, wife-abusing parasite. Granted, he's funny, in the line of insult comedy, as when he threatens the rent collector:

PERCY: Last time you hit me it cost you ten pounds in court.
ANDY: (menacingly) And I'm saving up again.

Courtenay was Andy to the life, but his mean-spirited antics were the opposite of charm. In "Don't Tell Me That Again," Price and Peacock created a genuine marital spat, true fury in music even in jest:

PERCY: I'm not going to stand here and listen to you shouting at your wife like that.
ANDY: Then I'll stand here and you shout at her.

But Percy leaves, and Andy tells his wife, "You're as ugly as a crow."

And that's when the public became fatally alienated. To advertise *Andy Capp* as "a musical" invited theatregoers primed for an enjoyable evening. With a little bite in it, perhaps, but nothing so purely bitter and life-denying. Price and Peacock were in a take-no-prisoners mood, and *Andy Capp* never did find its audience.

12

To Love Another Person Is To See the Face Of God

Pop Opera

We can date the emergence of the through-sung British musical—ultimately known as "pop opera"—from the afternoon of March 1, 1968, when parents (mainly mothers) of students at Colet Court School (at the time in Hammersmith) saw the original twenty-minute version of Andrew Lloyd Webber and Tim Rice's *Joseph and the Amazing Technicolor Dreamcoat*, as an end-of-term concert.

The audience had braced itself for something tiresome but "good for you," like medicine. Elgar or something. But when the catchy melodies began pealing out, the auditorium fairly jumped with pleasure. Composer Lloyd Webber was just short of twenty and lyricist Rice twenty-three, and the work itself was young, conceived for children (with the help of adult soloists) and as hip as biblical—Pharaoh was played as Elvis, the king of rock, here the King of Egypt.

Joseph was a sensation. The Colet Court mothers insisted on a repeat performance for the fathers, and, immediately, the two authors expanded the piece—a bit, later a bit more, and finally as a full-length show grand enough to hold the Palladium in a 1991 revival starring Jason Donovan.

By then Lloyd Webber and Rice had achieved the first phenomenon in pop opera's history in *Jesus Christ Superstar*. Every theatrical management turned it down. A musical about God? *Really*? So the work made its debut on a two-LP concept album (1970), so successful (in the US rather than the UK) that this "rock opera," as the release was billed, now seemed to cry out for a staging.

Lloyd Webber insisted it was an "oratorio," one "written from an album's perspective." That is, it lacked a cohesive narrative drive to marry the disc's separate musical bands. Still, it told of the last week before the Crucifixion; everybody knows that story. Just as the recording's listeners did, a staging's spectators could connect the dots, among, for examples, Judas' tortured fear that his Lord is becoming a professional celebrity; and Mary Magdalene's bewildered relationship with Him; and the local chieftains' anxiety about this heresy's turning into an uprising. The authors added just one number for use in the theatre, as Mary, so prominent in the work's first half, all but vanished in the second, with no more than a few lines in "Peter's Denial." Slipping in the beguiling "Could We Start Again, Please?" righted the balance.

Pop operas are known for establishing an elaborate production that haunts the show wherever it is done, but *Superstar* is protean; there's more than one way to do it. Launched as two different American concert tours, the work was then to be readied as a Broadway attraction, once the many American bootleg productions had been shut down, at a bill of $1 million in legal fees. Even nuns were sued.

Frank Corsaro was hired to direct the show because of his revisionist Personen-Regie stagings of potboilers at the New York City Opera, naturalizing relationships that had gone unexplored for a century. If Corsaro could make audiences accept *Faust* and *La Traviata* as living rather than museum art, he would be the one to make actors out of the rock singers the production would need.[1]

Corsaro's plans included substantiating *Superstar*'s cult obsession with a bank of television screens, the very glass of celebrity, but he was sidelined in an automobile accident, replaced by Tom O'Horgan, who had directed *Hair*. *Superstar*'s producer, Robert Stigwood, reasoned that *Hair* was a Zeitgeist show and *Superstar* was bound to be one as well, so O'Horgan was a logical choice.

Further, *Hair*'s hippies had been costumed as attractive freaks, and this would work for the inhabitants of Israel two thousand years ago, in effect updating the look from pastoral robes to Andy Warhol masquerade, the authentic "superstar" drag. Still, Stigwood was giving up a director, Corsaro, who could talk to actors for a director, O'Horgan, concerned only with how everything looked.

"I didn't know where to hide," says Lloyd Webber of his experience at *Superstar*'s Broadway premiere. He hated it—the opening "curtain" dipping backward as the chorus people clambered all over it during the overture; flying platforms out of Baroque opera; Jesus rising on a hydraulic lift as his

[1] Hal Prince telegrammed Lloyd Webber, asking to acquire the production rights to *Superstar*, but the composer didn't get it in time, to his dismay.

golden robe billowed out to fill the stage. The most sacred pages of the Bible were doing the hokey-pokey, in effect outplaying the central conceit of two leaders of a religious sect baffled by their shared destiny.

Thus, the events that founded Western Civilization were being—to some detractors—overthought, psychoanalyzed on the Shakespearean level, but to music suitable for the Top 40 chart. Very mixed reviews from the New York critics, seldom ready to embrace innovation, did not stop the production from lasting two years and paying off very handsomely halfway through the run. Whatever Lloyd Webber felt about what O'Horgan had done (Rice was more bemused than outraged), at least the cast was excellent: Yvonne Elliman (Mary) and Barry Dennen (Pilate) from the album, with Jeff Fenholt's Jesus and Ben Vereen's Judas. Luckily, they were all self-starters, creating their portrayals on their own while O'Horgan conjured up his pageant.

Did the controversy over rocking the Gospel distract from consideration of the work as art? A very different, somewhat coolly ceremonial staging by Jim Sharman for the eight-year London run starting in 1972 revealed how compelling the words and music are in themselves, accommodating any staging. This cannot be said of *Bitter Sweet*, *The Boy Friend*, or *Expresso Bongo*. But then, those are ethnically British, while pop opera tends to inspire works outside any national culture: international in flavor, they can be staged anywhere without mystifying audiences.

Superstar's power derives from each of its numbers catching the story at a high moment of its conflict, even at the Last Supper, when an agonized Christ turns against the apostles. They come off as idiots smug in their coming stardom because once they write the Gospels, "They'll all talk about us when we've died." The music is deliberately empty in contrast to the Lord's jangled despair; they sound almost like the students at the Colet Court *Joseph*: happy children.

Thus, *Superstar* is worthy of its historical role in establishing this new form of pop opera. Lloyd Webber's ability to compose consistently in a single voice (as in *Jeeves*) or to, so to say, eclecticize to teach the audience to navigate the action through musical signifiers (as in the panorama of pop forms pastiched in *Starlight Express*) has seldom been appreciated. And Tim Rice's ease in "conversationalizing" the bigger-than-life figures that pop opera delights in is similarly underrated, because he makes it look easy—creating, says Olaf Jubin, "the mistaken impression that anybody could have come up with these lines."

All the same, critics who regret the very invention of this format—"pop opera," they cry, "with its helicopters and chandeliers"—see "pop" as an assault on "opera," as an unruly urchin heaves a snowball at a grandee's top hat. Yet Lloyd Webber's rock is ofttimes uncanny, with sections in $\frac{5}{8}$ and $\frac{7}{8}$, altogether learned for street music. *Creative.* On the other hand, Rice does indulge in false rhymes, such as "apostle" and "Gospels," which could easily have been avoided, as "Gospel" (which nearly does rhyme) is colloquially used for the four books as well.

But there's no arguing with success, and now other "rock opera" double albums came along, including a pair on Joan Of Arc and Hitler that have disappeared from public memory. Something else: the music began to absorb more opera and less rock. Except for The Who's *Tommy*—which has been staged very successfully—no major pop opera has built its score entirely on hard rock.

As the music began to vary, so did the spirit of the shows. No longer were a serious tone and VIP protagonist de rigueur. There was comedy, for instance, when Tim Rice teamed with composer Stephen Oliver for *Blondel* (1983), a spoofy look at Richard the Lionheart's minstrel, here a savvy pop-tunesmith looking for a Big Hit as well as for his liege. As in *Superstar* and *Evita*, *Blondel* offered real-life figures known to fame, but soon enough pop opera moved into fantasy.

So *Metropolis* (1989), from Fritz Lang's 1927 film, found music for a futuristic city in which slaves are worked to death to keep the systems functioning for an elite of parasites. As in *Superstar*, three leads drive the tale: the city's ruler (Brian Blessed), who personalizes its technocratic oppressiveness (his establishing number is "The Machines Are Beautiful"), and his son (Graham Bickley), who falls in love with the slave children's schoolteacher (Judy Kuhn). Or no—there is a fourth, a robot (Judy Kuhn) designed to sow chaos among the slaves. Yes, that was Kuhn also as the robot, Futura, and one wonders if the idea of a musical with a robot was what enchanted the financial consortium that backed *Metropolis*, thinking it offbeat enough to become the next *Superstar*.

Blessed and Bickley were powerful singers, blazing at times, and Kuhn was at her most sensitive—essential qualities in a work so dependent on its vocalism. In a rock-cum-theatre-music program, the score allowed for more than a little spoken dialogue, but it was usually underscored, giving the impression that the music never stopped.

And that of course is the pop-opera recipe, one that the father of the form, Andrew Lloyd Webber, recommended, if only at first. He felt the alternating of speech and song a distraction, a series of roadblocks on the turnpike. And while he did eventually move into the book musical, pop opera deals with such high-strung characters that they almost have to keep singing. When a story of this kind makes its points—as in *Metropolis'* chorus "Hold Back the Night," with its big blocks of vocal harmony; or the main ballad, "[If] It's Only Love," it can only be in music.

So who wrote *Metropolis?* This is a curious footnote in pop opera's history, as most of the genre's composers were enthusiasts of music drama. Lloyd Webber was creating his own musicals on a toy theatre at a tender age, and there are comparable tales for many others. However, *Metropolis'* composer, Joe Brooks, had a background in American show biz that involved writing commercial jingles and producing the sort of films no one you knew had even heard of, such as *You Light Up My Life*, with its inane title song, the toast of the Karaoke parlors.[2]

Brooks' co-lyricist and book writer was English playwright Dusty Hughes, but as the start of rehearsals approached, it became clear that the score was not ready. Music director David Firman, who was to bear the credit of "Additional Material By," was asked "to work with [Brooks] on the missing moments." Yet more needed doing, and Firman (as he told me himself) was "commissioned to adapt and embellish some of the pre-existing material." Firman had as well to "compose new passages of music and new lyrics in the second act."

Necessarily a spectacle, to create visual cues for the two different worlds of laborers and elites, *Metropolis* seemed to call for a Continental touch, and the director was Jérôme Savary and the designer Ralph Koltai. The latter invented something new in his show curtain, which looked like a great stone wall that broke into four parts, the top and bottom sliding off vertically and the sides slipping into the wings. The workers' basement—in shades of grey—took up three complete stories of the Piccadilly Theatre's playing area, while the world of the parasites on the city's upper floors reveled in color. There were bullet-like elevators whooshing up and down, even below the deck, and Futura herself—again, Judy Kuhn, as a frozen-faced metal zombie—was an eyeful in her angry-red side-slit gown. Her exhibition "dance" for the grandees was

---

[2] It's not irrelevant to the case to point out that Brooks' arguably dodgy life culminated in his suicide when faced with some ninety charges for sex (and related) crimes, and even that his son was convicted of murder and is currently incarcerated.

a hoot, to music that deliberately suggested the mating of a cuckoo clock and a Slinky toy. Naturally, *Metropolis'* orchestrations were loaded with sci-fi sounds, which Firman recalls "were created in the band rehearsals by me and the [Synthesizer] Keyboardists."

The show ran only six months (and got Kuhn an Olivier nomination), but the notion of a musical version of Lang's bizarre movie and a complete recording on two CDs made *Metropolis* a cult musical. It is even revived here and there, though never as the monster show it needs to be. Really, one can't "small scale" an epic, especially without the Big Sing chorus the workers' desperation demands.

With a German source and designer, American and English authors, and a French-Argentinian director, *Metropolis* emphasizes the international character of the modern "British" musical—something, I repeat, that began with pop opera, as *Jesus Christ Superstar*'s inspiration was the universal language of rock rather than any ethnicity of narrative.

This is true as well of the biggest hit in this history—and it's another of those pop operas, *Les Misérables*. This show's saga starts when Alain Boublil sees *Superstar* and decides to write something comparable with composer Claude-Michel Schönberg. *La Révolution Française* (1973), like its predecessor, is a two-LP album billed as a "rock opera" and offering vignettes from a familiar story, here the Bastille, Talleyrand, the royalist revolt of the Chouans, Robespierre, and so on. Schönberg himself sang Louis XVI and Boublil's then wife, Françoise, played Charlotte Corday, who comes off as rather mild for the murderess of Marat.

Here is another title varying rock with smoother styles, but unlike *Superstar* and *Metropolis* it lacked a coherent narrative, instead featuring disconnected episodes. Yet *The French Revolution* proved stageable, at Paris' gigantic Palais des Sports, for a short run in a somewhat improvised production.

Then Boublil, in London, became entranced by an *Oliver!* revival. "When the Artful Dodger came on singing 'Consider Yourself'"—as Boublil told Margaret Vermette for *The Musical World of Boublil and Schönberg*—"the image of [Hugo's cocky street urchin] Gavroche came immediately into my mind [along with] all the characters from *Les Misérables* up there singing and living through . . . the joys and sorrows that defined their lives."

So the two authors, partnered by Jean-Marc Natel, constructed a *Misérables* album in the style of *The French Revolution*, the new work billed as a "tragédie musicale" yet still selecting episodes rather than amassing a finished adaptation. But the rock was gone in favor of theatre music fitted to character, as in the Kurt Weill flavor of the vamp to—and the insolent saxophone riff in—"La Devise du Cabaretier" (How To Run a Bistro), the villain Thénardier's establishing number, which instantly types him as a crook.

Besides being much shorter than the *Les Miz* we know, this first version has some different music. Fantine's big scene starts with music later reassigned to Éponine as "On My Own," then segues into "I Dreamed a Dream" backed by a women's chorus, much too "album" for a scene in a stage show. Yet this setting of Hugo's novel also played the Palais des Sports, in 1980, in a limited run that sold out the vast arena.

And there the saga would most likely have ended had not Cameron Mackintosh heard the album and realized what a great show the score could generate if it was expanded into a comprehensive and flowing narrative. No doubt he was attracted particularly by the opening measures of a repeated, descending four-note scale in the upper instruments, soon to be one of the most recognizable of the show's melodies.[3]

Setting in motion a co-production of *Les Miz* with the Royal Shakespeare Company, Mackintosh in effect turned a foreign work over to British auspices and, even partly, authorship. Yes, the source was the National Novel of France and the adaptation wholly French. But the piece now underwent a complete transformation by Britons.

Co-directors Trevor Nunn and John Caird laid out a scene-by-scene treatment for Boublil and Schönberg to follow as they filled in plot and character development, including such major numbers as "Bring Him Home" and "Empty Chairs At Empty Tables," crucial explorations of the feelings of Valjean and his incipient son-in-law, Marius, during the uprising sequence.

One odd revision switched the voice types of Valjean and Javert. Because French *opérette* (their term for "musical") prefers baritone heroes, the concept-album and Palais Des Sports Valjean took the lower line and Javert was a tenor. However, the RSC realized the Canadian tenor C. T. (later Colm) Wilkinson was their ideal Valjean—and they had in their company an actor with a valid baritone, Roger Allam, with a saturnine quality perfect for Javert, the implacable witch-hunter of the law-enforcement universe. So the two leads' vocal IDs were switched.

---

[3] Boublil and Schönberg called these "les notes magiques," and were dismayed when *Les Miz's* first English lyricist, James Fenton, advocated starting the story earlier than the authors had done, to introduce hero Jean Valjean and sadistic police inspector Javert—the story's central antagonists—and to follow Valjean's journey to redemption by the Bishop of Digne, an elemental part of Hugo's vision. Of course, this meant opening the show with the "Look down" theme and the grunting of the convicts rather than the airy, rhapsodic magic notes, among the two authors' favorite part of the score.

Few others of the RSC's acting base were suitable for this Big Sing event, which aroused critics' suspicions. Why was the RSC even singing in the first place? Still, there was a crucial link in that—as countless critics have pointed out—the RSC's very successful nine-hour adaptation of Dickens' *Nicholas Nickleby* was *Les Miz*'s matrix, for Nunn and Caird, designer John Napier, and lighting master David Hersey gave both shows a kinetic quality to bend all arts into one. Defining locales less by scenery than by lighting and quasi-Brechtian placetime chyrons in white lettering against black backgrounds (as in "Toulon 1815"), the creatives kept the playing area open to let the narrative run freely from place to place (aided by *Les Miz*'s revolving stage).[4]

Here is one example of how the staging worked. Early on, Valjean sings a monologue, "Who Am I?" (whose vocal line and accompaniment incorporate the "magic notes"), pointing him toward a court case that will threaten his freedom. He is alone on stage, spotlit in darkness, and as his solo reaches its very intense climax, the tribunal, the French flag, and the judges move into view behind him and others in the courtroom seem to materialize at the same time. Thus, Valjean hits the high-lying final phrase of his accursed prison number—"Who am I?" he cries, "24601!"—right in the courtroom without having taken a single step. In effect, he doesn't pursue the plot line: the story comes to him.

That RSC *Les Miz* (1985) marked a turning point in the pop-opera saga, as the form had been favoring the picturesque, the exotic, the dire doings of all but interplanetary folk, whereas Hugo's misérables are the unsung oppressed. Then, too, *Les Miz* is sensitive and touching in a way its more aggressive predecessors were not—and there was nothing in them to compare to the rousing finale of "Do You Hear the People Sing?," capping the transcendence of the dead Fantine and Éponine's greeting Valjean in the Beyond. The words as I write them sound sticky, but the moment onstage is thrilling.

So of course the critics blasted it. Yet the show caught on with the public almost instantly, to become the longest-running musical in history. A global phenomenon, it even took stage again in Paris, in 1991 at the Mogador, in French but in the form that Britain gave it. There are a surprising number of French pop operas that we never hear about, but, paradoxically, the famous one really isn't French anymore.

---

[4] Both shows also encouraged the cast to research the social character of the period involved, useful in the partly improvised *Nickleby* but something of an affectation in *Les Miz*, a work generated exclusively by its seven (Schönberg, Boublil, Natel, Nunn, Caird, Fenton, Kretzmer) authors.

13

With One Look I'll Be May

Andrew Lloyd Webber

"I've always wanted to change direction after each score," he told interviewer Sheridan Morley in the [London] *Times*. The Bible, P. G. Wodehouse, fascism, a backstager. "It's no good repeating yourself."

The music changes along with the topics, as Lloyd Webber commands many styles, freely moving from one to another within a single score. He writes classical fugues yet fancies the trendy rasp of the synthesizer. *The Phantom Of the Opera* dabbles in pastiche of vintage opera forms, yet its title song is disco. *Evita* opens with a choral requiem, dissonantly modern, but then Che turns around and addresses the audience in rock. And the through-sung scores set soothing melody right next to jagged recitative.

Lloyd Webber's music is a paradox, one reason why he has detractors. It challenges pundits who need to feel culturally insightful yet can't distinguish "The Riviera" from "The Lambeth Walk." So *Evita* was especially daunting to them, for *Superstar* was made of discretely self-contained numbers but *Evita* flowed, as themes popped up and vanished only to take over the score at a later point. And what about those strangely skewed musical dialogues, so aggressive yet pointedly inconclusive? What is the music *saying*?

Like *Superstar*, *Evita* wasn't a show at first. But *this* double-album was reviewing the unfamiliar topic of Argentinian politics in a depiction crammed with little twists. So it couldn't simply be placed on stage in the *Superstar* manner. When it was time to bring *Evita* into the theatre, director Hal Prince figured out what the characters should be doing in these often abstract scenes, and also what to emphasize as the busy narrative unfolded.

For example, Tim Rice had discovered that the real-life Che Guevara had tried to market an insectide—the revolutionary as capitalist, an irresistible proposition—and this was covered in a number on the album, "The Lady's Got Potential." The song also gave a bit of space to Perón and his rivals in the military, and Prince suggested Che become less the potentially confusing historical figure (insectide? Really?) and more a concept-musical emcee, gliding in and out of the continuity to mirror the public's dismay at Evita's ascension to power.

But more: Prince wanted Perón and the other generals to have their own number, and the authors gave them "The Art Of the Possible," staged as a game of musical rocking chairs. At each new round, a chorus man stepped out of the surrounding darkness to pull away one of the rockers while those remaining rushed from each available seat to the next to avoid being caught without a berth. At length Perón was the last man sitting, smugly puffing on a cigar.

Resisting spectacle, *Evita* played on a bare stage with a few projections as she slept her way up to Perón in "Goodnight and Thank You"; a wall of political posters coming down from the flies for "A New Argentina." Lloyd Webber's shows are music-driven, and he used plenty of Latin American rhythms here, but Rice's lyrics substantiated the story in a way few other pop opera's librettos do. Just the casual little hitch in Evita's play for Perón, when she sings "We'll . . ." and then, catching herself, restarts with "*You'll* [my italics] be handed power on a plate," naturalizes her pitch—but artlessly, colloquially. The music is tasting life.

And we have Rice's fascination with the data of the history to thank for a most provocative final line, new for the stage show. After Eva died in her hospital bed, Che "appeared" from out of David Hersey's mysterious lighting plan to tell the audience of a projected Evita mausoleum:

CHE: Only the pedestal was completed, and then the body disappeared for seventeen years.

He was speaking rather than singing, as occasionally occurred in this through-sung piece, another instance of the authors naturalizing the action. And while the public was absorbing this new information about the corpse vanishing, with everyone else on stage frozen in place around the bed and the open coffin, Che strode off and the lights went black.

Critics in London and New York scoffed, but theatregoers ignored them out of curiosity and then word of mouth, making *Evita* a vast hit and shedding bright light on its leading threesomes, London's Elaine Paige, David Essex, and Joss Ackland; and New York's Patti LuPone, Mandy Patinkin, and Bob Gunton. Yet this show marked the end of the Lloyd Webber-Rice collaboration. There was a bit more from them, including the little-known *Cricket* (1986), shown privately at Windsor Castle's Chapel Royal as a one-off. And wags pointed out that, as Jesus and Eva Perón had both died at thirty-three, a Lloyd Webber-Rice cycle was surely in process, promising such pop operas as *John Belushi, David Koresh*, and a certain smash hit, *St. Catherine Of Siena*.

But no. From now on, the composer worked mainly with Don Black and Charles Hart (among others), so this is a good time to post Lloyd Webber's chart:

Joseph and the Amazing Technicolor Dreamcoat (school 1968; West End 1993)
Bible fluff.

Jesus Christ Superstar (Broadway 1971; West End 1972)
The best-known story of all time, rocked.

Jeeves (1975; revised as **By Jeeves**, 1996)
The Wodehouse world, with libretto by Alan Ayckbourn, who had apparently never seen a musical and simply wrote a loooong and booooring play for Lloyd Webber to decorate with old-fashioned melody. A catastrophe at 38 performances.

Evita (1978)
The first pop-opera concept musical, as Che (Guevara? yes and no), not physically present in the story, is nevertheless onstage commenting throughout.

Cats (1982)
A revue with a throughline: Will Grizabella the Glamour Cat ride on a big tire? Yes.

Song & Dance, comprised of **Tell Me on a Sunday** (TV 1980) and **Variations** (concert 1978; both halves together 1982)
First, her side of it as a solo song cycle, then his (in company) in dance. The halves join forces at the end.

Starlight Express (1984)
Trains.

The Phantom Of the Opera (1986)
Lloyd Webber's most eclectic score, reaching even classical atonalism (in the Phantom's own work, *Don Juan Triumphant*).

Aspects Of Love (1989)

A modern *Così Fan Tutte*: a superb score lavished on trivial, inconstant characters.

Sunset Blvd. (1993)

Boasting one of the great diva leads of all time—but while she is an idiot, the role demands an actress of intelligence and resourcefulness in music that vivifies her as magnificent, creating a paradox at the show's heart.

Whistle Down the Wind (closed in US tryout 1996; West End 1998)

Lloyd Webber's second Christ musical (or is He just a wanted killer?), set in the American South.

The Beautiful Game (2000)

Soccer. A tragic show, as politics destroys the personal.

The Woman In White (2004)

Wilkie Collins' suspense novel played against ever mobile projections.

Love Never Dies (2010; revised Melbourne 2011)

Sequel to *The Phantom Of the Opera*. Good music, but we already collected these characters in the first show—and classy Raoul has changed into an angry boor, not remotely like the Raoul who sang the sweeping, generous "All I Ask Of You." Weirdly, the Phantom is now Don Juan Triumphant, Christine's "real" romance. I can't even.

Stephen Ward (2013)

On the notorious case of a man destroyed by the elites for letting the public learn how corrupt the elites are. A Captain Obvious book and a cheap-looking production doomed it, though it began smartly with the title character (Alexander Hanson) as a Mme. Tussaud wax model singing to snake-charmer flute and drums.

School Of Rock (Broadway 2015; West End 2016)

From the movie, on a high-school band.

After *Superstar* and *Evita*, any Lloyd Webber project attracted intense interest, and everyone regarded the forthcoming *Cats* as a folly. For one thing—as a Warner Bros. executive put it, "Half the world hates cats." And T. S. Eliot was the source of the lyrics? *That* T. S. Eliot? Why, this show isn't just fluff: it's arrogant fluff! Yes, and pop opera *itself* is arrogant fluff, so self-important with its cults and history! Oh, this one is a dance musical? With *British dancers*?

In his autobiography, Lloyd Webber admits that "conventional wisdom was that British musical theatre performers had two left feet." Yet isn't the problem more the limited choreographer pool than performers' abilities? Britain never developed a stable of dance directors comparable to Broadway's Robbins, de Mille, Fosse, Kidd, and the like; it wasn't West End dancers' fault if leadership lacked the imagination to create showpiece dances.

It's worth quoting Noël Coward's diaries on the chorus dancers in the London *Sail Away*: "Joe [Layton, the show's New York choreographer as well] has achieved prodigies with the dancers who are . . . actually better than our New York lot." Coward was a ruthless critic of his casts, and New York dancers are the best in the world, so his praise of the London ensemble is an arguably conclusive reply to the belief that Lloyd Webber referred to.

There was one British choreographer who stood within the top class back then (the situation is vastly improved now), Gillian Lynne. She was to stage *Cats'* musical numbers, and as the show is nothing *but* musical numbers, she was in effect *Cats'* director. However, producer Cameron Mackintosh had engaged Trevor Nunn for the top job, because Nunn's prestige work with the Royal Shakespeare Company would lend class to the project, in particular appeasing T. S. Eliot's battleaxe widow, whose imprimatur was legally sine qua non: without her approval, there could be no *Cats*.

So Lynne had to be content with an "Associate director and choreographer" credit just above Nunn's "Directed by." Still, many problems dogged the project—securing the New London Theatre, which had gone over to television and business conferences but offered the unique, proscenium-less "space" for a theatrical fantasy; completing the show's £450,000 capitalization, which Lloyd Webber effected by mortgaging his Sydmonton estate; placating the anger of designer John Napier when Lynne refused to ask her dancers to wear his elaborate costumes, which, says Lloyd Webber, Napier then "kicked . . . into the filthy gutter outside the theatre [and were never] seen again"; and replacing at a late minute Judi Dench (with Elaine Paige) as Grizabella, the show's key role (and the singer of its Big Hit, "Memory") when she snapped her Achilles heel during a rehearsal.

Add to this *Cats'* almost complete lack of story action—remember, it's a revue—which puzzled even enlightened minds. Speaking to Barbara Isenberg in *The Los Angeles Times*, Prince recalled hearing Lloyd Webber playing through the *Cats* score. Hmm, Prince thinks. Cats dance and then a tire? There must be more. "Is this about English politics?" he asked. They're not cats. They're really Queen Victoria, Gladstone, and Disraeli. Right?

Lloyd Webber then looks at Prince "as if I had lost my mind" and says, "Hal, this is just about cats."

The composer dreaded the first preview, knowing the usual "vultures" were there to hoot at a "catastrophe," but *Cats* proved irresistible then and after, in part because it turned pop opera joyful after the hieratic ceremonies of the two founding titles. *Superstar* has no comedy and *Evita's* "comedy" is really bitter irony. But *Cats* is all for fun, tempered only by the occasional solemnity.

On the other hand, *The Phantom Of the Opera* returned Lloyd Webber to his form's love of wayward personalities operating somewhere between the guiltless fiesta of fun showbiz and the knavery of melodrama. There were a number of lyricists, mainly Charles Hart but also Richard Stilgoe and Mike Batt. Add to this Maria Björnson's busy changes of scene and the magical effects the story demands, and *Phantom* appeared to mark an apex in the growing complexity of pop opera. Had the form become a monster, the greedy concoction of merchants, as its critics claimed it was?

But then, weren't these naysayers using pop opera—especially the madly successful *Phantom*, still playing *today* after some thirty-five years—as a straw man to beat on the musical in general? Much later, in 2018, responding to an announced television version of *Les Misérables*—the novel, that is—*The Guardian* let a writer share his relief that the adaptation would be entirely spoken. Here's his reasoning: "The worst part of any musical is the music . . . swelling up out of nowhere and killing the story dead for three minutes at a time so that some wobbly lipped non-entity can stumble on and warble about how sad they [*sic*] are in rhyming couplets." He concludes, "Musicals are the lowest form of entertainment."

This was the thinking behind the attacks on *Phantom*, because it was in effect the ultimate musical, the highest form of its kind, an eyeful and an earful. Hal Prince's staging emphasized the work's sheer bravura, its joy at being set free to do what musicals, uniquely, can do. When the leading sweethearts Raoul (Steve Barton) and Christine (Sarah Brightman) close the first act with a love duet, "All I Ask Of You," Prince is not shy about keying their movements to the music, all but sculpting their love in the rhythm of the orchestra's ebb and fall. Nor was Prince afraid to let the "opera ghost" himself (Michael Crawford) touch now and then on the poses of the transpontine thrillers (today we call it "silent-movie" acting), because musicals weren't invented to treat the everyday: this is a fantastical art form.

Phantom is filled with surprises, not only in those magic tricks—the now-you-see-him-now-you-don't mirror or the phantom's seeming to melt away into nothing at the show's end—but in the overall pacing. Pop opera is normally a stately enterprise, but this show races headlong through its story, except in the Phantom's scenes. These are fewer than one would expect (it's one of the shortest leading roles ever), and when they arrive they slow the playing tempo, as if the phantom were a deity for whom time stands still. His music, too, is on the adagio side, while the ensemble scenes for everyone else leap ever forward, such as "Masquerade," the second-act opening, with the cast (and a few costumed dummies to fill out the view) arrayed on a huge staircase that makes us wonder where Maria Björnson is keeping all that scenery when it isn't in use on stage.

Maybe the biggest surprise is how guiltlessly romantic the music is, with the gala, long-lined melodies that Lloyd Webber keeps pulling out like a magician producing his rabbit. One phrase of "All I Ask Of You," on "Say you love me ev'ry waking moment," is made of ninth and fourth chords that don't resolve for two whole measures, a kind of hymnody of storybook love. Thus, Lloyd Webber revives the musical's rhapsodic nature—its *Bitter Sweet*ness, so to say—which had gone into eclipse after *Jesus Christ Superstar* unveiled rock in opera.

Yet this ultra-musical show starts without music! Curtain up, an auction, cries of "Showing!" as the artefacts are displayed. There's a tiny bit of melody (the "Masquerade" theme) at one point, but not till the notorious chandelier is uncovered, lit, and drawn up into the auditorium does the "opera" truly begin. And like *Les Miz*'s revolutionaries' barricade and *Miss Saigon*'s helicopter, *Phantom*'s chandelier symbolizes—to those enemies again—pop opera's shallow grandiosity. However, in his memoirs Lloyd Webber revealed how slight *Phantom*'s scene plot really is: "All the sets are suggestions" using a few colorful pieces against a black-box stage layout, "curtains with one door frame," and so on.

One reason everyone thinks of the show's physics as elaborate is a single episode, Christine's first visit to the Phantom's lair, played as the two (impersonated in the darkness by doubles) seem to race down inclines upstage—first basement, second basement, third, at last into a boat gliding along a lake of lit candles as the Phantom urges Christine on to ever higher notes (on tape, to forestall mishaps). The "grandiosity" is an illusion.

But what could follow so imposing an attraction? As always changing directions, Lloyd Webber next offered a chamber piece, *Aspects Of Love*. Its source, David Garnett's novella of 1955, explores the fluid romantic alliances of a young man, his uncle, two women artists (an actress and a sculptor), and, late in the continuity, even the hero's underage cousin. Very little actually *happens*, so the musical would need extremely charismatic players. At least the hero, Michael Ball, was a splendid singer[1]—and he had the Lloyd Webber hit, "Love Changes Everything," which rises ecstatically from the simplest of phrases, of a Schubertian purity. The uncle was to have been the cinema's "licensed to kill" 007 Roger Moore—"licensed to sing!" the press chortled—but Moore couldn't handle the music and dropped out, replaced by Kevin Colson. Ann Crumb as the actress and Kathleen Rowe McAllen as the sculptress were capable performers, thought so essential that they, with Ball and Colson, led the cast on Broadway as well. But they weren't captivating enough to hold the silly story together.

Some writers think *Aspects Of Love* is Lloyd Webber's best score for its subtle interplay of melodic cells. Further, the dramatic continuity—the layout of the scenes—is the composer's own, so the show's innovative opening is presumably his idea: the curtain went up on Michael Ball alone on stage, singing that Lloyd Webber hit and moving—we think—inexorably toward a huge finish on a top B Flat. Yet just before the final phrase, Maria Björnson's huge screens turned to change the view to Something Completely Different: Ann Crumb and her fellow troupers in the final scene of *The Master Builder*. "The population of Montpellier had proved disastrously indifferent to Ibsen," Garnett writes in his novel, and after Crumb delivered the ecstatic final line, we heard the sound of about four hands clapping.

"The toast of the town!" Crumb bitterly carols. Penniless and without lodging, she perforce hooks up with Ball, which brings her into the circle of principals and, more broadly, the musical's theme that love really does change everything in one's life. The show is very faithful to Garnett's book, and that's the problem. These are not compelling characters, so who cares whom they love? Then, too, there is the show's constant repetition of major musical passages. By the time Ball gets to finish "Love Changes Everything" (now moving toward a high A), we could almost sing it along with him.

[1] In the novel, this character is Alexis Golightly, but Don Black and Charles Hart's libretto altered this to Alec Dillingham to avoid referencing the heroine of *Breakfast At Tiffany's*. While we're doing names: David Garnett's mother, Constance, was the go-to translator of classic Russian novels in the first half of the twentieth century. If you read *War and Peace* before Penguin offered a new version in 1957, chances are that you read Mrs. Garnett's Tolstoy.

This repetition of melody dogs also *Sunset Blvd.*, though here at least we have arresting characters in the has-been silent-film star and the struggling screenwriter she refashions as her gigolo. Nostalgic to a fault, the movie queen cultivates the hope of returning to the screen in a silent. Worse, her chosen vehicle is not age-credible but *Salome,* in her own scenario. She always gets a laugh when the writer asks how old Salome is supposed to be and the aged grandee replies, without a trace of self-awareness, "Sixteen."

That line isn't sung: *Sunset Blvd.*, has a lot of dialogue (by Don Black and Christopher Hampton, who collaborated on the lyrics as well). There's even a bit of dancing here and there, that essential element of the traditional musical that modern shows sometimes ban as being emotionally shallow, even as *Billy Elliot* made it thematically central to its utopian idealism.

Dance will make you free. Even: appreciating dance will make you tolerant. We used to speak of "song and dance" shows, but *Sunset Blvd.* is really a Big Sing event, especially in the numbers of the heroine, Norma Desmond. And the writer is Joe Gillis. Note the difference in tone, from the opulent (gala Norma) to the everyday (plain Joe). Kevin Anderson, who originated Joe in both London and New York, played a smartly nuanced hero, and made the most of his music, but it's impossible to stay even with the extravagant Norma, first Patti LuPone and in New York Glenn Close.

The Gaiety shows loved vivacious heroines and operetta favored sentimental ones, but pop opera needs titanic heroines, and the sheer glamour of Norma is unique. True, it's a phony glamour, the dangerous kind, of charisma without talent and power without focus. Thwart her will and she'll terminate you. Of her Salome, she says, "If she can't have him living, she'll take him dead."

LuPone's reflective characterization never quite captured the crazy soul of Norma; Close's mercurial approach was more to the point, now impulsive and playful and then lost and demented. It was as if LuPone's Norma was a human being who was no longer a movie star, while Close was a movie star who was no longer a human being.

Sunset marked the apex of Lloyd Webber's Big Sing format, as he would not enjoy that level of success in the form thereafter. Some critics observed that pop opera's era was ending—but its influence wasn't. Above all, its international popularity encouraged some songwriters to avoid "Anglicizing" their shows. They must appeal to everyone now. The joy of *Oliver!*'s first-night audience in discovering how "Consider Yourself" celebrated what was English in English entertainment—in being In the Moment when British art history was made—is gone forever. After pop opera got through with it, the musical as a form simply lost its nationality.

14

A Little Bit Naughty

The Last Thirty Years

As the pop operas continued to appear, *Chess* (1986), Tim Rice's collaboration with Benny Andersson and Björn Ulvaeus (the creatives of the Swedish pop group ABBA), was the classy one, centered on a rivalry of chess champions. ABBA's catalogue in the jukebox show *Mamma Mia!* (1999) creates a line-up of point numbers fitted into an innocuous story, but *Chess* tells of globally dangerous affairs of state and is very precisely musicalized with only one incongruous item, "One Night In Bangkok," which would seem to have been created solely to guarantee a Big Hit.

The two chess grandmasters are an American and a Russian, with a woman caught between them. Murray Head, Tommy Körberg, and Elaine Paige, respectively, sang the roles on the usual double-LP album and then animated the parts on stage in a production planned by Michael Bennett but executed after Bennett's withdrawal (because of the AIDS that would fell him) by Trevor Nunn. Still, it was Bennett's designs that Nunn worked with, most notably a playing area in the form of a chessboard mounted on hydraulic support to tilt this "stage" at dramatic moments. Memorably, the show began with an elegant prologue enacted by performers costumed as chess pieces moving around the board to "The Story Of Chess."

It was romantic and timeless, a stylized start to a realistic narrative steeped in Cold War antagonisms in an extremely rangy score. "Diplomats" presents the operatives overseeing this duel of the US and Soviet Russia in a pugnaciously conspiratorial rock gavotte (so to say), yet locale is established in "Merano," a modern version of the "merry villagers" chorus beloved of the Gaiety era. The Russian player, much more sympathetic than the American, offers himself to us, in "Where I Want To Be," in music suggesting someone teetering on a highwire spanning a gorge—a metaphor for the balancing act he must execute as a Soviet celebrity eternally under surveillance.

Then, too, *Chess* avoided the pestering musical reprises we hear in other titles of this genre while shunning also those mundane lines that sound so awkward when set to music. And this despite would-be collaborators skulking around the writers' workshop. "I bitterly regret altering massive chunks of the original album," Tim Rice confessed in his memoirs. Like his hero in "Where I Want To Be," Rice was a victim of success: with so much fame and money at stake, "too many cooks emerge."

True, it worked for *Les Miz*. But *Chess* is the most complex of pop operas, a love story caught in the war of tyranny against liberty. So rich a show gives interlopers too many opportunities to sabotage the authors' vision. Bizarrely, though the first production played London for three years, *Chess* has become the most revised of musicals, even taking on spoken dialogue (on Broadway) to clarify action that was already clear. Typical of this second-guessing was New York's transformation of "The Story Of Chess" from a beautifully spooky enactment of myth to a father's advice to his young daughter during the Hungarian uprising of 1956, which made the song frivolous. Aren't you two supposed to be running for your lives?

Claude-Michel Schönberg and Alain Boublil, understanding that the proper launching site for an international success was London or New York (with, of course, English adaptation of Boublil's lyrics), gave the West End their *Miss Saigon* (1989) and *Martin Guerre* (1996). The former used the characters of *Madame Butterfly*—a short story, play, opera, numerous movies, and even a point number in an American revue, "Poor Butterfly." So the tale is familiar to many, though now the heroine, originally a Japanese geisha married to and then abandoned by an American military man, was Vietnamese, working in a bordello, and there was a great deal of historical background in the Vietnam War, the Viet Cong invasion of the south, and the fate of "bui-doi," the children of mixed-race couplings, ignored by Americans and spurned by Vietnamese.

The most vital alteration of the *Butterfly* content was the expansion of a minor character, the marriage broker Goro, into the Engineer, the bordello proprietor, a grown-up bui-doi with but one ambition—to get to America and exploit its freewheeling economy with his expertise in finagling. Unappealing yet charismatic, he was a scoundrel who nevertheless made the story happen; everyone else was reacting to events while the Engineer was creating them. Jonathan Pryce made so much of the part that, when Actors Equity refused to allow Pryce to repeat his role in New York, producer Cameron Mackintosh threatened to cancel the production and its gigantic advance sale if the union didn't back down. And he meant it.

"I speak Uncle Ho and I think Uncle Sam," the Engineer explained, illus-trating how clever and unethical one has to be when surviving one of history's cataclysms, and *Miss Saigon*[1] linked the personal story and larger events most effectively. The two drivelines came together in the Spectacle Moment so be-loved of pop opera—the helicopter.

Far more persuasive than *Les Miz*'s rudimentary though sizable barri-cade (two halves moving in from stage right and left, each with one moving part inside it; big deal) and *Phantom*'s chandelier, *Miss Saigon*'s special-effect scene included an inside-hommage for devotees of Asian theatre. Director Nicholas Hytner established a scene of desperation: we in the audience were in effect inside the American compound in Saigon during the last minutes before the fall of the city. The Vietnamese who had helped the American forces and thus needed to get out before the Viet Cong arrived were upstage behind a fence.

Then, in a meme common in Kabuki and some other forms, the per-spective was reversed, so that the Americans were seen to be upstage be-hind the fence and the anxious Vietnamese were downstage. Now for the magic: through a combination of limited physical properties and genius lighting (by pop opera's go-to, David Hersey), the helicopter landed and took on passengers as the American Boy sought his Vietnamese Girl. However, though we saw her, frantically trying to signal him, he couldn't make her out in the melee, and reluctantly boarded the aircraft as the last ride to safety took off without the heroine.

This exciting episode may have been meant to front for the lack of inter-esting plot development in the second act, as a flashback to what chronolog-ically really belonged in Act One. The Engineer, too, had his big event late in the continuity, in "The American Dream," in which he extolled the material-istic benefits of capitalism as he rode next to the Statue of Liberty in a real-life Cadillac (in London, at least; the American staging used a smaller mock-up).

Further, the second act is vexed by one of the dullest principals in all pop opera—Ellen, the American Boy's new wife. In Puccini's version of the tale, she is wisely relegated to an "under five," little more than a walk-on; Schönberg and Boublil worked hard to enliven her, but she's essentially a maguffin, necessary yet irritating. And the rest of the cast, except for that

---

[1] This is a pun, at once an updating of "Madame Butterfly" and a reference to the sales-promotion contest the Engineer runs in his bordello, where American GIs vote for the girl they like the best, a miniature Miss America pageant. The show's logo was visual triple pun, blending a helicopter, a re-verse dollar sign, and a young woman's sorrowful face in a single drawing.

louche Till Eulenspiegel of an Engineer, don't project all that well, either. The heroine lacks everything but naive determination, and while Lea Salonga managed to vivify her, *Timeout London* asked, "Whatever happened to musicals with jokes?" The Boy has little more delineation, though the show's English-language librettist, Richard Maltby Jr., always thought that a good performer in the role made the whole evening pop.

In any case, *Miss Saigon* is one of the most successful titles in the pop-opera cycle. But *Martin Guerre* has struggled to survive in numerous revisions, because on one level it's like *Miss Saigon* without the Engineer. To repeat, pop opera is big theatre: it needs big characters. In that sense, it is opera, with its Toscas and Boris Godunofs and Tristans and Isoldes. No one in *Martin Guerre* is terribly compelling, even as the story itself is interesting: a husband returns home from the wars to general rejoicing, though he isn't in fact the husband. And then the real husband shows up.

That's something to work with, especially as this particular *Martin Guerre*—there are a number of adaptations—adds in a raging religious controversy that vastly affects the Guerre marriage. Still, besides the two men and the wife, every character in the show is an enraged Catholic, a solemn Protestant, or the village idiot, who in fact creates the tragedy to come by mistaking the fake Martin for the real one. Thus, all those revisions (which started *during* the original West End run) cannot repair the writing. It was broken from its very conception.[2]

Meanwhile, the Chichester Festival, far southwest of London, virtually on the Channel, offers original musicals as well as its stock-in-trade revivals, and one of its most singular offerings was Jason Carr's *Born Again* (1990), based on Eugène Ionesco's *Rhinoceros*. Set in a provincial French town, the play reflects Ionesco's experience as a Jewish Romanian in the 1930s, seeing friends and associates blithely rationalizing the growth of the Nazi-adjacent Iron Guard; then the entire nation turned into Nazis. So Ionesco filled his fictional setting with beasts, as, one by one, everyone becomes a rhinoceros, except Ionesco's protagonist (Jean-Louis Barrault in the 1960 Paris premiere, Laurence Olivier in London), the last human left, crying, "I will not surrender!" as the curtain falls.

Peter Hall directed *Born Again*, and in his and Julian Barry's libretto the action was moved to a unit set depicting various Los Angeles locales, especially

---

[2] Schönberg and Boublil also "fathered" *Marguerite* (2008) for the West End, updating *La Dame Aux Camélias* to Paris' Nazi occupation and featuring Ruthie Henshall, Julian Ovendon, and Alexander Hanson. But Michel Legrand composed it and Herbert Kretzmer translated Boublil's lyrics.

a shoppers' mall. Though through-sung, *Born Again* was not a pop opera but an opera opera, composed in classical style with occasional set pieces in pastiche idioms—the blues, for instance. Mandy Patinkin was the lead, with fellow American José Ferrer and Claire Moore as Patinkin's girl friend (with a lot more character than she had to work with in *Miss Saigon*).

Stagings of the Ionesco usually avoid showing the animals, but *Born Again* effected a coup de théâtre early in the continuity, when an elevator in the stage floor brought up a rhinoceros (actually two men in a rhinoceros suit, designed by Gerald Scarfe), which then rampaged all over the set and stormed off, a splendid exhibition. Carr brought the animals into the score, too, as in Ferrer's solo "I Want To Be a Rhinoceros," set to the stamping fury of a jungle creature. And here, too, came the blithe rationalization about how much better things are this way: no more psychology, manners, appeasing. "When a rhino don't agree, there's nothing to be said," Ferrer sang, to Carr's orchestration at once flighty and emphatic. "You just paw the ground and lower your head."

Because the theatrical year seemed starved for event and Carr was so young yet accomplished, *Born Again* became the talk of the arts world. Strangely, the production did not move to the West End (as some other Chichester stagings have done) and was not recorded, cutting off its future at the knees.

In contrast to *Born Again*'s innovative sound style were the shows using recycled music, with *Buddy—The Buddy Holly Story* reclaiming a key participant in the rise of rock and roll on one hand and the asinine sci-fi spoof *Return To the Forbidden Planet* on the other. Both appeared in 1989, but the difference between them is worth a century: *Holly,* a biography in a respectful if corny layout, was a very successful revival of a virtually forgotten (because so primitive) mode—the beat, the melody, and three chords. Further, American Paul Hipp (in London, then in New York) embodied Holly perfectly, no casual achievement as Holly had an oddly nerdy look for a rock and roller (think of England's more dynamic, camera-ready rock avatar Tommy Steele) yet was equal to Holly in musical expertise. By contrast, *Forbidden Planet* exploited comparable material in styleless renderings on a single set that may have cost all of fifty pence.

There were many others of these archeological musicals, but *We Will Rock You* (2012) was a stand-out, attracting those who normally skip musicals in favor of pop concerts. This one, however, they had to collect for its score made from the catalogue of Queen, including a grand finale of "Bohemian Rhapsody." The show looked at a dystopian world in which expression of any kind is outlawed—so of course rock, the essential defier of hall monitors in any age, becomes the instrument of liberation.

While *We Will Rock You* charged up its Queen jukebox quite faithfully, *Girl From the North Country* (2017) took liberties with its adopted inventory, the songs of Bob Dylan. They were respectful liberties, to be sure; none of the songs was denatured. Still, a few were mashed up to create new numbers, and tempos were often changed, quite radically. Thus, "Hurricane," Dylan's long narrative about boxer Hurricane Carter's controversial trial for a triple murder, is explosive, a true protest song, while *Girl From the North Country* renders it as a near-jaunty rhythm number, still serious in tone but something of a get-up-and-dance piece rather than a scathing narrative.

Most arresting is this show's singular use of the jukebox format, as this isn't exactly a musical. True, it has a full score of thirty different Dylan numbers (some used as incidental accompaniment, along with a smattering of Debussy's "Clair De Lune," all arranged by Simon Hale). But the songs aren't worked into the script as character or situation numbers. Instead, they're mood pieces, telling the audience not what the characters are thinking but how to feel about their roles in Conor McPherson's script.

McPherson didn't write a libretto (that is, dialogue needing lyrical enhancement) but rather a play (dialogue complete in itself). His setting is a guest house in Minnesota (Dylan's home state) during the Depression. Everyone's in trouble and a few are demented or criminals, as if McPherson wanted to mate Dylan with another American "outlaw" of art, Sam Shepard. For these characters and the way they express themselves have a Shepard feeling about them.

So *Girl* is something like a British version (McPherson is Irish) of an American show. It reverses the terms of Kern's *The Cabaret Girl* and Porter's *Nymph Errant*, which, we recall, were part-American-authored *British* shows. They couldn't travel to Broadway, but after *Girl*'s Old Vic and West End stays, it played New York's Public Theatre and even moved to Broadway. And just as *We Will Rock You* appealed mainly to rock audiences rather than to theatregoers, *Girl* attracted devotees of the drama, not the musical. It's an out-of-category format—and an amusing way to hear Dylan's repertory reinterpreted, with some wonderful singers replacing Dylan's raspy authenticity to give these pieces new life.

With such serious musicals as *Girl From the North Country* and the pop-opera cycle commanding the scene, musical comedy as such was becoming scarce, though *Spamalot* (Broadway 2005; West End 2006) showed the

comedy musical still capable of claiming a smash hit. This, too, was a somewhat transatlantic affair, based on *Monty Python and the Holy Grail* (and
other *Python* sketches and even adjacent works) and written by Pythonist
Eric Idle, co-composing with John Du Prez. But *Spamalot* premiered in the
US with a largely American cast (though Tim Curry played King Arthur),
directed by Mike Nichols. Surpassingly *Python* in feeling, the show nevertheless had an American musical's structure and drive, and one number, "You
Won't Succeed On Broadway," roamed far beyond *Python* borders in jesting
about the Jewish domination on the Rialto.

Many favorite bits from the *Grail* were drawn into the show just as they
were in the film, from the clopping coconuts to indicate horseback travel
to the knight who refuses to fall even when his extremities are hacked off.
All this would have made *Spamalot* too much the twice-told tale but for the
many new episodes, as when a raw youth (Christopher Sieber) became Sir
Galahad, to partner the Lady Of the Lake (Sara Ramirez). The lengthy scene
toyed with the incongruities that *Python* style doted on, though again the experience was very Broadway in tone, not least when the Lady's watery "Laker
Girls" threw off their diaphanous coverings to stand forth as cheerleaders
with pom-poms in bra and short skirt. Meanwhile Galahad and the Lady
rode forth in a boat suggesting the one the Phantom and Christine took to
the grotto, candles and all. And *this* led to "The Song That Goes Like This," a
parody of pop opera's power ballads with the raised key change. But this song
raised it a second time, as the two actors hurled imprecations at the show's
conductor, though Ramirez sailed up to a high B all the same.

Clearly, there was a public for a really funny musical; *Spamalot* ran four
years in New York, while at London's Palace (with Curry and Sieber again)
it managed two years and three months. Interestingly, Idle's old *Python* crew
told the press (in varying ways) that they didn't see the point in resuscitating
old work, though in all *Spamalot* was much advanced beyond the *Holy Grail*
movie. This simply reminds us that the people who don't get musicals *really
don't get musicals*, and their being artists themselves will never change that.

In any case, a new pair of British songwriters not only understood why the
gods created plays that sing but kept writing very funny ones, often adapting
children's tales: composer George Stiles and librettist-lyricist Anthony
Drewe. In such works as *Honk!* (regional 1977; London 1999), from *The Ugly
Duckling*; a new version of *Peter Pan* (concert 2001; regional 2007); an elabo-
ration of the movie score of *Mary Poppins* (2004); or *The Wind In the Willows*

(regional 2016), this team has brought imagination and craftsmanship to the ever more vanishing genre of more or less carefree musical comedy.

Children's tales always have villains, but Stiles and Drewe love (or are at least amused by) bad guys, no doubt because they really are no more menacing than the characters the audience talks back to at pantomimes. They're not really villains: they're drolls. So *Peter Pan*'s pirates get a banjo-thrilled salute to "Good Old Captain Hook," filled with encomiums to their chief, "worse than any other" yet "a credit to his mother."

Children's tales have as well a sense of wonder beyond that of the average musical, whether of bygone times like *Bitter Sweet* or in a new style like *Martin Guerre*. Thus, *Peter Pan*'s score rises to the poetic in "Never Land," Peter's advice to the Darling kids when he teaches them to fly. Following a newish tradition popularized by the Royal Shakespeare Company in 1982, Stiles and Drewe's Peter is played by not a hoydenish woman but an athletic young man, which gives an urgent "reality" to his instructions. The song's title is a pun, for Peter and the Darlings are headed for the Neverland but must remember to stay afloat: never actually land on solid ground. Rather, the Pan dream is of soaring above the cares of the earthbound, of commanding one's imagination. "Nothing equals the thrill," he assures them. "Just believe that you can, and you will!"

Perhaps Stiles and Drewe's most pleasing show is *Just So* (regional 1989; revised Boston 2002; Chichester 2004), from Rudyard Kipling's stories about how the animal kingdom developed its diversity. Thus, the crocodile closed its jaws on the elephant's nose and stretched it into a trunk, an event preserved at the musical's climax. Rather than hide the players in panto "skin" costumes, *Just So* dresses its cast to no more than suggest, with a horn on a hat or spotted clothing—and, truly, these are people with people problems, along with the Parsee (boasting an Indian accent) and his baritone Cooking Stove.

Cleverly marrying Kipling's episodes into a quest plot, the authors send the Elephant's Child and the flightless Kolokolo Bird to get the giant crab to stop flooding the world with his personal acquacade. There is a slight air of religious awe at the wisdom and power of the Eldest Magician (the Creator, of course), but the show derives its energy mainly from a cast of oddballs. This is a venerable musical-comedy trick, in use at least since Strauss' *Die Fledermaus* and at its apex in *Salad Days* and *Oliver!*: the protagonist (or sweetheart leads) will be basic while everyone else on stage is bent, one way or another.

Thus, *Just So* offers the Rhino, ashamed of everything about himself ("All I attract is the flies"); the Kangaroo, who learned to jump when chased by a hungry dingo; the Leopard and Jaguar, who, in "We Want To Take the Ladies Out [for dinner]," propose to devour some of the cast; and that Crocodile, sinister and hypnotic (and played, in superb irony, by the Eldest Magician). They all sing highly evolved lyrics (the Eldest Magician likes the Elephant's Child's "young inquiring mind," we learn, "a joie de vivre so rare to find") and are not above out-of-story gags. In one number, when the Zebra and Giraffe need to escape the slavering Leopard and Jaguar but pause to go into their dance, the Kolokolo Bird says, "Do we really have time for a tap number here?"

In all, *Just So* is that rarity, a family musical that is too smart to be a pantomime. One might say as much of *Billy Elliot* (2005), for its protagonist is a kid and there are plenty of other children in the cast for youngsters in the house to identify with. But this show is serious, set during the famous Miners' Strike of 1984–1985 protesting colliery closings during the Thatcher administration and based on Stephen Daldry's eponymous film. Lee Hall, who wrote its screenplay, wrote also the musical's book and lyrics, to Elton John's music, and Daldry then directed the show, thus locking up a tight adaptation.

And be it said that this story cries out for music. It tells of a working-class boy who wants to become a ballet dancer: to open up his life. Yet his birth culture is a closed society in which everything not compulsory is forbidden. For young lads boxing lessons are compulsory. Dancing is forbidden.

Yet Billy trades boxing for dancing—with a classful of girls, no less, and in the same place where the hated boxing is taught, for in this narrow world everything is jammed next to its opposite, liberty beckoning not from afar but right where you stand.

This is brought home in a marvelous number, "Solidarity," the toast of theatergoing circles because of the way song, dance, and dialogue drive the number through the plot and its opposed forces even while demonstrating how related everyone is to everyone else. As Daldry and choreographer Peter Darling laid it out, the men's chorus is broken into halves of cops and miners, natural enemies. Then there are the ballet-school girls, then Billy himself, gradually responding to the dancing by absorbing its principles.

Meanwhile—and there's a lot of meanwhile in "Solidarity"'s staging—the law and the workers explore their antagonism yet also, fantastically, switch "positions" while the ballet kids run in and out among them. The "Solidarity" vocal continues even as the men turn into ballerinas themselves, switch cop helmets for miner helmets (and vice versa), parade among and against one another, everyone mixed together. It's age against youth, the light of art against the dark of intolerance, the servants of the authorities against the independence of the human spirit. Yes, they *are* in solidarity *if only they knew it*, and the number is brilliant because it shows us that they don't. Then finally Billy executes a perfect series of fouettés. End.

But then Billy's ever angry miner dad (Tim Healy) appears, to berate him in fury for defying The Rules. Yet he will soften. Because, as the dancing teacher (Haydn Gwynne) tells him later in the show, "The kid's gifted! He's got a chance!" Then comes the killer point: "What do you got to offer him? Mining?"

Solidarity steals up on you, as we learn in the other of the show's famous numbers, when Billy dances a pas de deux with his older self, who attaches a hook to the boy's trousers to enable him to soar above the stage. And isn't this what dance is to Billy—escape from the bleak life of his tribe? Flight? It recalls what Stiles and Drewe's Peter Pan warns his adherents: Never land. Land is strikes and bitterness and The Rules. Flight is liberty.

No wonder *Billy Elliot* has proved so successful, despite an all but prohibitive need for extremely talented youngsters for the title part, three of them rotating from performance to performance. The musical has traditionally soothed our worries with happy endings, but, often, the happiness was simply applied rather than organic. Think of *The Boy Friend*'s Polly and Tony, who finally come together because he isn't a shop assistant after all. He's an aristocrat, too. Lovely. Billy Elliot, however, has to work for his reward, making his happiness more satisfying: justified.

How far we have come, too, from the kind of performers who functioned well in *The Boy Friend*. Musicals need *actors* now, even among the kids, and just as society has become more tolerant of those who defy their native culture, the musical has come along—or has the musical played a leadership role? In America, certainly, racial integration started in the theatre, when first of all Bert Williams, later Ethel Waters and the Nicholas Brothers, and still later Sammy Davis Jr. played leads in white shows.

Billy Elliot has its moment, too, for it ends as Billy, about to embark on his wonderful future, says farewell to his comrade, the ever-bicycling Michael:

MICHAEL: (as he rides in) Hoy! Dancing boy!
BILLY: See you, Michael.

Billy kisses Michael's cheek, a forgiving reference to Michael's interest in cross-dressing. Then Billy leaves—not only his past but the show itself, making his exit through the auditorium, as Michael watches and the curtain falls on the world in which men can't dance. But then the calls present a kind of *Billy Elliot* re-mix, as the whole cast gets into tutus, to see how it feels to dance for the sheer exhilaration of it.

Matilda (2010), from Roald Dahl's novel, also rotates young performers in the title role. Here the worrisome grownups are Matilda's abusive parents and the ghastly school headmistress, Miss Trunchbull (Bertie Carvel, in drag); the good ones are a librarian and a teacher, Miss Honey (Lauren Ward, wife of *Matilda*'s director, Matthew Warchus), who will end in adopting the little heroine.

Doesn't it seem as if all the interesting musicals are about revolts against tyrannies of various kind? It's worth noting that Dahl constantly identified himself as a kind of professional defier, through his most visible quality, even in his many children's stories, is a sadistic streak, as in Miss Trunchbull's throwing a student through the window (styled on stage through a trompe l'oeil maneuver) and forcing another student to eat an entire chocolate cake.

With a score by Tim Minchin and a book by Dennis Kelly, *Matilda* followed Dahl's tale closely in Rob Howell's design of an empty stage taking in furniture as necessary (blackboard and desks, library stacks, park swings) but bursting with alphabet blocks that exploded beyond the proscenium into the house: the blocks of learning, of reading, of imagination. The bad grownups are hostile to them, but a good grownup, hearing a little girl re-count her stories, will say something like, "What happens then?"

As we learn from *Matilda*'s key art of a young miss posed arms akimbo with an air of command, what happens is that all the bad grownups are defeated and the nice schoolteacher learns from her pupil. Like Billy Elliot, Matilda is a quietly indomitable creative force, even developing the power of levitation, though we mainly remember her amusing sense of justice in punishing her hateful father by adulterating his hair tonic to dye his head green. "Sometimes you have to be a little bit naughty," she explains, in music snappy and syncopated. (Minchin marks the number "Swing.") Reasoning it out as she juggles Minchin's triple rhymes ("do a lot, you . . . / . . . little stop you / get on top, you . . .") she tells us, in "Naughty," that bad guys will set the narrative unless you fight back.

Minchin's music and lyrics dive-bomb wonderfully into the heart of this charming story. It's a fully fledged theatre score, wedded to the action—"Loud," the credo of Matilda's vulgar mother; "The Hammer," underlining Trunchbull's love of physical power, the better to intimidate everybody; "Telly," a credo now from Matilda's father, "educated" by the airwaves. Most beguiling is the Swing Number, "When I Grow Up," from Matilda's schoolfellows, looking forward to sweets without end and conquering monsters hiding under the bed. It includes a solo for Miss Honey, apt because she is in effect as unseasoned as the kids, not yet really grown up. And most attuned to the drama is a pair of adversarial numbers: "The Smell of Rebellion" as Trunchbull senses a mutiny, and "Revolting Children" for the kids themselves, "living in revolting times," so they "sing revolting songs"— and note this quaint conceit—"using revolting rhymes." And Trunchbull is right, because the mutineers will win, and sic semper tyrannis.

In *Matilda's* published song folio, Minchin's foreword reveals an ur-chord he uses throughout the score, basically an $F^{13}_{\ 7}9$ without a bass grounding; Minchin employs it with different bass notes, inventing a few very wild harmonies. One can actually hear something of this in the vocal lines, and there is a cute moment in Miss Honey's self-deprecating "Pathetic," when she hesitates to knock on Trunchbull's door out of fear and Minchin pulls off an hommage on the recitative for "It's just a door; you've seen one before." The wording and vocal line sound exactly like Stephen Sondheim—but it's set to the *Matilda* ur-chord, and it makes us too, ask, "What happens then?"

This must be the era of kid musicals, though *Everybody's Talking About Jamie* (2017) catches youngsters on the high-school level. Here there are more good grownups than bad, but like Billy and Matilda, the protagonist, Jamie (John McCrea), needs all the help he can get, as his dream is not to dance or explore the intellectual life but to be a drag queen.

Jamie outlines his ambition to us in the First Number, set in the classroom (for vocational guidance); Jamie's mates sit facing upstage where Miss Hodge (Tamsin Carroll) reigns. In one of the most ingenious musical stagings I've ever seen, for the effervescent "And You Don't Even Know It," Jamie lets us into his imagination as he leads the kids in a wild dance rampage, set by choreographer Kate Prince to hip-hop steps, acrobatics, and role-playing, as the boys brag and the girls cast doubts. Overtly effeminate—because that's how nature made him—Jamie dances atop the desks as if commanding the fashionista catwalk and the place explodes (even Miss Hedge takes part) in a rave-up devoted to the joy of teens celebrating life before it gets serious (i.e., grown up) on them.

So composer Dan Gillespie Sells and librettist-lyricist Tom MacRae wrote *Jamie* from the kids' point of view. There are important roles for Jamie's very supportive mother (Josie Walker), who gives him his first pair of Totally Fabulous Shoes—big red heels; for Jamie's bigoted father (Spencer Stafford, whose track in the show includes playing also a drag queen, Laika Virgin); and for a former drag artist who now runs a dress shop (Phil Nichol). Still, the action focuses on Jamie, his pal Pritty (Lucie Shorthouse), and the class bully, Dean (Luke Baker), who at least is only verbally, not physically, aggressive. Perhaps the show wouldn't work unless the authors took us right into Jamie's dream on his terms, because all we hear about is cross-dressing but what we're thinking about is yet another individual wants freedom.

Yes, the familiar story. And the show's structure is traditional, a linear narrative with useful song spots and no twisty paradoxes of the W. S. Gilbert kind in the plotting. Interestingly, Jamie's father never comes around, blackhearted to the end. But the rest of Jamie's woes are easily lifted: Miss Hedge tries to bar him from attending a school dance in full kit but finally gives in. And Dean then shrugs off his former hostility and walks into the dance with Jamie.

But enough of fathers! Now for wives, especially those of Henry VIII in Toby Marlow and Lucy Moss' *Six* (Edinburgh Fringe 2017; West End 2019), seventy-five minutes of mostly song about who these women were but treated in strictly millennial style. The six multicultural performers are dressed in black-and-white short skirts and (usually) matching tops with hand-held mikes and a lot of trendy prancing. It's Tudor glam, exuberant and busty, arguably the most *now* musical of all time. Neither music nor lyrics attempts to define the ladies as individuals; rather, the score defines the Zeitgeist. It's not about Back Then, because Then is so sixteenth century. It's really more about Anna of Cleves referring to her disastrous courtship-by-diplomats with "You said that I tricked ya," because she "didn't look like my profile picture."

The lack of dramatic portrayal has not fazed *Six*'s vast and appreciative public, who respond to the clever "spontaneity" of the piece; it's so tactlessly merry that the cast could almost be making it up as they go. Then, too, *Six* has the air of a concert more than a theatre piece: it derives power from its performing energy rather than character interaction.

This marks such a break with tradition of the British musical that for stability's sake we're going to close with one of the most traditional of the form's titles, *Half a Sixpence* (1963; revised 2016). Another of the many adaptations from H. G. Wells' novels, this one, specifically from *Kipps*, brings us back to the days when many of the best British musicals did not cross the Atlantic because they were thought too English—parochial, even exotically so. In fact, *Half a Sixpence* did get to (and made a hit on) Broadway. Still, this was mainly because of its star turn by Tommy Steele as the draper's clerk who comes into a fortune, is taken up by a highborn woman and fleeced of all he has by her family, only to return to his childhood sweetheart and contentment.

This combination of Cinderella and social critique is typical Wells, not typical musical comedy, and many enjoyed the show without noticing how corrupt the high hats are, how smoothly—professionally, almost—they divest the guileless protagonist of his treasure and then slip away unpunished. Is this a Marxist musical? One doesn't get many of those, especially not with a very tuneful David Heneker score and a chorus of gents in striped jackets and boaters partnering the ladies with their parasols tipped just so.

Appearing in the wake of *Oliver!*'s habilitation of musicals drawn from old novels, *Half a Sixpence* wasn't as creative a production; Loudon Sainthill's sets and costumes were at times fanciful but not revolutionary in the Sean Kenny manner. We do note with surprise that John Dexter, celebrated for his work in scenically elaborate social drama and then opera at the Met, was the show's director. Perhaps the Wellsian politics attracted him, as his plays, such as *Chips With Everything* and *The Royal Hunt Of the Sun*, dealt with what Germans term *Faustrecht*—the "right of the fist" but, roughly, "The powerful should cheat to win."

So *Half a Sixpence*, with a book by Beverley Cross, faithfully followed Wells' division of caste. At bottom was the Steele role, Arthur Kipps, his fellow drapers' clerks, and his sweetheart Ann (Marti Webb). Above them was the draper himself, Mr. Shalford (Arthur Brough), so grumpy that he gets a laugh when a photographer taking a group picture asks him to smile:

SHALFORD: (Looking like an Easter Island statue) I *am* smiling.

Higher yet is the Walsingham family—Artie's other sweetheart when he comes into money; her dreadful mother; and the brother who "manages" Artie's fortune by speculating it into nothing and then fleeing. Somewhere in the center of it all is Chitterlow (James Grout, thought so essential to the eccentric Wellsian atmosphere that he came over with Steele when *Sixpence* went to Broadway), a playwright and thus "classless," as theatre people have historically been, forbidden church burial in some cultures yet knighted in others.

Chitterlow's main role is as deus ex machina, as Artie has capitalized Chitterlow's play and the play is a hit. So there's some financial comfort after all, though by play's end Artie has learned not to care about it. He and Ann, married with a baby, run a little bookshop, all thought of "la-di-dards" behind them. The show's title is money—a sixpence piece broken into halves as love tokens—yet the last thing we see is the Kippses settling in for a quiet domestic evening, Ann knitting and Artie taking up his pipe:

KIPPS: I was just thinkin' what a rum go everythin' is.

And as he lights up, the curtain comes down.

Add to this narrative a rich series of songs and dances and a book that plays well even though Artie and Ann win each other in the middle of Act Two, leaving some thirty minutes to fill with more plot to keep the machine running. In fact, the climax comes too early, when Artie bumps into Ann, the parlor maid of a Mrs. Botting, one of the Walsingham gang. Botting is bragging about how she enforces discipline among the help:

MRS. BOTTING: I stopped [Ann] a month's wages and I've kept her in [during] her last three half-days—to remind her of her place.
MRS. WALSINGHAM: I think you've been too lenient.

Monsters. Artie gives it all up then and there, as he and Ann celebrate with the sentimental "Long Ago," which actually tries to rationalize something we've been worrying about: Why did Artie desert Ann for Helen Walsingham? True, Helen was glamorous and Ann was . . . Ann. "We were far too shy," Ann and Artie sing. "Much too scared to try." As they leave the basement kitchen of Mrs. Botting's, all the call bells in the house angrily start jangling—and the orchestra takes this up, turning them into wedding bells. And shouldn't that lead to a bride-and-groom finale?

But Act Two is just getting started, with a little slew of songs, including production numbers. Doesn't this throw the whole show off kilter? But then, this was David Heneker musical, and his music and lyrics supply the drive missing in the clumsy storytelling. Most of the numbers turn on the worldview of characters just out of their teens—buying a banjo, praying for good weather for an upcoming date—and Tommy Steele, after all, was still known at the time as Britain's outstanding rock and roller, the ultimate kids' music.

It was easy to see how someone so youthful (Artie is twenty; Steele was a persuasively juvenile twenty-six) could make Artie's mistake in getting involved with the Walsinghams. Further, though Steele has his detractors for his high-energy performing, that outside-the-box personality is part of Kipps' charm. "Don't you understand?" said Helen to her mother as she sadly left Artie forever. "I loved him. And I loved him just the way he was."

Half a Sixpence was such a big hit, at 677 performances in London though just 511 in New York, that it went Hollywood in the typical sixties "overproduction." It was a creditable job, but it came out when audiences had tired of Big Hollywood Musicals, and the film banked so poorly that it hurt the show's prestige. It remained famous over the years but had been degraded to amateur-society fare till Chichester put on a heavily revised version in 2016, with a new book by Julian Fellowes and new songs by Stiles and Drewe.

Good Arties are hard to come by, but Chichester more or less discovered a perfect song-and-dance jeune premier in Charlie Stemp. But did the *Sixpence* score need a revision? In the event, the alterations amounted to no more than smart housekeeping: cutting the now outdated or unnecessary numbers such as "The Old Military Canal" (which covered scenery movement and gave Tommy Steele time to effect a costume change); re-centering Artie's interest in Ann by starting off with the title song, their key duet; giving Helen Walsingham more to sing (she originally had just her part in a hymn) so we could better understand how she was affecting Artie. Comparably, Artie's baffled "In the Middle There's Me" clarified his attitude toward his pair of damsels, because he can't figure out how the love thing works when there's two of it.

In all, the *Sixpence* score became longer and, yes, better: more complete. Further, every one of Heneker's surviving songs now sported new lyrics here and there, generally an improvement. In a way, the Chichester revisal recalls the old saw that British musicals were prim while American musicals were dynamic, for this *Sixpence* was souped up with that American verve.

Thus, in 1963 the show opened with a book scene presenting trade on the floor of Shalford's emporium, with the boss barking orders and customers browsing, the whole thing culminating in a ballet. After a change of set, Artie and his fellows, in the waltzy "All In the Cause Of Economy," simply added a few details to what we had just seen, extraneously. The 2016 *Sixpence*, after first establishing Artie and his Ann, then set the Shalford trade scene to music, in "Look Alive," a much more direct and concise way to launch the action.

And yet. Some of the numbers in 2016 were too raucously staged. A new piece, "Pick Out a Simple Tune," found Artie charming the swells with his banjo playing. This was a ritzy party, with a highly spiced dress code, the men in tails and the women in the latest thing from Paris. Yet as Artie coached them in a melody that would not have disgraced a Slade-Reynolds farrago, the fancy folk turned into wild animals. They went simply mad, my dear; one man hung from the chandelier as if he'd never heard music before.

But these people are stylish if nothing else. And they *are* nothing else—so why picture them losing their poise? This is Artie's "Lambeth Walk" moment, and we remember how that number (in the original 1937 *Me and My Girl*) did allow one old fool to humiliate himself carrying on with Teddie St. Denis. But the Chichester *Sixpence* offered a stageful of such nonsense. Yes, musicals are fantasies, but they still have to honor character logic.

Further, "Flash Bang Wallop" was laid out with such abandon that we constantly lost sight of Charlie Stemp amid the support and extras. Hiding your star in chaos is nothing but bad planning; this is not how star shows work. We aren't attending *Girl From the North Country,* where there is no protagonist and everyone shares the storyline. We're at *Half a Sixpence,* where the exhibition lead gets the exhibition spots.

It is true that the 1963 *Sixpence* would not have aged well; it was already virtually a twenties musical, a *Mister Cinders* with a dancing star. This new *Sixpence* left many in the audience ecstatic at the return of something intrinsic to the British musical that had somehow gotten lost between *Oliver!* and *Jesus Christ Superstar*: charm. We find it in countless titles from *The Geisha* to *The Boy Friend*, now tilted to the eccentric side, now to the sentimental. When Noël Coward delivered the aforementioned curtain speech at the premiere of *Cavalcade*, he might have been thinking especially of the stage when he said it was "pretty exciting to be British," not least because, all his life, Coward was deeply involved in the creation of musicals—a form that, contrary to a certain legend, was invented and developed by Coward's people.

Discography

HMV (Past Classics CD) made two 78 albums of the 1920 *Beggar's Opera* in what became the standard version by Frederic Austin, who also sings Peachum and conducts. The performance is as antique as a peruke, but HMV (Pearl CD) took down also the 1940 Glyndebourne staging, rather more vital, with Michael Redgrave's Macheath. His tone is thin, but he hits the notes—and the Peachum, Roy Henderson, makes a formidable opponent, reminding us that Peachum is really the show's anchor personality.

Later albums include dialogue, and Decca's all-star opera-spoof rendition under Richard Bonynge gives us Joan Sutherland (as Lucy) in the most dramatic utterance of her career, in her second-act scene with Macheath (James Morris) on the line, "A *husband*?" Douglas Gamley's eclectic orchestrations are as funny as the script. While Frederic Austin ended "Before the Barn Door Crowing" (Gay's parody of the Handelian "simile" aria) with a lusty cock crow, Gamley quotes Rimsky-Korsakof's *The Golden Rooster*.

To follow the transition into G & S comic opera, try William Shield's *Rosina* (Decca), with a wonderful cast; note Monica Sinclair "manning" up her contralto in a trouser role. Then try von Weber's *Oberon*. Is it opera? Or, rather, is it what people who liked musicals went to before "musicals" as such existed? Only Decca gives us the score in the English it was composed to; luckily, the young Jonas Kaufmann sings Huon. Actor Roger Allam, the original Javert in the RSC *Les Miz*, narrates. Closer in style to G & S is Michael Balfe's *The Bohemian Girl*, the most popular whatever-it-is of the Victorian Age. Not till 1991 was there a complete reading (Argo) of this disjointed, silly work. It's a toy opera. Richard Bonynge, always a champion of the offbeat, leads a dull cast, but we're unlikely to hear another.

Let's reduce the massive G & S catalogue to *Ruddigore* alone. HMV's first-ever, an acoustic set from 1924 (Sounds on CD), is virtually the cast album of a "premiere"—the revival of the show after thirty-two years of exile. Savoyards love its heavy complement of D'Oyly Carte players—Bertha Lewis and Darrell Fancourt actually enliven the dreary "There Grew a Little Flower." One lead who was not with the company—George Baker in the patter role—is so stylish he's more Carte than the Carters.

Still, I find HMV's 1931 remake (Arabesque CD) more vivid, and Decca's LP *Ruddigore* (Naxos CD), featuring the last generation of great G & S stylists, is better yet, as conductor Isidore Godfrey sparks it up with fast tempos. Ann Drummond-Grant (Godfrey's wife) is the best Mad Margaret on disc, exercising dainty tact when Sir Despard speaks of being "a dab at penny readings" and she has to reply with "They are not remarkably entertaining." A unique delivery.

Decca's stereo *Ruddigore*, again under Godfrey, pulls an amusing stunt in the patter trio, "My Eyes Are Fully Opened," which Sullivan set without breathing spaces, so singers always fudge notes and words. These singers are jammed up against the microphone, to sing in half-voice and thus fly through their phrases in a single breath. Also, Decca included "The Battle's Roar Is Over," not heard since HMV's acoustics and necessary in establishing the tenor's romantic side. Decca threw in a bonus of *Ruddigore*'s original overture, poorly designed to give away the quodlibet from Act One, though it does conclude gaily with the long-lost sing-song finale. On CD, Decca adds a complete *Cox and Box*, dialogue and all. It was supposed to be the older of two Carte performances, but early pressings accidentally programmed the later performance. No matter: they're both excellent.

Meanwhile, EMI had opened its own G & S inventory under Malcolm Sargent using opera singers such as Elsie Morison and Owen Brannigan, and the music has never sounded better. These are not theatrical readings, but the *Ruddigore* works well except for George Baker, back from the dead in the patter role.

Now for some history, for TER recorded *Ruddigore*'s 1887 original, proving G & S were right to make the cuts. The ghosts scene drags horribly, and the hero's patter song, "For Thirty-Five Years I've Been Sober and Wary," broke the fourth wall:

> I played on the flute and I drank lemon-squashes,
> I wore chamois leather, thick boots, macintoshes,
> And things that will someday be known as galoshes . . .

A character from the past conversant with the future? Fie, Gilbert!

We're not including DVDs in this already overburdened survey, but let's take note at least of two movie bios. Mike Leigh's *Topsy-Turvy* doesn't explain who anyone is; you have to submerge yourself in the experience as if in an operetta version of *The Matrix*. Less well known, *The Story Of* [in America: *The*

Great] *Gilbert and Sullivan* is a color film from 1953 with Robert Morley as the irascible Gilbert and Maurice Evans as a peace-making Sullivan with a lot of onstage assistance from the D'Oyly Carte company, including a miniature *Trial By Jury.* The music covering the "judge's note" business I mentioned in the text is cut, but sharp eyes will spot the note in the plaintiff's hand just after—again, a meme that may lead directly back to Gilbert's stage direction one hundred fifty years ago.

In the Edwardian Age, Hyperion offers *The Geisha,* beautifully sung by Lillian Watson, Christopher Maltman, Sarah Walker, and Richard Suart under Ronald Corp. If your pet mouse can read you the tiny (and faint) lettering in Hyperion's synopsis and text, you'll get a good sense of ancient musical comedy as a composition. In performance, however, the singing was less finished than it is here. For proof, try Opal's collection of the 12 original-cast (OC) cuts of *Florodora,* one-sided seven-inch 78s with piano accompaniment. The choruses are utter cacophony, given the tech available in 1900, but the solos are listenable; Ada Reeve's "Queen of the Philippine Islands" comes over nicely. But note that everyone tends to speak at least some of the vocal lines—and these are not rich voices to begin with.

HMV took down an acoustic *Merrie England* with the same house talents heard on their first G & S sets. Yet here they sound more vital, perhaps because Edward German, conducting, mustered his crew before each session. Tenor John Harrison, in "The English Rose," has more flair than the best-known D'Oyly Carte tenor of the time, Derek Oldham, even if Harrison dodges the optional B Flat at the number's end. Coincident with the 1960 Sadler's Wells revival, Decca produced an Edward German LP with one side devoted to *Merrie England,* using the singers who were trying to music their way through G & S over at EMI. At least Alexander Young rises to the B Flat. The classic *Merrie England,* a catalogue perennial, is EMI's stereo set led by June Bronhill.

EMI put out also two *Arcadians* LPs, each borrowing from the other to fill out CD reissues. The Cynthia Glover disc is bonused with Gwen Catley's vapid renditions of old British show tunes, a must miss. But the June Bronhill *Arcadians* offers fillers with some of the original cast, mainly the flavorsome Florence Smithson, somewhat free and *intime.* Bronhill is as always exceptional; her leading of the first-act finale (on both CDs) reminds us how much rare art lies in these old "musical comedies." Ohio Light Opera's complete *Arcadians* (Newport), with heavily cut dialogue, is capable, energized only by comic Daniel Neer's wild-eyed Simplicitas.

Gertie Millar's best numbers, along with a few by George Grossmith Jr., were on a World LP; Leverage has a comparable CD, misspelling Gertie's name as "Miller." Next, jump over to any music-hall compilation—ASV Living Era has a fine one—to see how vastly the halls depended on radical personalities. Next to Millar, someone like Marie Lloyd is a subversive.

The 1910s and 1920s bring in some famous titles, and a busy industry in full-scale OC albums left us with José Collins herself in *The Maid Of the Mountains* (Palaeophonic CD). She's wonderful even in acoustic sound. There's a modern *Maid*, though. Producer Emile Littler, who never met an operetta he wouldn't revive on the cheap, brought *The Maid* back in 1972, and it, too, got an OC (EMI). The performance is coarse—but note that, finally, someone noticed how unbalanced the maid's romance was: she duets with The Guy Who Sings yet runs off with The Guy Who Doesn't. Here the latter gets the big tunes and two interpolations. Lyn Kenington delivers a great "Love Will Find a Way," acting it as if just now discovering what it means and capping it with a high A so resounding it sounds like a C. In the end, listeners will prefer Hyperion's *Maid*, a performance on the grand scale under Ronald Corp; he uses a generous edition with more music than one finds in the published score. As for that other wartime long run, *Chu Chin Chow*'s well-sung World LP got onto CD (West End Angel), with bass Inia Te Wiata covering six different roles. (The CD doesn't credit the conductor; the LP names him as Michael Collins.)

Two works by foreign composers shed light on the very varied state of West End vocalism back then. Columbia's fifteen OC 78 sides (Opal CD) of Messager's *Monsieur Beaucaire*, written for London in 1919, offer an unsatisfying First Couple in the poor diction of Maggie Teyte and baritone Marion Green's terrible singing. But the Second Couple's John Clarke is superb in "Honour and Love," capped by a ravishing pianissimo high A. *Lilac Time*, the British version of the Franz Schubert bio-musical, claims eight Vocalion cuts (Pearl CD) with just the three leads. Soprano Clara Butterworth is fine, but Courtice Pounds and Percy Heming are labored. The first *Lilac Time* LP (World) again used just the three leads, and while Jacqueline Delman, *The Crooked Mile*'s John Larsen, and later Covent Garden Rigoletto Peter Glossop justify this marvelous music, not till June Bronhill (CFP CD) led a full cast with a more complete program did the work come alive, albeit in overly modern orchestrations.

With Noël Coward, pride of place goes to EMI's fancy box set of Coward's HMV 78s, from the 1920s into the early 1950s and taking in essential discs with Gertrude Lawrence, the definitive Coward partner. In these early years we hear Coward's "dying dove" (as playwright John Whiting put it) sound in ballads and, in comedy, his brisk yet whimsical approach, an idiom all his own.

When Columbia's Goddard Lieberson was running his series of vintage shows, he included *Bitter Sweet* and *Conversation Piece*. The former is fascinating, with a passionate Portia Nelson and somewhat wan Robert Rounseville but taking down many of the ensembles, ignored on the rival *Bitter Sweet* LPs, and an authentic Viennese cembalom for "Zigeuner." But Coward hated the tapes and the release was canceled. TER took down a complete *Bitter Sweet* from a revival, though Martin Smith's baritone and very English manner is wrong for the hero, a tenor and Continentally exotic. Valerie Masterson rather smothers him when they duet.

HMV caught eight OC numbers from *Conversation Piece* (EMI), but Lieberson's two-LP Columbia set (Must Close Saturday, which *just* fits the whole thing onto one CD) is "complete" with (heavily cut) dialogue. Coward himself appears opposite Lily Pons, who ends the show with Lucia Di Lammermoor's high E Flat. Coward also wrote and delivers rhymed couplets for narration. "What elegant language they discoursed in," he chants of his Georgian people, and "If you're in doubt, just read Jane Austen." It rhymes if you're English. In place of a chorus, Coward sings the scene-change numbers himself, though two, the Fishermen's Quartet and "Mothers and Wives," were omitted. The young Richard Burton, well ahead of his fame, plays the Boy, but the role is small and dull.

Let's jump ahead to *Sail Away*, good enough on Broadway (Angel) but New Yorkers Stritch and Dale and the West End cast (Varese Sarabande CD) give a more theatrical report. Stritch's opposite, David Holliday, is terrific, suave on "Go Slow, Johnny" and burning hot in the last A of "Don't Turn Away From Love." The whole recording has a live-on-stage feeling; when Stritch sarcastically suggests concluding "Come To Me" with "one fast chorus of 'Beyond the Blue Horzon,'" the stewards break into it—they don't on the New York disc. Coward taped his own solo voyage of the score with Peter Matz's little jazz group (Capitol LP), unmemorably, and Harbinger has released a CD of Coward's demos including two cut numbers, to piano only, in poor sound.

The many Coward recitals, from Bobby Short to Ian Bostridge to Christine Ebersole, can't capture Coward's crisp delivery, as essential as the notes and harmony. Everyone's too moist and expansive; Coward is tight and dry. Worth mentioning (because it's so offbeat) is EMI's *Twentieth Century Blues*, in the trendy genre of unlikely covers—the Pet Shop Boys in "Sail Away"; an "I'll See You Again" from Sting, with a harp; and the alt-rock band Suede in "Poor Little Rich Girl" in techno-pop with a wailing vocal ritornello. Imagine the Duchess' feelings. But far more stylish is Joan Sutherland's Coward (Decca), a lovable disc with the imprimatur of the author, talking his way through two duet scenes. The diva is in great voice, amplifying the scales in the intro to "I'll See You Again" and soaring over Douglas Gamley's habitual apocalyptic scoring. A more theatrical Coward is reviewed in the OC of *Cowardy Custard* (Victor)—so easy to like that even The Master approved.

Ivor Novello's operettas all got OC 78 sides, and EMI recorded a studio *Dancing Years* (CFP CD, with other Novello bits) headed by a committed Anne Rogers. Mezzo Ann Howard, in the Olive Gilbert track, is sensational, especially in one intense last line over the chorus in "When It's Spring In Vienna."

The Dancing Years even has a cast album, from the 1968 revival, no doubt because June Bronhill was in it. Hear, in the verse to "Waltz Of My Heart," how uniquely she presents "Joy fans a fire in me," with an emphasis that is acted yet vocal as well. And our calendar of *Dancing Years* sopranos now reaches Valerie Masterson in TER's complete reading on two CDs. The set underlines how little vocal composing Novello's operettas had, as there's a ton of incidental and dance music. This is not to mention the performance numbers confusing the plot, so dramatically irrelevant that TER brought in Janie Dee to narrate.

We can visit Vivian Ellis in his two characteristic modes, musical comedy and "light opera." Of the former, the *Mr. Cinders* revival got three different discs, all from TER. First came the King's Head cast (with piano), then the Fortune Theatre transfer (with a little band), and at last the Highgate School production. The youthful cast and ten-man pit (with bright new orchestrations) do well enough for unseasoned amateurs, and the Jim is polished. Contradicting the second TER LP's note on the authorship of "Please, Mr. Cinders," the Highgate back insert credits it to Vivian Ellis alone.

Ellis' smash operetta, *Bless the Bride,* never got an OC. Ellis' memoirs tell us that the "libraries" (the ticket agents who could support a show by buying up seats to sell) and dance bands ignored the piece—but BBC radio aired a large sampling of the score by the cast (AEI; Sepia). A studio group (MFP LP) offers the excellent Mary Millar and Roberto Cardinale in too short a selection, though the performance does observe the original vocal arrangements. Note how the squared-off "English" music on Side One gives way to the seductive "French" music on Side Two when the action moves across the Channel.

On the cycle of seamy naturalism, *Expresso Bongo* (AEI) is notable for the cynical tone that infects almost all the numbers, and James Kenney's Bongo really catches the brainless glee of early rock and roll. Writing such ditties in the real world is how Lionel Bart made his entree, and his first music-and-lyrics show, *Fings Ain't Wot They Used T'Be* (Bayview) was recorded live, underlining the semi-amateur tone of its staging. More professionally, there was an all-star studio disc (HMV LP), with Joan Heal, Adam Faith, Sidney James, Alfred Marks, and even Bart himself. When Tony Tanner rips into "Contempery," he outdoes Wallas Eaton on the OC for sheer mean-streets polish (if you know what I mean), and at the song's takeoff on A. A. Milne's poetry, when Alice (Christopher Robin's nanny) is mentioned, someone says, "'Ere, is she still on the game?" (There's an ad lib there on the OC, too, but it's impossible to make out.)

For the musically-advanced wing of the cycle, *The Crooked Mile* and *Johnny the Priest* (both Must Close Saturday CDs) are essential, and *Oliver!*, brings us to a joyfully primitive score. The OC is a classic, preserving Peter Coe's music-hall informality. Note the cat's yowl during "I Shall Scream" at a sight gag as Mr. Bumble treads on the animal; American cast albums omitted these theatrical bits, but British recordings "souvenired" a production exactly as was. One quirk: "Oom-pah-pah" is missing its quodlibet section.

Oliver!'s Broadway cast is actually that of the long pre-Broadway tour, with a different Dodger. Eric Rogers doubled his London scoring for thirteen players at David Merrick's insistence, cleverly maintaining the original charts to expand them at climaxes. The Israeli cast, in Hebrew (CBS LP), is a copy of London, because Peter Coe directed it himself, no doubt eager to work with Rivka Raz. Yes, the beloved star of your and my fave Middle-Eastern musical, *It All Started in a Shtetl*, plays Nancy. The Fagin is Shraga Friedman, who co-wrote the translation (and, incidentally, made a Yiddish version of *Fiddler on the Roof* that was used decades later in the production seen in New York in 2019). Excellent conducting and engineering allows us to hear more of Rogers' detail—and note, again, the cat's yowl. Fun fact: the liner notes (in English) report that the cast "discovered quite a number of old friends among the songs," presumably the street vendors' cries in "Who Will Buy?" and possibly "Boy For Sale," as Bart might indeed have "made use of some old Hassidic tunes . . . from his childhood in Whitechapel."

There are plenty of *Oliver!* discs. Capitol released an English studio cast headed by Stanley Holloway and Alma Cogan, with more elaborate orchestrations than Rogers'. The reading lacks drama, and Tony Tanner's Dodger is well past his urchin days. But the disc does something arresting with the "Oom–pah–pah" quodlibet. Nancy typically get drowned out when she sings against the ensemble, but here *they* suddenly duck into a pianissimo, so we can hear both melodies at once.

One *Oliver!* number is missing on all of the above, the near-hysterical reprise of "It's a Fine Life," tiny but narratively vital. However, a TER studio disc includes it, along with the Nancy of opera soprano Josephine Barstow, the only vocalist to get truly inside "As Long As He Needs Me" after Georgia Brown. Many disagree with me, including TER's chief, John Yap, who reissued the disc with a new Nancy, Sally Anne Triplett.

Each new *Oliver!* expands the scoring, and the 1994 Palladium disc with Jonathan Pryce (EMI) is so *concertante* that every instrument seems to be going off at once. There are elaborate choral charts and dance arrangements, too, as well as (new) incidental music. Interestingly, we get a reminder of the original dire end of Act One, when Mr. Brownlow indicates to the constabulary that Oliver is a thief. (In 1960, he just nodded; here he has a spoken line.) The orchestra then played the first three notes of the title song vastly disguised in discords, though this production plays only the last of them.

For Sandy Wilson: *The Boy Friend* lacks a proper OC, as it's severely truncated. (The first release was on 78 and a ten-inch LP.) Sepia's CD reissue bonuses twenties cast recordings of numbers Wilson may have had in mind when conceiving the score—an imaginative gesture from this always enterprising label. The first Broadway *Boy Friend* (Victor)—"now with Julie Andrews," as the ads might have phrased it—is much better than London's, not least in the jazz band that replaced the original piano-only pit, and London's 1984 revival (TER), newly orchestrated even more jazzily, is very atmospheric, with a fine cast. Wilson's petite charmer gets a grand reading here, as when, at the end of "It's Nicer In Nice," Rosemary Ashe's Hortense rides over the chorus, culminating in a high D. Interestingly, this production used the New York version of the A strains in "The Riviera," re-composed by co-producer (and unofficially the director after he pushed Vida Hope out of the way) Cy Feuer, fearing that Wilson's hommage had cut too close to the bone of *Good News!*'s "The Varsity Drag."

Valmouth and *Divorce Me, Darling!* both claim OCs and Chichester revival discs; the latter, both on TER, are better, *Valmouth* for a more complete reading and *Divorce Me* for a more scintillating cast. Note how the few pastiche numbers in *Divorce Me* marry the rest of the score so well that the effect is of an evening full of thirties hommages. For example, is Bobby's "Someone To Dance With" pure Wilson or was he channeling songs Fred Astaire sang?

Julian Slade's *Boy Friend, Salad Days*, also suffers an incomplete OC (Sepia CD), and one is constantly aware that this is a regional cast, not indigenously West End, as when Jane wonders who will give the parties after they leave college and Timothy answers, "There won't be any *parties*," accenting the wrong word. The 1976 revival (TER) is no improvement, but EMI competitively offers a starry cast and the entire score, from overture to play-out. This was a BBC radio broadcast, with bits of dialogue to keep the listener notified of the continuity, though many of the lines are invented and the non-musical scenes in the beauty shop and fashion house are missing. Simon Green's Timothy gets that remark about parties wrong, too, and note the cover photograph of the original production's Bob Harris with Minnie the piano, ironic in that Harris played Troppo, a mime who obviously isn't on the disc. Still, the picture at last tells us Minnie's make: she's a D'almaine.

Sepia's CD reissues of later Slade bear bonus tracks of his earlier work in Bristol, a key to the ID of the postwar British musical as so much of it originated—like Slade's Bristol shows—as part of a regional company's regular season and was taken to London almost as afterthought. Sepia's *Follow That Girl* (reverse the booklet if you want your CD to replicate the look of the original LP) preserves the quixotic "Life Must Go On," for two bons vivants, so gay that the song was apparently dropped after the opening and isn't in the vocal score.

Slade's one spectacle, *Vanity Fair,* has no OC, but a small company revived it in 2001 (Bayview) with an added Slade number, "La Vie Boheme," whose A strain has the flavor of the tunes Marguerite Monnot wrote for Édith Piaf. The song is another quodlibet, as if every composer with an urge to prestige needed to refer back to Arthur Sullivan, who habilitated the practice in musicals. *Vanity Fair* opens with a "singing man" hawking his ballad—the show's title song—bringing us back to the musical's beginnings in ballad opera. But this is dead music. Next to an ever-expanding talent such as Lionel Bart, Slade seems limited.

Speaking of Bart, *Blitz!* (EMI) and *Maggie May* (Bayview) are essential listening; both CDs add in the numbers originally issued only on appendix 45 EPs. *Maggie May* boasts two magnetic stars, but *Blitz!*'s unknowns are even so a vital crew, and the sound effects (contrived especially for the disc) and the stereo separation are superb. In "We're Going To The Country," you can hear the children crossing the stage, and Amelia Bayntun spends "So Tell Me" pacing the floor with worry.

Monty Norman's *Belle* (MCS CD) seems to have two separate casts—the rambunctious music-hall squad and the somewhat pallid "real" characters, making us wonder what the show is saying about art (the music hall) versus life. Now for an experiment: we play first the Saga studio cast of David Heneker's *Jorrocks* (Stage Door CD), led by Barry Kent in a character role, an odd choice for the hunk who had just finished playing Lancelot in the Drury Lane *Camelot*. But British studio casts always favored "smooth" vocalism, also, sometimes, lame orchestrations, and this *Jorrocks* is the worst example.

Then we move to the *Jorrocks* OC (EMI), everyone seizing the story as if still on stage. Even the very timbre of soubrette Cheryl Kennedy bears a sort of plangent determination, very right for the character. (Note future Lloyd Webber lyricist Richard Stilgoe in a minor role.) The heroine of *Ann Veronica* (Stage Door CD) is also determined, but Cyril Ornadel composed her as a soprano, for even as late as the 1960s the British musical favored the "operetta" sound in leading ladies. The belt heroines, such as Pat Kirkwood, are the exception, though pop opera finally overturned the tradition because of its roots in rock. Even when it moved on to pure theatre music, the chest-voice heroine was the norm, as with the protagonists of *Evita* and *Miss Saigon*.

We should note as well, in the British tradition of recording composers in medleys of their scores, Ornadel's own *Ann Veronica* LP (CBS), a garishly vapid runthrough with a Howard Johnson's chorus and a naggy harpsichord continuo. This genre had featured, for instance, Vivian Ellis (a superb pianist) playing his music concerto-style with an orchestra. But this *Ann Veronica* is a disgrace.

The prize score of the 1960s is Ron Grainer's *Robert and Elizabeth*, so dramatic yet so musical. American tourists bringing back a London cast album (because the discs weren't available in the US) was a "thing" that started with

Salad Days and continued with *Oliver!*, *Blitz!*, and so on, but it really took off with *Robert and Elizabeth* (WE Angel). John Clements, as the despotic father, got first billing, but operetta dotes on sweethearts, and Keith Michell and June Bronhill own the program in ten big numbers, with dialogue bits piecing the story together. A Chichester revival (First Night) gives us a vigorous Mark Wynter and a game Gaynor Miles. The smaller orchestra lacks a full string section, but the CD includes more music, including Browning's "Long Ago I Loved You," which isn't in the vocal score. The show is musically so grand that full-out numbers—"Want To Be Well," "What's Natural," and "Under a Spell"—have yet to be recorded.

In the era between *The Boy Friend* and *The Phantom Of the Opera*, try comparing *Peg* with *The Hired Man*: the charm score vs. the dramatic one. The *Peg* OC (TER) preserved the show's only outstanding element, David Heneker's score. The disc does give us a rare chance to hear Martin Smith, his voice opening up gracefully on the high phrases of "Peg O'My Heart." In the Cole Porter revue *A Swell Party* (Sylva), Smith sang "Rap Tap On Wood" to his own piano accompaniment and even tap-danced at the keyboard. YouTube has Smith's turn as Jean Valjean, worth a detour. Sadly, he was cut down by AIDS at thirty-seven.

The Hired Man's OC (Polydor LP) never made it to CD, but most of the leads are on the two-disc concert (TER) and, lo, we have another Highgate School cast on a private CD produced by TER. The kids are hopelessly over-parted (as they weren't on their *Mr. Cinders*), proving just how dramatic the vocal writing in these modern operettas can be.

For pop opera, we can explore the form's evolution from the first *Joseph* recording (Decca LP), very much in the well-intentioned amateur mode, with extra music added. Tim Rice unveils his Elvis imitation as the Pharaoh; later punters more authentically capture The King's uniquely seductive rustication of urban rhythm and blues. For Final *Joseph*, with even more music—including the pastiche numbers (Parisian nostalgia, calypso, et al.) that Lloyd Webber has such fun with, the Palladium cast (Verve), with Jason Donovan and narrator Linzi Hateley, is the best of a huge list.

Try then the *Jesus Christ Superstar* concept album (best remastered on Verve), more agonized than any other reading in its Personen-Regie, because this was pure rock while the many later *Superstar* recordings are theatre-based. They also employ the more homogenized scoring of a theatre pit, while the original maps all over the geography of orchestration.

The comparably silken *Sunset Blvd* has collected cast albums from Helen Schneider (in German) and Diahann Carroll (in Canada), but most listeners will wonder about the Normas of London and New York, both on Polydor. The West End's Patti LuPone has the stronger vocal command, Broadway's Glenn Close the feral quicksilver of the truly demented. The discs of course cannot convey the latter's zesty plastique, such as her blissful little kick during the dance in "The Perfect Year," helping us understand how wonderful Norma must have been in silents, when portrayal was exclusively visual.

LuPone's Norma lacked such bonnes bouches, but she soared through the big moments like a trapeze artist, while Close had to husband her resources. Nevertheless, she made the music work for her, somewhat as opera soprano Hildegard Behrens did when singing Wagner's Brünnhilde, identifying so intensely with the music that, despite an underpowered instrument, she became the Brünnhilde of the age.

While we're making opera comparisons: Puccini mischievously gave the tenor in *Gianni Schicchi* an impossible-to-sing long E vowel on two high B Flats at the end of his aria, knowing that this vowel and extended big notes are incompatible. Similarly, Lloyd Webber ended Norma's "With One Look" on a comparable note. The unconquerable LuPone sings it dead-on, but Close has to make an adjustment, singing, "With one look, I'll be *may* [instead of *me*]." In effect, this only adds to the mystique of Norma Desmond, a riddle wrapped in a mystery inside an enigma (to recall Churchill on Russia). Norma confounds comprehension right up to the show's last seconds, when—at least in the original staging—a curtain dropped down to receive a projection of the very young and unspoiled Norma, innocent of the corruption of fame.

Les Misérables counts an unusual discography, starting with that small-scale concept album released only in France (Ais CD). This is a very different *Les Miz*, with much less music and a small band, though the performers are passionate. The London OC (First Night) is superb, though missing a lot of the music that was written specifically for the RSC mounting. The Czechs must identify with the show's rebelling students from their own oppression by the Soviets, as there are no less than three Czech recordings. The one on three discs is note-complete, as is *Les Miz*'s so-called Symphonic Version (First Night), with an expanded orchestra. It can be thrilling to hear all those strings, but the performers, drafted from various *Les Miz* companies, are not consistently competitive with the OC.

In 1991, the RSC version was produced at the Théâtre Mogador in Paris (Trema, the label that released the concept LPs), and it's odd to hear Boublil having to translate from Herbert Kretzmer's English when Boublil had already written (different) French words for many of the numbers. Much is lost, as always with translations. "At the End Of the Day" 's first line is now "Quand le jour est passé" (When a day is at end), which loses the pun on the English idiom meaning "After all's said and done." And in "I Dreamed a Dream," Boublil once wrote of the misery of the poor; now he had Fantine's vision of love to deal with, and a superb line such as "He took my childhood in his stride" becomes "En m'ayant volé mon enfance" (While having stolen my childhood), giving up Kretzmer's (or James Fenton's) poetic image of the alpha lover acquiring a human bauble as he stalks the earth. Louise Pitre, Broadway's first Donna in *Mamma Mia!*, plays Fantine; like the cast generally, she is quite good but does not leave her mark on the music. The London OC remains the great one.

Many changes large and small have affected the show—at one point cuts were instituted to avoid overtime, and les Thénardier get more cartoonish at every staging. But one thing has remained constant: the show's official orchestrator, even for the first French album, has always been John Cameron.

Bibliography

The first history was Ernest Short's *Fifty Years Of Vaudeville* (Eyre & Spottiswoode, 1946), taking the musical from Hollingshead's and Edwardes' two Gaiety Theatres up to "The Lambeth Walk." (Short uses "vaudeville" and "variety" as synonyms for "musical," common usage in the old days to distinguish the likes of *Mister Cinders* from the "operas" of Gilbert and Sullivan et al.) This is a useful work, enlivened with anecdotes.

Derek and Julia Parker's *The Story and the Song* (Chappell, 1979) runs from 1916 to 1978 and gets a lot wrong, though it does tell us that Julian Slade's great role in his college acting days was Lady Macbeth. Sheridan Morley, bless his heart, gets even more wrong in *Spread a Little Happiness* (Thames & Hudson, 1987), but he was personally close to some of his subjects (indeed, one of Noël Coward's godsons) and his book is bountifully illustrated.

Kurt Gänzl's gigantic two volumes of *The British Musical Theatre* (Oxford, 1986) are formidable, as each year (starting in 1865, well in time for G & S and not signing off till *Starlight Express*) gets, first, a show-by-show assessment and, second, the production credits, taking in even cast replacements and alternate stagings. Two fine books on pantomime are A. E. Wilson's *King Panto* (Dutton, 1935) and Gerald Frow's livelier *"Oh, Yes It Is!"* (BBC, 1985). Both are illustrated most pertinently; Frow's photo of Dan Leno and Herbert Campbell costumed for *The Babes In the Wood*, Campbell in monstrous drag and the two of them holding a piglet by the trotters (and the pig is in drag, too) captures late-Victorian panto in full true.

On the other hand, *Immoment Toys* (Benjamin Blom, 1945), a collection of critic James Agate's reviews of musicals, is all but useless, as Agate jams away at length about nothing before giving just a few lines to the work at hand. Thus, on *The Fleet's Lit Up*, as late as the second paragraph Agate writes, "In [Théophile Gautier's] *Mademoiselle de Maupin* occurs this passage: 'Three things are dear to my heart: gold, marble, purple . . .'" and so on for sixteen more lines and yet another paragraph about Gautier, the whole mentioning in passing two members of *The Fleet's Lit Up*'s cast. What does Theophile Gautier have to do with a comedy musical on a nautical theme?

Adrian Wright's *A Tanner's Worth Of Tune* (after a song in *Johnny the Priest*) and *Must Close Saturday* (both from Boydell, 2010 and 2017), covering postwar musicals are more focused than Agate. Still, they spend too much time talking around the shows, such as quoting the notices rather than describing these entertainments experientially. Wright sounds like someone who saw more or less everything, yet his discussions are curiously absentee. He does, however, include plenty of photographs of actress Judith Bruce for her fan club.

On the creators of the art, Hesketh Pearson's *Gilbert and Sullivan* (Penguin, 1950) is brisk and fair, with good stories; then try Gayden Wren's superb *A Most Ingenious Paradox* (Oxford, 2001) for analytic G & S deconstruction. Vivian Ellis' *I'm On a See-Saw* (Michael Joseph, 1953) is very personal except about his sexuality, still illegal when the book appeared. Noël Coward's *Diaries* (Little, Brown, 1982), edited after his death by confidants, are brutally honest about everyone but himself. Philip Hoare's Coward biography (Simon & Schuster, 1996) is the best in the line, and for a Coward treat try his volume in the *Treasures* series (Deutsch, 2012), a pictorial adventure including tucked-in replicas of Coward artefacts—the original *Cavalcade* program, letters and cables, lyric manuscripts in his brisk and frosty hand, artwork, even a contract for "Master Noel Coward" for a walk-on part in 1911.

On specific shows, Edward Behr treats *Le Miz* (Little, Brown, 1989) and Marc Napolitano *Oliver!* (Oxford, 2014), thoroughly researched and good companions for your next visit. Michael Walsh does the shows of Andrew Lloyd Webber in coffee-table format (Abrams, 1989), going up only to *Aspects Of Love*, while John Snelson (Yale, 2004), rich in smart musical analysis, reaches *The Beautiful Game*.

Lloyd Webber's own *Unmasked* (HarperCollins, 2018) complements Tim Rice's *Oh, What a Circus* (Hodder & Stoughton, 1999) in their conflicting personalities, as the composer is prone to micromanage (at times intensely) while the lyricist is friendly and easy-going. Typically, Lloyd Webber's recollections are more precise in what happened, but also more wide-ranging, as he devotes some pages, for example, to a section-by-section recap of his Paganini *Variations* (as in "Variation 5 became the full company song at the end of [*Song & Dance*] with the title 'Unexpected Song'"). He also brings in personal matters, as with the near-death ailment of his first wife, whose National Health doctor ignored the symptom of excessive thirst, a sign of onset diabetes known even to medically ignorant laymen, and self-righteously insisted that it was only "stress." Lloyd Webber is open, too, about how fiercely he defends his vision of what he wants his works to be. So were Beethoven, Verdi, Wagner. They're the creators; it's their right.

On the academic side is *British Musical Theatre Since 1950* (Bloomsbury, 2016), in which three critics examine numerous shows from a social more than artistic perspective—though the two are really intertwined in the end. A sampling: Robert Gordon deals with *Salad Days*' "subversive gay context." Millie Taylor considers the latent anarchy in *The Rocky Horror Show*. And Olaf Jubin argues that pop opera—his term is "the spectacle musical"—might be uniquely derived and thus not precisely a musical as we have come to understand the term.

All three writers meet again in the huge *Oxford Handbook Of British Musicals* (2016), which runs from *The Beggar's Opera* to *Matilda*. The essays take in Robert Gordon on *Billy Elliot*'s "Politics Of Class and Sexual Identity"; Carolyn Williams with—in effect—the same approach to G & S; David Cottis on the Newley-Bricusse shows as concept musicals; Miranda Lundskaer-Nielsen on Cameron Mackintosh; and Dominic McHugh on Noël Coward, still the most prepossessing figure in the entire saga despite his musicals being almost reclusive by now. Even the *Sail Away* script—and this title is especially suited to amateur groups—wasn't published till some fifty years after the show closed.

Index

Brough, Arthur, 200
Brown, Georgia, 125, 130, 147, 212
Bruce, Judith, 147
Brunskill, Muriel, 116
Bryan, Dora, 86, 87
Bryant, Johanna, 168
Buccaneer, The, 132
Buchanan, Jack, 56, 57, 62, 65, 74, 76, 77,
    142, 164
Buckingham, Roy, 116
Buddy—The Buddy Holly Story, 191
Bugsy Malone, 163
Bull, Peter, 152
Burke, Alan, 117
Burnand, F. C., 11, 15, 16
Burton, Richard, 209
Butterworth, Clara, 47, 208
By Jeeves, 56, 180

Cabaret Girl, The, 44, 45, 57, 192
Cahill, Marie, 75
Caird, John, 176, 177
Cairo, 52
Calthrop, G. E. (Gladys), 99
Camelot, 214
Cameron, John, 217
Candide, 107
Canterbury Tales, 151, 154
Cardinale, Roberto, 211
Careless Rapture, 64, 67
Carmen, 121
Carr, Jason, 190, 191
Carroll, Diahann, 216
Carroll, Lewis, 20
Carroll, Tamsin, 198
Carson, Jean, 108
Carte, Bridget D'Oyly, 14
Carte, Richard D'Oyly, 14, 16, 22, 23, 28,
    205, 207
Carte, Rupert D'Oyly, 14
Carter, Desmond, 45, 47
Carter, Hurricane, 192
Carvel, Bertie, 197
Carvey, George, 41
Caryll, Ivan, 30, 31
Cat and the Fiddle, The, 73
Catley, Gwen, 207
Cats, 51, 180, 182, 183

Cavalcade, 101, 203
Cavalleria Rusticana, 38
Cellier, Alfred, 26
Chalmers, George, 5
Chamberlain, Neville, 90
Champion, Harry, 37
Chancellor, Robin, 112
Charig, Phil, 43, 57
Charles, Pamela, 86, 87
Charles II, 4
Charlie Girl, 152
Charlot, André, 62, 74, 91
Cherry Girl, The, 30
Chess, 187, 188
Chilton, Charles, 150
Chinese Honeymoon, A, 32
Chrysanthemum, 112, 113, 138
Chu Chin Chow, 50–52, 73, 208
Churchill, Winston, 216
Cilento, Diane, 111
Cinderella, 57, 110, 152
Cinderella At School, 28
Circus Girl, The, 30
Clare, Malcolm, 127
Clarke, Cuthbert, 34
Clarke, Jeremiah, 3
Clarke, John, 208
Clement, Dick, 164
Clements, John, 157, 215
Cleopatra, 52
Cliff, Laddie, 43
Close, Glenn, 186, 216
Coates, Edith, 107
Cobb, Will D., 35
Cochran, Charles, 41, 46, 52, 74–76, 83–
    85, 87, 91, 96–98
Cochran, Fred, 122
Coe, Peter, 113, 114, 127, 128, 151–
    153, 211
Coffin, Hayden, 27, 33
Cogan, Alma, 212
Cohan, George M., 41, 42
Cole, 160
Cole, Nat King, 118
Collins, Dolores, 50
Collins, José, 48–50, 61, 72, 208
Collins, Michael, 208
Collins, Wilkie, 181